THERAPEUTIC PERSPECTIVES ON WORKING WITH LESBIAN, GAY AND BISEXUAL CLIENTS

THERAPEUTIC PERSPECTIVES ON WORKING WITH LESBIAN, GAY AND BISEXUAL CLIENTS

Edited by
DOMINIC DAVIES
and
CHARLES NEAL

OPEN UNIVERSITY PRESS
Buckingham · Philadelphia

Open University Press
Celtic Court
22 Ballmoor
Buckingham
MK18 1XW

e-mail: enquiries@openup.co.uk
world wide web: http://www.openup.co.uk

and
325 Chestnut Street
Philadelphia, PA 19106, USA

First Published 2000

A catalogue record of this book is available from the British Library

ISBN   0 335 20333 7 (pbk)   0 335 20334 5 (hbk)

Library of Congress Cataloging-in-Publication Data
Therapeutic perspectives on working with lesbian, gay, and bisexual
  clients / edited by Dominic Davies and Charles Neal.
      p.   cm.
   Includes bibliographical references and index.
   ISBN 0-335-20333-7 (pbk). — ISBN 0-335-20334-5 (hbk)
   1. Psychoanalysis and homosexuality Case studies. 2. Gays—
Counseling of. 3. Bisexuals—Counseling of. 4. Psychotherapist
and patient. I. Davies, Dominic, 1959– . II. Neal, Charles,
1948– .
RC451.4.G39T476   2000
616.89'14'08664—dc21   99-30665
                                                                CIP

Typeset by Graphicraft Limited, Hong Kong
Printed in Great Britain by Biddles Limited, Guildford and Kings Lynn

To those scouts who dared go ahead, search and report back, as well as to those brave ones who are now prepared to take this knowledge on and deepen our connections, one tribe with another.

Contents

Notes on contributors

Denis Bridoux is a psychother*artist* and licensed NLP trainer based in Yorkshire. He is a member of Kink Aware Professionals, an international body supporting the needs of the S/M and sexual edge community. Secretary of Halifax Area Gay Group from 1982 to 1992, he was involved with HIV voluntary organisations in Yorkshire from the mid-1980s and was AIDS/HIV coordinator in South Humberside from 1991 to 1995. He runs licensed NLP courses for health-related professions with Post-Graduate Professional Education and for gay men as Outcome. He also offers coaching over the telephone.

Dominic Davies is a BAC accredited and UKRC registered independent counsellor and therapist and has been practising in the person-centred approach for 20 years. He was a founding member and former co-chair of the Association for Lesbian, Gay and Bisexual Psychologies UK and co-editor with Charles Neal of *Pink Therapy* (Open University Press 1996). Dominic is in private practice in London, as a therapist and supervisor, and runs an international training consultancy developing sexuality training for therapists and other helping professionals in Europe and Australasia. He is a Visiting Fellow of Nottingham Trent University.

Dr James Gray is a chartered clinical psychologist working for Brent, Kensington, Chelsea and Westminster Mental Health NHS Trust at the Chelsea and Westminster Hospital and the Kobler Clinic. He specialises in working with people with HIV and sexual health problems, and the majority of his casework is with gay and bisexual men.

Deirdre Haslam lectures in counselling at Anglia Polytechnic University. She is a UKCP registered psychotherapist and a supervisor accredited by the Roehampton Institute. She works in private practice and in the voluntary sector. At present she supervises for the East London OUT Project and the Stockwell Centre, Colchester. Her research interests include working with difference and diversity and interactive learning within complex systems.

Susannah Izzard is a psychoanalytic psychotherapist in private practice, and Lecturer in Counselling at the University of Birmingham, where she runs the MA in psychodynamic counselling. Her research interests include personal development in counsellor training, gay and lesbian issues in psychoanalytic work and training, and gender identity in women.

Martin Milton is a chartered counselling psychologist and UKCP registered psychotherapist attached to the University of Surrey and the Kingston and District Department of Clinical Psychology. He is a professional member of the School of Psychotherapy and Counselling at Regents College and is a member of the Society for Existential Analysis. In addition he has been Chair of the Standing Committee for Professional Affairs of the Division of Counselling Psychology (1994–8), sat on the Executive Committee of the Division (1997–8) and is currently on the committee of the newly established British Psychological Society section for lesbian and gay psychology.

Charles Neal is a UKCP accredited humanistic and integrative psychotherapist, a supervisor and trainer in private practice. He is founder of the Association for Lesbian, Gay and Bisexual Psychologies UK and co-editor (with Dominic Davies) of *Pink Therapy* (Open University Press 1996). Charles is also a Co-director of Transform Consultancy – 'an agency for change' – and has special interests in creativity, intimate relationships and sexualities.

Graham Perlman is in clinical training in transactional analysis. He works as a therapist in South London in a private practice for gay men, as well as training in personal development skills. He lives with HIV and his current interests include the transference implications of gay and HIV identity in the therapeutic relationship, and holistic perspectives on well-being. He co-facilitates the Healthy Life Programme for Camden and Islington Health Promotion Services – a programme for HIV+ men to improve the quality of their lives by integrating exercise and psychological well-being.

James Pett worked as a university lecturer in the Middle East and developed young men's support groups before training as a therapist and supervisor in the UK. He has worked for both voluntary organisations and for a local authority in the fields of HIV/AIDS and drugs, and has many years' experience working with gay men. He has written on therapy and supervision and has trained counsellors. He has a particular interest in transcultural counselling and the role of language and imagery in the therapeutic process.

Keith Silvester qualified as a psychotherapist at the Institute of Psychosynthesis, London, where he is a training supervisor. Formerly, he trained as a community worker and worked as a freelance training consultant. He is accredited as a counsellor with the British Association for Counselling and is registered as a psychotherapist with the United Kingdom Council for Psychotherapy. He is on the complaints committee of the British Association for Counselling. Since 1993, he has been employed as Student Counselling and Advisory Service Coordinator at the Central School of Speech and Drama, London.

Gail Simon works as a systemic and social constructionist therapist and has a special interest in the politics of therapy. Gail works with The Pink Practice, Leeds and London and for the Airedale NHS Trust. She is a UKCP registered psychotherapist, a Kensington Consultation Centre registered systemic supervisor, a BAC accredited counsellor and a UKRC registered independent counsellor.

Martin Weaver is a trainer and psychotherapist who has been involved in NLP since 1991. His work with gay men and counselling dates back to 1983 when he volunteered to work with the Terrence Higgins Trust, where he took the first call on the helpline in 1984. He worked for 11 years in the NHS as a senior manager working on sexual health and team development issues from the late 1980s to 1997. He now runs the Martin Weaver Health Consultancy. Martin will gain UKCP registration as an NLP psychotherapist in the year 2000.

Gwyn Whitfield is a founding member of The Pink Practice in Leeds and London where she works as a social constructionist therapist. She has worked in the field of counselling, community and organisational development for over 20 years and is particularly interested in systemic and social constructionist therapy with individuals. Gwyn is a UKCP registered psychotherapist and a Kensington Consultation Centre registered systemic supervisor.

Acknowledgements

Dominic Davies would like to thank:

- My life-partner Lee Adams, and former foster son David for their love, support and encouragement to undertake and continue with this project through some very difficult times.
- The goodwill of my co-editor Charles Neal and all the contributors to this volume for managing to work within the restrictions placed on them due to my living and working in Australasia for several months. I am grateful that most were accessible via e-mail or fax, without which the whole project would have been impossible.
- My close friends and colleagues: Jinny Gray, Oran Kivity, Bill Logan, Richard Murphy, Allan O'Leary, Malcolm Pearce, Fiona Purdie, Steve Quick, Jo Roebuck, Alison Seymour, Keith Tudor, Bob Trett and Fran Walsh for their wonderful emotional, physical and spiritual nourishment, support and encouragement.

Charles Neal would like to thank: my life lover, Jeremy Cole, my sons Sam and Jago and my sister, Carole Lott; my guides Rex Bradley, Terry Cooper and Jenner Roth; my healers Edie Freeman, Ron Marx, Kevin Murphy, Wendy Copeland and Delcia McNeill; and my loving friends who have all helped me keep going through a terrible and painful year, especially Fran Livingstone-Ra, Jacqueline Hockings, Warren Evans, Liz Veecock, Marion Russell, Debs Burch, Jill Gabriel, Giles Collinge, Tom Cooper, Claudine Meissner and Jeff Lane. I feel extraordinarily blessed to share life with you.

The editors would like to thank:

- Michael Jacobs, consultant editor for Open University Press for his feedback on drafts of each chapter.
- Dr John Gonsiorek who kindly agreed to write the Foreword for this volume. His support for the development of gay affirmative therapy in Britain is extremely helpful.
- Rozanne Leppington and the *Human Systems Journal of Systemic Consultation* for permission to include a diagram in the chapter on social constructionist and systemic therapy.

| JOHN GONSIOREK

Foreword

Reading this volume on the western side of the North Atlantic, the first thing that strikes me is the prominence given to different 'schools' of therapy; this focus is in fact, the central organising principle of this book. While theoretical schools were important in American psychology only a few decades ago, the landscape is now different: eclectic approaches predominate. Rather, I should say 'integrative' approaches are the norm. It is not easy to discern much difference between the two, except perhaps that 'eclectic' became such an imprecise term as to cause embarrassment. 'Integrative' suggests a more robust and busy approach to synthesising perspectives, and in fairness, recent theoretical attempts to actively integrate schools of therapy have been more substantive than earlier ones. In clinical practice, however, I suspect that most mental health practitioners in the USA are as much 'eclectic' as 'integrative'.

The nascent gay/lesbian affirmative psychotherapies in the USA have shared this bias and most are so thoroughly integrative that this aspect usually remains an unspoken assumption. The exceptions are the psychoanalytic traditions, which have historically taken great pains to keep themselves distinct from the crowd of therapy schools. Even approaches that are labelled as a 'school', such as feminist therapies, tend themselves to be highly integrative; they are a school more in socio-political stance than psychological theory.

This volume takes a distinctly different approach. A variety of schools of psychotherapy are explored for their theoretical understandings of sexual orientations and shortcomings in this area. The chapters then focus on clinical applications, usually with case examples. Most give a sense of the historical development of that theory's views on sexual orientations.

This is not done with a postmodern sense of irony and distance, but with a literal seriousness and a level of engagement which communicates that the authors 'believe in', or are passionate about, their theories. The contrast with affirmative approaches in the USA is considerable; and I believe it can illustrate a number of intriguing features of how these approaches have developed to date.

Part of the recent de-emphasis of psychological theory in the USA may stem from the insidious effects of 'identity politics', and its resulting Balkanisation of intellectual activity and civic life. Particular client populations are assumed to be so unique as to at least warrant separate discussion, if not constitute virtual subsets of therapeutic endeavour. Despite all the talk about 'different ways of knowing', there has been little substantive, formal theory that details these allegedly different paths. I suspect this is related to the peculiar manner in which 'diversity' has been construed in American identity politics: diversity of people is sacrosanct, while diversity of ideas is initially ignored, and then seen as subversive and reactionary when asserted. Diversity of people, operating within prescribed, limited intellectual activity and homogeneity of ideas, used to be called 'empire'. Any theory that operates on a broad psychological bandwidth is eagerly dissected to reveal what 'isms' it harbours. Any theory that strives for universality is summarily dismissed. However, instead of each identity group giving rise to its own elaborated theoretical school, a handful of cultural snapshots and caveats are superimposed upon the overcooked, weakly differentiated stew of integrative, American-style therapy. Identity politics does not seem to result in identity-based theories, and seems resentful of any intellectual force that might require an amelioration of its political agenda. After dividing people from each other into increasingly separate, alienated, and numerous fragments, the identity politics of the American academic offers only the thin palliative that diversity must be respected – somehow.

The economics and politics of health care in the USA may also play a role in this process. As health care, including mental health services, becomes 'corporatised' through the imperatives of managed care, theory – and intellectual activity – become suspect. Results alone, preferably in the shortest time frame possible, are valued, and theory and technique are seen as relevant only to the extent that results are quickly facilitated. Theory is ultimately suspect because it might provoke clinicians to act with agendas other than quick 'results'. Profit is indeed a jealous god.

A juggernaut, then, has developed in mental health care in the USA. Health care corporations, and the academic Left have become strange but increasingly familiar bedfellows. The shattering of the body politic into myriad 'diverse' fragments is an imperative of identity politics, and a marketing opportunity for corporations. Both forces distrust independent and critical thinking, preferring homogeneity of thought and world view. Both operate invisibly, and tend to censor by dismissive denial, then outraged vehemence, when criticisms are openly voiced.

Lesbian/gay affirmative perspectives in American psychology partake of these failings no more than psychology in general – but also no less. This volume serves as a tonic for this weakness. As the authors examine their theoretical orientations for distortion and limitation regarding sexual orientation, and re-tool them for clinical practice that respects and values sexual minority clients, the entire effect is freeing. Affirmative psychotherapy practice becomes not just another colour in a mythic rainbow of diversity, but a powerful lens that can illuminate a variety of intellectual and clinical traditions, singeing them a bit if need be.

The volume goes further: it avoids the pitfall of becoming 'other' – a trap American affirmative psychotherapy has been flirting with for some time. As an identity politics perspective is implicitly adopted, affirmative theory and practice with lesbian, bisexual and gay clients becomes a 'specialty', an enclave, a ghetto, weakly connected with mainstream psychological theory and practice. This is a great vulnerability. Most specialised, separate enclaves in psychological theory and practice will have short, undistinguished lives. Peruse a text reviewing schools of therapy from 60, 40 or even 20 years ago; many are no longer with us, or exist only as quaint remnants on the margins of mainstream theory and practice. It is a more strenuous, but I believe wiser and more productive investment in the future, to transform existing orientations to be free of theoretical bias and rendered into clinical usefulness for lesbian and gay clients. The dalliance with self-ghettoisation is a prescription for obsolescence. The forces which continue to be arrayed against lesbian and gay people and bisexuals are formidable enough, without such self-defeating indulgence.

The hard work of analysing a preferred theoretical orientation that the authors endeavour in this volume is an exercise in genuine critical thinking. This is a valuable contribution in its own right, and especially welcome since this activity has fallen into disfavour in American affirmative psychology as it has become increasingly influenced by postmodern, identity politics and social constructionist perspectives. In America these perspectives tend to view describing and criticising the underlying assumptions of a viewpoint as equivalent to critically analysing it: once the subject has been dismembered, no reassembly is necessary. These perspectives also maintain an arm's-length distance from the material analysed, as a sense of commitment to or passion for the thing analysed is disdained. Simply stated, it is very difficult to think critically while remaining so disengaged and smugly certain that the material studied is illusory or flawed. Ironically, despite the decidedly social constructionist bent to European thought, and British thinking in particular, the contributors in this volume are fully engaged, passionately involved with their theoretical schools, and determined to understand and remedy them. Many in the USA would do well to emulate this stance.

The authors in this volume also capture another currently lost gem in the USA – a sense of history. Schools of psychotherapy always retain tell-tale traces of their particular origins – the world views of a specific time and place – with their unique preoccupations, lacunae, flashes of brilliance, biases and idiosyncrasies. These can serve as an easy entry into the hard work of critical thinking, as the traces of particularity and obsolescence in a therapy school are reasonable first guesses (though by no means certain ones) of where the ground may have shifted, and the perspective needs to be reappraised.

An appreciation of the history of schools of therapy can also teach humility: a valuable lesson for all therapists who remain, despite much protest, contrary aspiration and discomfort, ultimately in their traditional role as agents of social control. A sense of history impels a recognition that many if not most of our cherished theories and techniques will acquire obsolescence, perhaps foolishness, and maybe even scorn from future practitioners, researchers and theoreticians. Perhaps even more galling, history can teach us that we are unlikely to discern which of our ideas will retain brilliance and relevance for another time and place. This bitter humility, I believe, is a necessary corrective to the arrogance and self-importance of psychotherapists and psychotherapies.

Readers from many countries will find here, I believe, much of substance, and stimulation to think in new ways about their work with gay and lesbian clients. North America may have led the way during the 1970s and 1980s in the development of gay/lesbian affirmative psychological perspectives; but has become increasingly encumbered through the 1990s by the broader malaise in American psychology and intellectual life. This British volume, and work being done in other parts of Europe, may well help inaugurate the next phase of affirmative psychology: one that is politically conscious without being politically driven; one that embraces and implements diversity of thought, not only diversity of people; one that is passionately engaged in theory and practice, not removed in an ivory tower of academic irony; and one that is critically thinking, not dogmatic.

Clinicians in particular will be well-served by this volume in discharging their primary duty of operating in the best interests of their clients, and in further freeing themselves from their historical legacy of serving as the heel of society's boot on the necks of lesbian and gay people. After all, 'Do no harm' comes first.

John C. Gonsiorek, PhD
Clinical Assistant Professor in the Department of Psychology
University of Minnesota, Minneapolis, Minnesota, USA
March 1999

DOMINIC DAVIES AND CHARLES NEAL

Introduction

How this book came about

In 1996 we edited *Pink Therapy: A Guide for Counsellors and Therapists Working with Lesbian, Gay and Bisexual Clients* for Open University Press. It was an amazing success both in terms of sales (it sold out within the first five months and needed to be reprinted) and in the perception of reviewers and colleagues in the field who welcomed a practice text with a British focus in a much neglected area. We discovered how eagerly clinicians and researchers wanted more affirmative theoretical and practical materials. As a result we committed ourselves to two further volumes.

This volume is the second in the series. In this volume, we wanted to explore what is unique about each of a range of theoretical models and so set our contributors four tasks. We asked them: What has been the history of your model's approach to homosexuality and how have lesbian, gay and bisexual people been explained and treated? What are the unique strengths of your approach in working with lesbian, gay and bisexual clients? What are the theoretical difficulties that need to be surmounted when working affirmatively within your approach? We then asked them to illustrate their ideas with clinical and practical examples.

As the field of 'gay affirmative' theory and practice is still very young, we thought it would be particularly interesting to explore 'pure' theoretical models and, while many people practise integrative or eclectic therapy we sought to identify some of the differences and similarities inherent in the major core theoretical models. Contributors were drawn from our professional contacts; most often these were members of the Association for Lesbian, Gay and Bisexual Psychologies UK.

However, we regret this volume is incomplete. A chapter on Gestalt therapy was to be included and unfortunately could not be finished in time for publication. We regret the lack of this perspective and we apologise for it. The reader may notice other theoretical models also missing – this volume simply reflects (a) those major counselling and therapy trainings in whose fields we knew someone who was willing and able to write about them and (b) we had space for. It is not a complete nor exhaustive collection, and we would not pretend otherwise.

What we found

The core message from most chapters seems to be that the therapist needs to have done a considerable amount of personal awareness work on their attitudes to homosexualities and to lesbian, gay and bisexual people. To be an effective practitioner in any of the models, each of our contributors would ask of the therapist, *know thyself*!

It has been interesting to see how much is shared across theoretical orientations and both of us have enjoyed learning more about the differences between us and what we might learn from these. We were also fascinated to see how each contributor seemed to reflect their therapeutic methodology in their writing style and description of their subject. In this way, this volume demonstrates a respect for diversity.

Pride

Much is made within the lesbian, gay and bisexual communities of the term 'Pride'. This is usually used in the context of our annual marches and festivals. Many lesbians, gay men and bisexual people describe this event as their equivalent of Christmas. The London event used to be known as Gay Pride and then became Lesbian and Gay Pride: most recently it has been Lesbian, Gay, Bisexual and Transgendered Pride. It then lost all the labels and became simply Pride. Are there lessons here about the gradual development of separate identities and their changing significance?

An understanding of the cultural significance of this event in the lives of lesbian, gay and bisexual people is important. It will of course mean many things to different people, but the event comes as a response to society treating homosexuality as shameful, and as a refusal to be shamed. For some it is a political rally, for others a celebration and occasion to party, for still others a public expression of their sexuality. For most of us these dimensions have a different weight at different times.

It is not a British cultural norm to feel proud. 'Pride goeth before a fall' as the saying goes. We are told one must not 'blow one's own trumpet' yet it is seen as a sign of positive mental health that one should feel good about one's achievements and have strong self-esteem. As editors, we feel an immense sense of pride when we consider this series of books:

- we are proud that while many of the contributors have never written for publication before, all have submitted thoughtfully argued chapters of interest and value;
- we are proud that through writing, contributors discovered new aspects of their professional selves and many have expressed a desire to write further professional articles – as the field of British gay affirmative therapy writing is still extremely small, we are delighted to have encouraged this development;
- we are proud to be associated with high-quality, ethically sound clinical work, and that contributors have demonstrated themselves to be not only skilful practitioners, but also able theoreticians;
- we are proud to be making a contribution to improving the quality of therapy and psychological services available to people from sexual minorities;
- we are also proud of helping to improve the quality of therapy training – each chapter in this book will be of use to therapy trainers and students in exploring and debating effective work with sexual minorities.

Language

Sexual minorities

As in *Pink Therapy* we have tried to avoid the overuse of 'lesbian, gay and bisexual' and have referred wherever possible to the population under discussion simply as 'clients'. We aim to be inclusive wherever possible while remaining aware of the need for the acknowledgement and valuing of different experiences of sexuality.

Of great importance is self-definition and a move away from medical pathology. Some of us have attempted to counteract stigma by using previously pejorative terms, describing ourselves, for example, as 'dykes' and 'queers'. It is important for therapists wishing to establish constructive working relationships to use the terms that clients have adopted for themselves. We are all learning more in this area and we appreciate that some people may feel offended or excluded by terms used here for which we apologise in advance.

Therapists and counsellors

We use the term 'therapist' as shorthand to describe psychotherapists and counsellors of any theoretical orientation. The term is also intended to embrace advice workers, health professionals, social workers and other helping practitioners whose interest in these matters includes them in our readership. We continue to be fascinated by the vast range of work of related interest we are hearing about.

Case examples

We use clinical examples to illustrate theoretical material. These are usually composite from a number of clients stories (unless otherwise stated) and have been thoroughly disguised. We hope all examples serve as helpful illustrations of the points being made. All contributors have made every effort not to describe clients as if they were different from ourselves in their issues, struggles and experiences.

This is a rich and exciting area with considerable energy and commitment and we hope this volume and its two companions will stimulate readers' further involvement in and contributions to its future development.

It is increasingly obvious that what we have had to call 'gay affirmative' therapy is, in reality, affirmative therapy *per se*. For not until all clients are treated as unique, integral, valuable individuals without the prejudices attaching to particular types and categories of people will any of us be truly safe, respected or healed.

DEIRDRE HASLAM

Analytical psychology

Individuation is a natural necessity inasmuch as its prevention by a levelling down to collective standards is injurious to the vital activity of the individual . . . a serious check to individuality, therefore, is an artificial stunting. It is obvious that a social group consisting of stunted individuals cannot be a healthy and viable institution; only a society that can preserve its internal cohesion and collective values, while at the same time granting the individual the greatest possible freedom, has any prospect of enduring vitality. As the individual is not just a single, separate being, but by his [sic] very existence presupposes a collective relationship, it follows that the process of individuation must lead to more intense and broader collective relationships and not to isolation. Individuation is closely connected with the transcendent function . . . since this function creates individual lines of development which could never be reached by keeping to the path prescribed by collective norms.

If a plant is to unfold its specific nature to the full, it must first be able to grow in the soil in which it is planted.

(Jung 1953–77, vol. 6: 448–9)

Introduction

Any attempt to assess Jungian psychotherapy from a gay-affirmative perspective must take into account the complexity of Jung's own attitudes towards sexuality and gender, and separate these to some extent both from the theory which he developed and the methodology of analytical psychology as practised in the consulting room today. This chapter attempts to tease out the different strands of Jung's views on homosexuality, which often contradict each other, as well as assesses the extent to which contemporary Jungian depth psychology could function in a gay-affirmative manner. First, does it affirm the individual's right to choose a homosexual or bisexual lifestyle, accepting it as psychologically normal and healthy? Does it recognise that the problems (including self-hatred) that this person may bring into therapy are as likely to stem from the homophobia of family and society as their own psychopathology?

Second, to what extent does the contemporary Jungian practitioner acknowledge that their own attitudes towards homosexuality and bisexuality will become part of their work with clients and that being a therapist will involve continuously working on their own shadow projections?[1] Are they also willing, as a practitioner, to join in a more overtly political challenge to the heterosexism and homophobia endemic in our society?

Jung and homosexuality

Jung's pronouncements on homosexuality are few, given the copiousness of his writings. Hopcke (1991: 13) suggests that this is partly owing to the relative lack of importance that sexuality in its literal, observable aspects (as opposed to sexual symbolism) had in Jung's developing theories once he had moved away from Freud. However, this is not to say that he was not interested in sexuality nor that he ignored it in his clinical work. Far from it. The few examples of references to homosexuality are often in relation to individual casework with particular patients.

Hopcke (1991) divides Jung's writings and development of a theoretical framework into three periods. The first is from 1908 to 1920, when Jung was still influenced by psychoanalysis. During this period he sees male homosexuality as arising out of a disturbance of the parental relationship (an approach close to Freud's idea of a pathological identification with the mother as being at the root of manifest homosexuality). In the second period from 1920 to 1927, when Jung was developing and consolidating his own theories, he sees homosexuality as a person's response to the collective unconscious and an identification with the contrasexual archetype, the *anima* in the case of a man or *animus* in the case of a woman (see below). Between 1936 and 1950 is the period of what Hopcke calls Jung's mature thought, where he 'puts forth characteristically Jungian ways of approaching homosexuality clinically and theoretically' (1991: 14). By then Jung sees homosexuality as a manifestation of a search for wholeness and a connection to the archetype of the Self, albeit of a wrong-headed kind. It needs to be reiterated that this discussion still refers solely to male homosexuality. Woman's search for the Self is not mentioned.

To summarise Hopcke further, he identifies four attitudes that Jung held towards homosexuality: 'social tolerance, placement of the phenomenon in a historical and cultural context, distinction between a patient's homosexuality and other aspects of his or her personality, and especially the presumption of meaning' for the individual man or woman (1991: 56).

It is not entirely clear what Jung means by his term 'contrasexual'. Does he refer merely to psychological phenomena derived directly from biological sexual differences between men and women? Is he talking about the internalisation of gender differences present in culture? Sometimes Jung comes close to the modern feminist perception that socially constructed behaviours become seen and experienced as 'normally' associated with men or women just as if they were biologically determined (and hence unchangeable) behaviours. By not being explicit his analysis conflates arguments, which must be kept separate if we are to make sense of them.

In any event Jung argues that the manifestation of contrasexual tendencies in individuals during the first half of life must be seen as a regression. This would be because younger people are so literal about sexuality. A male would quite literally strive to become a female rather than accessing unconscious potential, which might be, or be symbolised by, something apparently female. In the second half of life an exploration of what is symbolised by the 'opposite' sex is a necessity if the individual is to progress towards individuation, the natural goal of wholeness towards which all human beings are tending as if driven by an instinct or drive (Jung 1953–77, vol. 5: 300). Thus the same behaviour is viewed differently, depending on the age of the individual. It also has to be reiterated that while Jung's discussion is quite coherent when applied to heterosexual males, it does not have the same smoothness when applied to heterosexual women or, indeed, to homosexual men and women. Jung himself recognises this and struggles to adapt his argument, but it remains awkward and difficult to follow (vol. 6: 470).

Jung's own beliefs about 'normality', including sexual 'normality', led to considerable confusion about what he had to say concerning homosexuality, and this remains embedded in much Jungian theorising today. Nevertheless there is also compelling evidence, perhaps most powerfully articulated in the quote which begins this chapter, that Jung also believed in the imperative of individual freedom in the Self's journey towards individuation; that to be constricted by collective attitudes was injurious both to individual development and to the healthy functioning of society.

However, the attitudes towards sexuality and gender that informed the development of psychological theory during the first half of this century in the West remained virtually unchallenged by Jung, particularly in the early years as he began developing his own theories. Struggling to develop a culturally sensitive psychology, his attitudes were based on a narrow definition of objective truth, which took a Swiss, white, male, heterosexual perspective as the norm. He blew it, but he was trying.

The dominance of this paradigm in the development of psychological theories has led to a lack of clear awareness of the significance of difference arising out of class, gender, race, sexuality, etc., which has only seriously been challenged in the past 30 years. As a result these variables become problematised: either they get ignored or they are cobbled onto the existing theory, in a manner which demonstrates an awkward attempt to include that which, by its very essence, actually calls into question the validity of existing theory (Simon 1996). Jung's attempt to adapt his theory of contrasexuality is an example.

In spite of these provisos, Jung did recognise the problematic nature of subjectivity and the impossibility of writing from a purely objective stand-point: 'the subjective factor has all the value of a co-determinant of the world we live in, a factor that can on no account be left out of our calculations' (1953–77, vol. 6: 375). And on the subject of women he writes:

> Are we not all involved in some programme or experiment, or caught in some critical retrospect that clouds our judgement? And in regard to woman, cannot the same questions be asked? Moreover, what can a man say about woman, his own opposite? I mean something sensible that is outside the sexual programme, free of resentment, illusion and theory. Where is the man to be found capable of such superiority? Woman always stands just where the man's shadow falls, so that he is only too liable to confuse the two. Then, when he tries to repair this misunderstanding, he overvalues her and believes her the most desirable thing in the world.
>
> (1953–77, vol. 10: 113–14)

In principle, then, Jung acknowledges that personal bias, based on a projection of one's shadow onto the other can fatally interfere with a dis-passionate analysis of the 'facts'. Nevertheless this does not prevent him from writing of the male 'pathological homosexual who [is] incapable of real friendship and meet[s] with little sympathy among normal individuals' (1953–77, vol. 10: 107). Or, if the individual is a woman, he writes that her 'attitude to men is therefore one of disconcerting self-assurance, with a trace of defiance. Its effects on [her] character is to reinforce [her] mascu-line traits and to destroy [her] feminine charm' (vol. 10: 108). Since Jung sees self-assurance and assertiveness as being constitutionally masculine he views a woman with such traits as having become possessed by her *animus* (see below) and as having lost sight of her identity as a woman. This is a clear example of the way his own prejudices interfere with his clinical judgement. Indeed, Jung's sentence following this suggests that consider-ably more is at stake than a dispassionate observation about homosexual women in general, giving the impression that it stems from a personal experience of rejection: 'Often a man discovers their homosexuality only when he notices that these women leave him stone-cold' (vol. 10: 108).

Throughout the *Collected Works*, when writing about sexuality gener-ally, it is clear that for Jung what he is writing about is male heterosexuality unless he specifically states otherwise, as, for example in *Symbols of Trans-formation* (1953–77, vol. 5: 160). Here, in his discussion of the Upanishad he makes no comment on the fact that in Hindu mythology gods and goddesses are frequently bisexual/hermaphroditic. It seems, therefore, that while for humans such sexual fluidity is an anachronism, at the level of myth it is accepted without comment as the norm. Human heterosexuality as norm is never seriously challenged by Jung, even when he acknowledges from his own clinical observations that homosexual experiences are 'more common than is generally admitted' (1953–77, vol. 10: 105).

This acceptance of heterosexuality as normal means that homosexuality becomes abnormal: homosexual men and women are variously described as being in an immature stage of sexual development, possibly as a defence against the perceived dangers of heterosexuality (1953–77, vol. 7: 88); as suffering from 'a defective adaptation to external reality and a lack of relatedness' (vol. 6: 471); as being morbid (vol. 6: 472) and a danger to young people (vol. 10: 107); as having become identified with the contrasexual element which, for a man means identifying with the *anima*, the archetype of the feminine and, for a woman, identifying with the *animus*, the archetype of the masculine. Either of these leads to unattractive behavioural traits and mannerisms (vol. 10: 107). Yet elsewhere, Jung argues that homosexuality might be constitutional (vol. 19a: 199). The problem with this last hypothesis is that it can lead in two directions: either it means that homosexuality is normal, and therefore not pathological, or it indicates that the homosexual individual is innately bad and fundamentally flawed.

On the other hand, by the early 1920s Jung is already differentiating between types of homosexual activity: that which is 'the order of the day among the younger age groups' and that which is 'a higher and more spiritual form which deserves the name "friendship" in the classical sense of the word' (1953–77, vol. 10: 107). He recognises that homosexuality between older men and younger boys can be of lasting value to both, citing Greek society to support his thesis (vol. 7: 106), and that female homosexuality can lead to social and political emancipation as well as allowing women to develop both emotionally and intellectually (vol. 10: 108). He also acknowledges the significance of culture on attitudes towards same-sex unions and gives the example of Anglo-Saxon countries where passionate friendship among women is seen as socially acceptable (vol. 10: 108).

By the early 1940s Jung's use of case study material makes clear that he sees individual neurosis as symptomatic of the effects of socialisation on the individual psyche (1953–77, vol. 7: 265). He argues that homosexuality is a product of environmental damage stemming from parental, specifically maternal, inadequacy (vol. 7: 191). Homosexual fantasies arise out of an unsatisfied need for love from an overambitious, masculine mother which leads to a craving for love from teachers 'of the wrong sort' (vol. 17: 126–7). What he means by this Jung does not say. It certainly conflicts with his earlier description of a homosexual man whose brilliant educational gifts stem from his homosexuality (vol. 10: 107).

In 1950, in a further reflection on a patient, Jung suggests that his homosexual object choice enables him in this way to remain true to his mother; he refers to the myth of the marriage of mother and son, which suggests a continuing acceptance of a different standard for judgement when dealing with myth.

By 1954 Jung seems to be bringing together two strands of his thinking about the meaning of sexuality: the mythic and the psychological. He suggests that rather than viewing homosexuality as a psychological perversion, it is more likely to be as a result of incomplete detachment from the hermaphroditic archetype. Indeed he suggests that by preserving the archetype of the Original Man the homosexual man is holding onto a richness that has to some extent been lost by a one-sided sexual being (1953–77, vol. 19a: 71). He further suggests that no useful conclusions about a person's sexuality can be reached by citing the mother complex as playing a role: typical effects of a mother complex are homosexuality, Don Juanism, impotence or a great capacity for same-sex friendship (vol. 19a: 85). In other words it can lead to the heights of refinement or the depths of depravity, to a homosexual or a heterosexual object choice.

Thus we have seen Jung move from a position of defining homosexuality as a manifestation of regressed sexuality, caused by an inadequate relationship with one or both parents, towards seeing it as possibly constitutional, or finally as a manifestation of a person's connection to a divine archetype. However, it is also important to remind ourselves that Jung emphasises the need for diversity in society if it is to remain healthy and continue to develop. His practice as an analyst and his keen observation of social behaviour led him to question society's condemnation of homosexuality as either a sin on the one hand or pathology on the other, and of individuals as bad or mad. He makes clear his belief that both these diagnoses are faulty and destructive.

I began this chapter with a quote that clearly demonstrates Jung's belief that the individual's prime purpose in life is to seek individuation. This means that the most important thing for a person to do is to break from identification with socially imposed norms in order to find their own way of connecting to the divine, however individuals may perceive this.

Jung, the man, may continue to have ambivalent attitudes towards those who are sexually different from the social norm. His approach is Eurocentric in that he ignores (most probably because he was unaware of) the role that same-sex relationships have in tribal cultures, invariably described as 'primitive' by him. Nevertheless I submit that Jung, the first exponent of analytical psychology, recognises that homosexual life choices can be one way of attaining individuation.

How has history informed practice?

The difficulties of presenting a coherent or comprehensive view of analytical psychology, as it is practised today by Jungian depth psychologists, stem from the fact that the different schools within analytical psychology hold widely different views about individual development, pathology and the path to individuation. This will depend on whether they accept a developmental view (derived from psychoanalysis) of human growth and development (the developmental school), or whether they foreground Jung's preoccupation with mythology and symbols of the Self (the classical school).

Inevitably, any theory based on a reductionist explanation of human development, which seeks to find causes in the past to explain human misery, must pathologise a homosexual object choice to some extent, since reductionism is based on the notion that there is such a thing as normal, healthy human development in opposition to pathological, unhealthy development: 'the etiological project is utterly implicated in a psychopathological project' (Samuels 1993: 197).

Certainly the majority of psychoanalytic training institutes in London until very recently refused to accept lesbian women or gay men for training, since they considered that their sexual orientation was a manifestation of immature development. Indeed I interviewed a woman in 1996, who had not even discussed her lesbianism with her Jungian analyst, since she feared that this would lead to her failing to be accepted as a Jungian analyst herself. The training that she was doing never once addressed homosexuality or bisexuality theoretically, and these subjects were never discussed during seminars.

The most recent book containing contributions from Jungian analysts belonging to the Society of Analytical Psychology, *Contemporary Jungian Analysis* (Alister and Hauke 1998) does not contain a single indexed reference to homosexuality or heterosexuality, although Colman's chapter, 'Contrasexuality and the unknown soul' does refer to both in his discussion of *anima/animus* (1998: 201). Presumably it was not considered significant enough to index these references.

However there is one chapter (Beebe 1998) in *Post-Jungians Today* which considers the implications of an analysis between a heterosexual analyst and a lesbian patient, and makes clear that it is not her homosexuality *per se* which is the problem but the homophobia of society. Things are changing, if only slowly.

A further book, *Same-Sex Love and the Path to Wholeness* (Hopcke *et al.* 1993) explores same-sex love from a Jungian perspective. It provides personal accounts by individuals of the particular ways in which women loving women and men loving men can lead to transformation through the experience of sameness. It explores homoeroticism in the arts and then tentatively offers theories on homosexuality from a Jungian perspective.

Apart from this there is very little in the post-Jungian literature which looks specifically at the particular needs of the lesbian, gay or bisexual client. Kulkarni (1997: 98) refers to Claire Douglas' (1990) description of two categories of Jungian theorists who do, the conservators and the reformulators, and adds a third, the radicals.

The conservators attempt to retain Jung's theories and do not question them, although they expand on them. At worst, Kulkarni suggests, these theorists retain the homophobia of Jung; at best they are liberal in attitude but nevertheless still write from within a heterosexist paradigm. Among this group Kulkarni places those who are attempting to reclaim the goddess, who call for 'a restoration of the feminine' (1997: 99). She sees this as yet another attempt to stay within a gendered paradigm, which inevitably pathologises homosexuality and bisexuality. I suggest that while this group may stick to the letter of Jung's law, they are in fact ignoring his spirit. He always maintained that he was not interested in initiating a school, although in practice he drew a band of devoted followers around him in Zurich, including many strong and articulate women. But his stated aim in his work was always to encourage his analysands to find their own path towards individuation.

The reformulators attempt to deal with the problematic areas of Jung's theory by redefining it, but the basic theory is not really challenged. Kulkarni (1997) differentiates three subgroups in this category: the first comes from a mainly feminist perspective, but nevertheless does not challenge the heterosexism inherent in Jung. The second does not claim a feminist perspective and seems intent on holding onto gendered concepts such a masculinity and femininity, which I discuss below; if they refer to homosexuality at all it is usually pejoratively. The third group consists not only of lesbian and gay theorists, but also of some heterosexual writers engaged in 'gay-affirmative' research. Kulkarni also sees their approach as doomed, since it is still framed in gendered language and seems intent on holding onto concepts which in her view need to be radically rethought or discarded altogether. In effect Kulkarni regards all these approaches as merely tinkering at the edges: while they may question they do not actually challenge the heterosexism embedded in the theory. My own view is that to hold onto gendered concepts of the *anima/animus* (masculinity, femininity and contrasexuality, see below) in their original form of necessity leads one into a mire of contradictions, which do not help anybody, heterosexual or homosexual.

Kulkarni (1997) reserves her full approbation solely for the last group, the radicals. These theorists, few in number, 'Are intent on taking Jung in entirely new directions, beyond himself (and usually in spite of himself). They are the iconoclasts, the freethinkers, the agitators, the renegades. They are on the cutting edge, as I see it, of Jungian feminist thought' (p. 105). The radicals have questioned a number of sacred cows of Jungian theory, namely issues of gender, contrasexuality, the *anima/animus*, and the 'feminine' and 'masculine' principles. They consider that these categories need to be drastically reconstructed if not discarded from the theory altogether. Samuels, for example, stresses the importance of holding onto the idea of gender confusion, which he sees as 'liberating us from the rigidity of gender stereotyping' (1989: 97). For example, if women are seen as embodying something that can be defined as 'the eternal feminine', and men as embodying something that can be defined as 'the eternal masculine', we are inexorably drawn into unhelpful debates about normality. Elsewhere, in a discussion about 'fathering' and 'mothering', where he deliberately questions 'the limits of anatomy and biology when it comes to parenting', Samuels welcomes the confusion that such questioning creates, since this also 'challenges the primacy of heterosexuality as the overall frame in which these kinds of subjects are discussed' (1993: 132).

In my view it is this group and those analysts and therapists influenced by them which offers the most to individuals interested in Jungian therapy. In practice, however, whatever individual Jungian analysts might think about working with lesbian women, gay men or bisexuals, the reality is that the majority working at present in Britain have not had a training which has validated bisexual or homosexual experience, either theoretically or in terms of clinical supervision. Thus they may not necessarily have a background which adequately prepares them for working gay-affirmatively.

Why seek Jungian therapy?

A Jungian approach has the potential to offer much to lesbian, gay and bisexual clients who seek therapy, in that the central focus of the work is towards enabling an individual woman or man to achieve wholeness (individuation in Jungian terms) – it takes a *whole life* perspective. By this I do not mean that the aim is for everything to be sorted out and for the person to live happily ever after. The concept of wholeness includes confusion and chaos, dark as well as light. Most importantly it includes an acceptance of a person's shadow. By this is meant that the individual has come to accept those aspects of themselves that have been denied or feared, and might well include positives as well as negatives. For example, a conscious fear of failure or envy of another's success might well be blocking an unconscious fear of succeeding and of becoming visible. Writer's block, which I certainly experienced with this chapter, is a manifestation of this. In this sense, a Jungian approach attempts to move beyond a mere understanding of opposites in the psyche to holding 'the tension between claims of and tendencies towards unity and claims of and tendencies towards diversity' (Samuels 1989: 4).

In my own clinical practice I have often found that the experience of this tension in me has led to a feeling of deadness, disorientation and an inability to concentrate. It is as if the struggle in my client between their need for closeness and the equally strong need for separateness leads to an inner paralysis that gets communicated in the transference and leaves me feeling equally paralysed. Over the years I have taken this to supervision and tried to find ways of dealing with it, since it invariably leaves me feeling guilty and inadequate. I have tried fighting the feeling, usually by going up into my head and working hard to interpret, but that has never been successful. I have tried simply to endure it. On occasion I have even risked sharing my state with my client, once I have escaped from it. Invariably this has been helpful to some extent, since they recognise it as something that they are also feeling. But I have never really felt satisfied with any of these alternatives.

It was only recently that I discovered a more meaningful interpretation of what was going on. It was as if a light had been switched on in a dark place. Jung's use of the metaphor of alchemy as a means to understanding the relationship between analyst/therapist on the one hand and analysand/client on the other, stresses the sense of equality between them: it is an I/Thou relationship, to use Buber's phrase (Buber 1994). The therapeutic process itself becomes a '*vas alchemicum*', a sacred space, in which both analyst and client share the experience of relationship and thereby become transformed and experience transcendence.

Schwartz-Salent, in *The Mystery of Human Relationship* (1998) explores the significance of this for the analyst and maintains that she or he must be prepared to go into their own 'mad part' if they are to meet the 'mad part' of their clients. This is only possible if they are willing to let go of being the one who knows and to stay with not knowing. In this process a third area – the field – becomes constellated, in which something new, which belongs to neither the client nor the therapist, emerges. It is their joint contemplation of this third thing which leads to a greater understanding of what has until then been denied – the shadow, if you like – and which has contributed to the client's distress. Schwartz-Salent stresses that it is the analyst's willingness to forego being in authority which paves the way for the process of transformation to occur. Or as Samuels puts it, summarising Jung's attitude in his video discussion with Michael Jacobs: 'You can exert no influence unless you are subject to influence' (1997).

It was my reading of Schwartz-Salent's text that helped me to make sense of the disorientation I described above. The following example illustrates my experience of this.

Case example 1

I have been working with Annabel (not her real name) for about a year and we meet once a week for an hour and a half. She feels comfortable about her sexuality as a lesbian. She has 'always known' that she was a lesbian since adolescence, although she did not come out until she went to university. Her family knows but it is not openly talked about at home. She is, however, frequently criticised for 'being difficult'. Although her sister, to whom she is close, accepts her sexuality (in my experience this is a very common scenario).

Annabel's reason for seeking therapy was that she has a history of failed relationships. She longs for closeness with another woman but is equally terrified of it. The pattern of her relationships is for them to start full of passion and to end, usually quite suddenly, just as she feels a desire to commit herself. At this moment her girlfriend will either tell her that she no longer loves her, or might begin an affair. For Annabel, this is a devastating moment. As I listened to her describing this pattern, the image of someone being either in prison or on the run came to me. Annabel agreed that this is how it often feels for her.

In the past six months or so in our work together, I have found myself increasingly falling into the trance-like state, which I describe above. To begin with I tried to ignore it, working extra hard to deny it and continue as if nothing untoward was happening to me. By doing this I was becoming increasingly out of touch with the reality of disconnectedness in the room between us. But this was not brought up or worked with. By doing this I was, in effect, acting out the silence and lack of connectedness in Annabel's reality, which she encountered with her family.

On one occasion I said something, which in my trance-like state made perfect sense, only to be jerked out of the trance when Annabel looked at me in astonishment and asked me why I had said that. I found myself wondering the same thing myself, but since I could no longer remember what I had said nor get back to the state in which it was a logical response, I could not give an explanation that made sense to either of us. After fumbling for a while, trying not to acknowledge that I had no idea, I finally admitted that I had been having difficulty in concentrating and that the statement made no sense to me any more. We continued somewhat uncomfortably with the session and no more was said about it.

In a later session when the same thing began to happen, I attempted to ask Annabel if she ever felt out of touch with reality and she replied that she often did. So I admitted that I had been feeling that way in the session, which interested her greatly. I also felt better that the truth of my experience was now out in the space between us, but I was not very sure where to go with it. I did not at that stage make the connection with Annabel's family's reaction to her lesbianism, or to her own fear of closeness to me as a lesbian woman.

It was at this point that I began reading Schwartz-Salent's (1998) book and saw my experience mirrored for me in the examples he gave from his own practice and in his struggles to cope with the resulting counter-transference feelings evoked in him. I felt as if I were being rescued from drowning.

Since then I have tried to stay with the feelings of deadness when they occur, which I call 'becoming the stone woman' and I have been able to share this image with Annabel, without attempting either to explain it or interpret it. It is a huge relief to me that I no longer try to escape the discomfort of not knowing what to do and it seems to help Annabel to know that I too can feel the sort of deadness that she so often feels. Together we have contemplated what it might mean, making the connections with her family relationships. As a result our relationship feels more real and this is enabling us to explore what happens to her when she gets close to somebody in a sexual relationship.

Therapy as an alchemical journey involves the coming together of therapist and client in a *coniunctio* or 'sacred marriage'. While acknowledging the heterosexism of this image, it nevertheless symbolises the warring of opposing elements which finds a resolution in their interconnectedness and it is, thus, a powerful metaphor for the therapeutic relationship as it is experienced in the consulting room. This is inevitably followed by a descent into the *nigredo*, the darkness of disconnection. Schwartz-Salent reminds us that this process of alienation and the experience of despair are an inevitable, normal and healthy stage in the journey of the Self towards individuation. Therapist and client must together have the courage to stay in the *nigredo* and experience the darkness of separation, the death of the soul, for out of this death comes a rebirth.

By surviving this ongoing cycle of closeness, followed by disconnectedness many times both therapist and client can gradually withdraw their projections onto the other, thereby lessening the pain of separateness. This process of integrating the shadow, coming to terms with those aspects of the Self that have long felt unacceptable, is an integral part of the search for individuation.

Culturally in the West we are bombarded with messages that exhort us to deny our sense of disconnection and of alienation. It is hardly surprising, therefore, that so many people suffer from stress and mental ill-health when they are told that it is a sign of their pathology to feel what they feel rather than a sign of the splits in society. Their pain and despair is put down to there being something wrong with them which can only be put right with drugs or a more manic consumption of material goods, in order to make them feel 'better'. I suggest that it is society's madness which is being denied, not their own. An alchemical approach to psychic pain allows for, indeed is based on, a confrontation with this despair. Rather than fleeing in terror from the shadow, we turn round and go to meet it instead (Haslam 1997).

Jung believed that a person's truth is shaped in the context of both their personal history and that of the collective. In its recognition of the importance of taking into account the social and cultural context in understanding a person's pain a Jungian approach brings together both inner and outer reality. It moves beyond a merely literal understanding and interpretation of that person's history to making sense of it in terms both of their ancestral heritage and what Jung called the 'collective unconscious'. In this sense it connects the individual to something larger than her or himself.

Jung's insistence on the valuing of individual and cultural diversity – on pluralism (Samuels 1989) – means that a person's ethnicity or sexual orientation is, in theory, not pathologised, and this allows for an exploration of the way society scapegoats those who are different or who challenge the status quo as a way of denying aspects of itself: 'This Other is a creative other and needs nurturing for it is closely linked with another other – the convenient receptacle for prejudice and projection, the subject of fantasies of superiority' (Samuels 1989: 5).

Jung's theory of archetypes can be enabling as well as disabling. An archetype is a deep structure in the psyche, a noumenal hypothetical pattern[2] (Samuels 1997) which profoundly affects the experience in consciousness of images that are known from the culture. Where archetypes suggest an exploration of a person's inner world which goes beyond personal history they can liberate the individual. For example, I suggest that the reason many lesbian women and gay men responded so profoundly to the death of Princess Diana in 1997 was precisely because she embodied for us the archetype of the Outsider, who took up the cudgels on behalf of other outsiders, not least people with AIDS and landmine victims. If, on the other hand, archetypal theory is used to pathologise them by reference to eternal psychological verities then it is unhelpful (see below).

My reference to Diana as an archetype should not be understood as an attempt to fit an individual into a preconceived structure. Rather it is a quest for personal meaning making. It is 'a quest to understand whatever phenomenon [lies] before [therapist and client] by accepting it on its own terms' (Kulkarni 1997: 166). Jung's theory of psychological types could be seen as just such an attempt to fit people into preconceived structures. Nevertheless it is different from labelling people according to heredity or as a result of particular parenting. It is a way of identifying individuals according to character structure, which recognises that we are different in our approaches to experience, without reference to our sexuality or gender. It is a theory of consciousness, which seeks to identify an individual's basic responses to the world, according to whether they are more extroverted or introverted. In addition Jung identifies personality according to four functions: the so-called rational functions, thinking and feeling; and the irrational functions, sensation and intuition. (By 'feeling' Jung meant something other than an emotional response; rather it concerns a person's ability to judge and evaluate the appropriateness of a thing.)

One element of a Jungian therapy is to identify the ways in which the tensions in a person between their thinking and feeling functions on the one hand, and sensation and intuition functions on the other, create difficulties both for their relationship to the Self and to the outside world. Jung suggests that a person has a dominant way in which they respond consciously to the world. The inferior function is buried in the unconscious and can usually only be identified and brought into the light of consciousness through therapeutic work. This is the function that can cause the individual difficulties, because it is denied. Like a child, who feels herself to be invisible, it creates chaos in a person's life in order to gain attention. One of the aims of therapy is to bring this inferior function into consciousness, in order to facilitate a path to wholeness, or the development of integrity (Beebe 1998: 53).

This is well illustrated by fairy tales of the Fisher King, an ailing old man with three sons, who are sent out into the world to find a way of rescuing the kingdom from desolation. Invariably it is the youngest son, the 'dummling', seen by everyone as stupid and naive, who brings back the treasure. This youngest son is the symbol of the buried inferior fourth function, which brings back health and vitality to the kingdom. In spite of the sexist nature of this depiction, the symbol of the weakling, who will rescue the kingdom, is an apt metaphor for what therapy seeks to do in enabling the inferior function first to be identified and then brought into consciousness.

Mary Loomis in *Dancing the Wheel of Psychological Types* (1991) has made a connection with Native American teachings about the medicine wheel, which I have found fascinating, particularly since my interest was previously aroused by my learning of the important place that women who love women and men who love men have in the spiritual and cultural life of the community. Loomis weaves the two systems together in a way that is enlightening and helpful.

A final point to be made is that ideally a Jungian approach is based on a willingness on the part of the therapist 'to dispense with theoretical knowledge' in order to approach 'the task of understanding with a free and open mind' (Jung 1953–77, vol. 10: 495) in order to help people 'get a hold on their own lives' (Kulkarni 1997: 177).

Aspects of Jung's theory which are unhelpful in a gay affirmative approach

The fact that so much of Jung's theory is based on an assumption of innate, biologically-based characteristics of femininity and masculinity means that it is all too easy to assume that there is only one right way of being a woman or a man:

> as the mediator between outside and inside, the persona is the place in the personality in which a compromise must be forged between collective values and individual needs. Since patriarchy and heterosexism typically assume anatomically specific behavior patterns for boys and girls at birth, a masculine or feminine face comes to be pasted on children according to gender, with heterosexuality indiscriminately expected as the developmental norm.
>
> (Hopcke 1991: 149)

For example, Jung's theory of the *anima* and the *animus* instantly leads us into trouble, not least because of the sexist nature of this pair of opposites. It is quite clear that for Jung the *anima* is a more positive inner figure than the *animus*, which is invariably seen pejoratively. In addition the *anima* as soul is not the opposite of the *animus* as spirit. One might well ask whether this implies that men have no spirit and women have no soul.

Post-Jungians have repeatedly attempted to redress this imbalance by suggesting that maybe both men and women can have an *anima* and *animus*, and that they merely represent those qualities of otherness that we project onto another, usually when we fall in love. Colman, for example, suggests that the *anima* as soul might 'turn up in same-sex guise for homosexuals' (1998: 104). Samuels (1997) describes the *animus* and *anima* as carrying the unlived potential of the individual, which must be liberated if she or he is to live a full life. Kulkarni (1997) rejects all attempts to salvage these images of contrasexuality, precisely because they are so embedded in gendered thinking.

Nevertheless, the concept of *anima* and *animus* as mediators between a person's conscious and unconscious and as basically sexual in nature is a useful one. Hopcke (1991) argues that society's assumptions of heterosexuality have an effect on the way that individuals present themselves in the world, as any lesbian woman, gay man or bisexual is likely to attest. In the same way, the images that emerge into consciousness through dreams are likely to be infected by the culture's attitudes towards behaviours, which are associated with one or other gender. The following example of a dream illustrates this:

> I am in a boat, sailing swiftly along a fast-flowing river. Suddenly the river dries up, but the boat continues on its way, because it has developed a row of little wheels along the keel that enable it to keep upright. As we hurtle along the, by now, dry riverbed I hear the captain of the boat, in the guise of an ex-supervisor of mine, singing lustily above my head. The boat magically stays upright in spite of the lack of water, until we suddenly emerge into open sea.

It seems to me that the meaning of this dream is quite clear. When I am in a tight spot and flying along by the seat of my pants, so to speak, it is my *animus* that keeps my spirits up with a song. The fact that it appears in the guise of a man is, frankly, less important than the fact that it affirms my ability to hang on in there when the going gets rough.

If the individual experiences an inner emptiness, which they seek to compensate for by finding completion through relationship to another, the concept of *anima* can be valuable as a way of understanding this loss of soul. The need to take back this projection and recover one's *anima* from the shadow can then become one of the tasks of therapy.

Case example 2

Jeannette is a young African British woman who has been coming for counselling for about 14 months. Her presenting problem was a deep, at times almost suicidal, despair. There were many contributing factors to this, including a difficult relationship with her partner and an extremely problematic relationship with her family, who do not know that she is lesbian. We have spoken much about the impossibility of her coming out to her extended family because of the strong homophobia that she would encounter if she did. Her despair is a response to her sense of alienation from her community and her equally strong sense of being an outsider in the white world, in particular the gay community which can be very racist in its attitudes towards people from ethnic minorities (Mason-John 1995). We could, therefore, describe her inner emptiness as indeed a loss of soul. Much of our work has been concerned with reconnecting with the soul. By this I mean enabling Jeanette to find a way of holding onto her cultural and spiritual roots while at the same time valuing herself as a lesbian, even when she encounters hostility from the outside world.

Jeanette's relationship to her *animus* has been equally difficult. She has feared to be assertive, because she is terrified of her own rage, fearing that it could annihilate others. As a result she has been passive and unable to protect herself from the tyranny of others, including her partner, who used to be prone to violence with her. However, as she has learned to integrate her *animus* and value the energy it releases in her, she has been better able to prevent others from violating her.

Jeanette is quite clear that the relationship with me, in which she can feel held as she encounters her inner emptiness, has been instrumental in keeping her out of psychiatric hospital. Both she and I know of others who have fallen between the cracks of two cultures, experiencing homophobia in the one and racism in the other, without the kind of support that could have made sense of their inner splits, and whose lives have been devastated as a result.

Key issues that need to be addressed in working affirmatively

Clearly the first issue is that of the potential for the therapeutic relationship to be abusive, when a therapist's need to be in authority is challenged by a client, or when their clients force them to face some unexamined prejudices. This can happen in many ways.

It may be hard for the therapist to let go of their need to remain hidden from their clients about such issues as where, how long and in what way they have trained and what supervision arrangements they may have. I believe it is important for these issues to be talked about if the client so wishes. This includes the right of clients to know the sexual identity of the therapist. A therapist must be willing to disclose this and to work with what it might mean in the course of the therapy, without interpreting it as a manifestation of the client's neurosis or a desire to challenge some earlier taboo about family secrets. These issues must be brought into the *vas alchemicum* and worked with.

It follows from this that the therapist needs to be willing to own and to work on their own issues brought up by the therapy outside the therapeutic relationship, either in their own therapy or supervision. Otherwise there is a danger of their projecting their own insecurities and/or hostilities around same-sex love onto their clients, by pathologising them as immature or the result of an identification with a contrasexual archetype, or, if they are bisexual, by living this out literally rather than symbolically.

At the same time they need to be ready to work with the reality of desire within the therapeutic relationship and what it might mean for both, without acting this out, which is always abusive. Lesbian and gay therapists will confirm that sexual desire is a live issue in their work with their clients and this includes sexual feelings aroused in the therapeutic relationship itself.

Another issue is the extent to which one discloses personal history. There is a fine line to be drawn here and I am finding that I need to be sure that my reasons for disclosure are to further the work rather than to fulfil my own needs for empathy, or as a seductive way of seeking my client's approval. In other words I need to remember that I am 'in it' along with them.

An image I find myself using to share this sense of reciprocity with my clients is that of a voyage into the unknown, where I see myself as a kind of co-pilot, who knows the ropes, has done quite a lot of sailing and has brought along her charts, but who has not been on this particular voyage before. The important thing for us both to remember is that we are bound to hit squalls and may well be in danger of capsizing. We might even find ourselves in places labelled on the old maps 'here be dragons'. It is at those moments, in particular, that survival depends on our trust in and reliance on each other.

The first time I suggested this and admitted that I was at the outer limits of my competence as a therapist, my client, a lesbian woman who had already demonstrated enormous trust in me in spite of earlier mistakes which we had had to negotiate, looked astounded. It had never occurred to her that I might be out of my depth or floundering in my work with her. And yet she had pushed me to go to the outer reaches of what I knew as a result of her own needs. My willingness to acknowledge this led to a real deepening of our relationship, which meant that the final six months were a time where, between us, much was achieved as we learned to trust each other in this joint enterprise. What I am really talking about here is my own countertransference feelings, which I have to process in my own therapy and/or supervision rather than acting them out on my clients.

The therapist also needs to demonstrate a sense of receptivity towards whatever a client might bring, including issues around their sexuality. If a therapist does not consider the possibility of there being an alternative to heterosexuality, this is likely to manifest itself in their responses to the cues they may get from their clients, who will undoubtedly pick up this lack of awareness and consequently feel unable to disclose their anxieties around their sexuality. I am now certain that the premature ending of sessions with one of my early clients was as a result of my not picking up such cues, largely because I had still not come to terms with my own lesbianism, and thus I ignored the signals emanating from her. It follows from this that there is a danger of using heterosexual relationship patterns as the norm, thus ignoring the potential for alternative forms of relationship and lifestyle for lesbian women, gay men or bisexuals: 'The existence of a thriving gay community undermines a social system that deploys heterosexism to maintain control of women' (Samuels 1993: 197).

Finally, the therapist must be clear that not everything that a client brings can be put down to a problem of their sexual orientation. We have other issues as well, that are to do with aspects of our lives that may have nothing to do with our sexuality. The therapist also needs to recognise that some problems may be a response to racist and/or heterosexist oppression, or to cultural expectations about how to live the good life and be successful. Such expectations lead to internalised oppression, which will need to be worked with in the therapy. This means that the therapist must have a political awareness about the nature of such oppression (Samuels 1993).

In my view an approach which seeks to enable the individual to become more fully themselves must be valuable for lesbian women, gay men and bisexuals. Jung's insistence that the therapist must put aside their own prejudices and values in order to understand their clients' perspective means that in principle we should be well served by entering into a Jungian therapy. Unfortunately the reality is less rosy.

Individuals who are interested in exploring a Jungian approach, which as I have demonstrated has much to offer, need to be clear about their needs and to be ready to question any potential therapist about their own attitudes before embarking on this journey. They need to pay attention to their gut and to ask themselves whether they can trust this person as a companion on their path in search of the *lapis* – their journey towards the Self.

Notes

1 Pathologically, a rejection of instinctuality, hence a depotentiating of the personality, or a projection of unacceptable facets of the personality onto others. It is also possible to identify with the shadow – a form of negative inflation such as self-depreciation, lack of self-confidence or fear of success (and a peculiar

'analytic' state in which everything is put down to dark and nasty unconscious motivations) (Samuels 1985: 93).

2 In this context *noumenal* means a hypothetical pattern which is intuited rather than being provable by recourse to observable, material existence.

References

Alister, I. and Hauke, C. (eds) (1998) *Contemporary Jungian Analysis: Post-Jungian Perspectives from the Society of Analytical Psychology*. London and New York: Routledge.

Beebe, J. (1998) Toward a Jungian analysis of character, in A. Casement (ed.) (1998) *Post-Jungians Today*. London and New York: Routledge.

Buber, M. (1994) *I and Thou*, trans. R. Gregor Smith. Edinburgh: T&T Clark.

Colman, W. (1998) Contrasexuality and the unknown soul, in I. Alister and C. Hauke (eds) *Contemporary Jungian Analysis: Post-Jungian Perspectives from the Society of Analytical Psychology*. London and New York: Routledge.

Douglas, C. (1990) *The Woman in the Mirror: Analytical Psychology and the Feminine*. Boston: Sigo.

Haslam, D. (1997) Myth, legend and fairytale in therapeutic work with lesbian and gay clients, *Self and Society*, 24(6): 8–11.

Hopcke, R.H. (1991) *Jung, Jungians and Homosexuality*. Boston and London: Shambala.

Hopcke, R.H., Lofthus-Carrington, K. and Wirth, S. (eds) (1993) *Same-Sex Love and the Path to Wholeness*. Boston and London: Shambala.

Jung, C.G. (1953–77) *The Collected Works of C.G. Jung*, vols 1–20, trans. R.F.C. Hull, (eds) H. Read, M. Fordham and G. Adler. London: Routledge and Kegan Paul.

Kulkarni, C. (1997) *Lesbians and Lesbianisms: A Post-Jungian Perspective*. London and New York: Routledge.

Loomis, M. (1991) *Dancing the Wheel of Psychological Types*. Wilmette, IL: Chiron Publications.

Mason-John, V. (1995) *Talking Black: Lesbians of Black and Asian Descent Speak Out*. London: Cassell.

Samuels, A. (1985) *Jung and the Post-Jungians*. London: Routledge & Kegan Paul.

Samuels, A. (1989) *The Plural Psyche: Personality, Morality and the Father*. London and New York: Routledge.

Samuels, A. (1993) *The Political Psyche*. London and New York: Routledge.

Samuels, A. (1997) *Michael Jacobs in Conversation with Andrew Samuels: Jung and the Post Jungians* (video). Leicester: University of Leicester, Department of Adult Education and Audio-Visual Services.

Schwartz-Salant, S. (1998) *The Mystery of Human Relationship: Alchemy and the Transformation of the Self*. London and New York: Routledge.

Simon, G. (1996) What is gay affirmative therapy? Conference paper, Association of Lesbian, Gay and Bisexual Psychologies Conference, University of Nottingham, 16–17 September.

Cognitive-behavioural therapy

Introduction

This chapter describes the cognitive-behavioural approach to psychotherapy with lesbians, bisexuals and gay men. Outlined in the first section are theoretical aspects: the generic cognitive-behavioural therapy (CBT) model and its features; the CBT attitude to 'homosexuality'; and later developments of particular relevance to this client group. The second section focuses on the clinical use of CBT with lesbian and gay clients and outlines a number of case examples (based on composites rather than individuals). The chapter finishes with some recommendations for good practice.

I will not focus on the exclusively behavioural tradition, which is based on radical learning theory. This has not been able to give an adequate explanation of complex human behaviours and therefore has little relevance for CBT practitioners in this area. This chapter is based primarily on clinical work with gay men, and so caution should be exercised in generalising to bisexuals and lesbian women. However, since the model is a generic one, the framework is similar with all client groups, although particular issues may be different.

Theoretical aspects

Overview of the CBT model

CBT is a psychotherapy approach that looks specifically at the links between emotions, thoughts, behaviour, physiology and the environment. Particular attention is paid to conscious thoughts, biased and distorted thought processes, unhelpful beliefs, and their link with emotional distress. The therapist helps clients to examine such unhelpful thought processes and to learn other, more realistic and helpful ways to formulate experiences. Behavioural tests are used to explore predictions based on 'irrational' beliefs and to examine whether, even if the feared event took place, this would be catastrophic and the person would not be able to successfully cope. This element of behavioural testing provides the 'B' in CBT.

In Britain, however, 'CBT' is largely synonymous with the most widely-practised form of cognitive therapy, that based on Aaron T. Beck (1976, 1988; Beck *et al.* 1990). An older form of cognitive therapy, rational emotive therapy (RET, which was later renamed REBT, with the addition of 'behaviour') was established by Albert Ellis (1962). However, this has not taken off to the same extent with, for example, Dryden (1996) reporting that a minority of mental health practitioners have adopted its principles. RET will not, therefore, be the primary focus of this chapter (Wolfe 1992 gives an account of working in such a way).

Beck was a psychoanalytically trained psychiatrist who became dissatisfied theoretically and clinically with this approach. He was also aware of the emerging findings on information processing from cognitive psychologists. His model of emotional disorder is that distress results from the activation of negative beliefs that lead to biased and distorted thoughts about the self, the world and other people, and the future (the 'negative cognitive triad'). Such distortions include all-or-nothing thinking, catastrophisation and personalisation. These can lead to a misinterpretation of the world and one's place in it, with resulting misplaced emotional responses. CBT initially focused on depression and anxiety problems. However, the approach has been applied and found to be effective in an ever-increasing range of areas such as with couples (Beck 1988), people with personality disorder (Beck *et al.* 1990; Young 1990), and people with low self-esteem (Fennell 1997). There is a long tradition of empirical evaluation of CBT, and it has proved to be an effective treatment for many specific problems.

Features of the CBT method

The cornerstone of CBT is guided discovery using Socratic questioning techniques (see page 30). This is done in the context of a collaborative relationship – a partnership that is as equal as possible. The therapist is viewed as having expert psychological knowledge and the client is seen as being the expert on themselves. The therapeutic alliance is important but not all-important – i.e. not the main vehicle for change. All five interacting systems (cognitive, affective, behavioural, physiological and environmental) are addressed but usually the emphasis is on the cognitive as this is an accessible point for psychological intervention and the cognitive-affective link has empirical support. The focus is primarily on the 'here and now', especially factors that maintain the problem. The past is relevant to the understanding of current difficulties in that it is here that the foundation for the belief system has been laid.

In the first few sessions an individualised conceptualisation of the person's problems is formulated and explicitly shared. Homework tasks are also central to CBT whether they are reading, thought monitoring and challenging, or behavioural tests. The goal is for the client to become their own therapist and to learn enduring skills. CBT is generally brief, focused and time limited (typically fewer than 20 sessions).

The radical behavioural tradition

As mentioned in the introduction, this chapter does not focus on the purely behavioural approach. Reviews and critiques of behavioural therapy aimed at 'conversion' to heterosexuality may be found in Bancroft (1974), West (1977, Ch. 9) and Silverstein (1996). Clinicians have variously employed aversion therapy using electric shock, drugs or the imagination to 'extinguish' homosexual desire; systematic desensitisation to 'overcome' heterosexual anxiety; and guided masturbation and fantasy to condition sexual behaviour. Behavioural approaches to sexual orientation such as these are not practised in mainstream psychology today due to both the evolution of ethical awareness and their extremely limited therapeutic success (e.g. see Haldeman 1994). However, their usage may still be seen with other sexual minorities such as 'transvestitic fetishists' and paedophiles, although again with extremely limited success and ethical disquiet about such procedures.

Attitudes to homosexuality

> [CBT] is *uniquely suited* to assist clients in accepting and dealing more adaptively with their same-sex sexual orientation.
>
> (Kuehlwein 1992: 255, italics added)

> Cognitive therapy seems an *ideal* therapy approach for helping lesbians develop a positive self-identity because of the influence of individual and social beliefs on this process. By helping women test out these beliefs . . . they can come to more balanced views of the possibilities of lesbian relationships.
>
> (Padesky 1989: 155, italics added)

Comments such as these may arise for some of the following reasons. As there is no explicit tradition within Beckian CBT of pathologising gay and lesbian sexuality as deviant, there is no need to adapt or conveniently overlook aspects of the theory. Indeed there are no references in Beck's writings to sexual minorities. CBT comes from a stance of humanistic empiricism and therefore takes a morally neutral standpoint on sexuality. With its emphasis on a collaborative relationship and guided discovery, CBT can also be seen as a feminist therapy (Padesky 1989).

A criticism that can be levelled at most psychotherapies is that they can individualise societal problems into intrapsychic difficulties. CBT pays attention to the role of environmental factors and looks at maladaptive coping patterns as 'survival strategies' rather than due to some psychopathology of the client. The individualised conceptualisation of difficulties and the use of therapeutic 'curiosity' in guided discovery make CBT ideal for the heterogeneous problems presented by clients – there is no 'off the peg' formulation of sexual orientation and attendant difficulties.

Case descriptions of CBT with lesbian, bisexual and gay clients include: attaining and maintaining a positive lesbian identity (Padesky 1989, and from an RET perspective, Wolfe 1992); developing a positive gay male identity (Kuehlwein 1992); couple therapy with gay men (Ussher 1990); and a number of gay men referred to an HIV setting (George 1993).

Another reason why CBT has no explicit homophobic history could simply be a reflection of the relative youth of the approach. With the older RET there has been more of this homophobic and heterosexist tradition. Ellis trained and practised from a psychoanalytic tradition and published accounts of the treatment of 'severe homosexual problems' (Ellis 1956). In this paper he makes it clear that while he considers homosexuality itself to be normal, 'The abnormality in homosexuality consists of the *exclusiveness*, the *fear*, the *fetishistic fixation* or the *obsessive-compulsiveness* which is so often its concomitant' (1956: 191). The treatment advocated was an active form of psychoanalytical psychotherapy which, by 1965, Ellis had further developed into the RET approach. He believed that homosexual behaviour arose from irrational and self-defeating beliefs, which needed to be brought into the light, and challenged. Attention was focused on the accompanying neurotic disturbance, with sexual orientation left to change of its own account (treatment being the removal of heterosexual fears and a reduction of the 'obsessive' need for homosexual outlets as opposed to the eradication of all homosexual interests).

Ellis seems to have adopted the stance that, although homosexual behaviour was universal and normative, *exclusive* homosexuality was pathological: 'most fixed homosexuals, I am convinced, are borderline psychotic or outrightly psychotic' (Ellis 1965: 81). His arguments were based on his opinion that as everyone was innately bisexual, and as there was so much prejudice towards gay people, nobody could rationally choose to live a gay lifestyle! Ellis later revised his view to the position that people may rationally choose an exclusively homosexual (or heterosexual) life, but they may be irrational when they absolutely insist that they cannot under any conditions enjoy any kind of heterosexual (or homosexual) behaviour (Dryden and Neenan 1995). Heterosexual fear may still be seen as one of the 'causes' of homosexuality. For example, Campbell (1985) takes the stance that while homosexuality *per se* is not disordered, in many instances it is a result of a pathological motivation and a way of avoiding the stress of pursuing heterosexual relationships. However, he also states that no authoritative statements can be made regarding this subject due to the lack of research. Interestingly, Ellis himself as an adolescent and young adult was too scared to approach women, an anxiety that he treated by a self-directed exposure programme (Yankura and Dryden 1994).

An additional controversial area for CBT is treatment of men for 'sexual addiction' or 'sexual compulsion'. CBT models have been applied to this area, for example Scragg (1996) on cottaging (having sex in public toilets). While there is acknowledgement of the fact that only a minority of people who cottage find the experience negative (Church *et al.* 1993), Scragg focuses on this minority who experience distress and a feeling of being out of control. Such commentaries on compulsive sexual behaviour show uncomfortable parallels with earlier descriptions of gay people presenting for treatment. As Silverstein (1996: 8) points out: 'What these [gay] men and the patients volunteering for treatment to be cured of their compulsive sexuality have in common is that they have been taught to be ashamed of their sexual desire'.

Nevertheless there is a need for consideration of the distress and social impairment that can accompany the behavioural patterns of such people presenting for treatment. Perhaps CBT can help engender the self-acceptance that actually enables a more full and varied expression and enjoyment of that sexual desire (see case examples at page 31). In addition, in CBT there are specific techniques that may help tackle 'compulsive' cottaging. These include focusing on removing barriers to gay socialising (cognitive restructuring and techniques of systematic desensitisation), identifying antecedents to cottaging, learning how to tolerate negative emotions and guilty feelings, and using 'flashcards' to improve resolve during high-risk situations.

Schema-focused cognitive therapy

As CBT has continued to develop, recent work has been done at the level of the 'schema', the most fundamental level of psychological organisation. Straightforward CBT proved not to be so successful with the more complex cases of enduring and 'characterological' problems. Young (1990) talked about 'early maladaptive schemata' (EMSs) which are the persistent dysfunctional core beliefs believed to underlie enduring psychological problems. EMSs are seen as unconditional, self-perpetuating, dysfunctional (leading to distress), triggered by the environment, linked to high affect, and laid down in the first few years of life. Examples would include fundamentally-held views of the self as worthless, bad, unlovable, or unacceptable, the world as a terrifying, uncontrollable place and other people as dangerous, abusing, or absolutely necessary for security. Schema have been likened to prejudices, in that both have similar resilience, distorting and self-perpetuating properties – they 'fight for survival'. Work on changing them is described by Beck *et al.* (1990), Young (1990) and Padesky (1994a).

Schema-focused cognitive therapy (SFCT) may have particular relevance for working with lesbian, gay and bisexual clients seeking therapy. Hanson and Hartmann (1996) describe how feeling 'different' is a central feature of many gay men's early experience. This difference may begin as early as conscious memories and predate any feeling of being *sexually* different. Familial and societal reactions to expressions of nonconformity may be extremely negative. Self-schema that may be particularly relevant for these clients are hypothesised to include: social isolation and alienation, undesirability or defectiveness (see Young 1990). EMSs are formed not by isolated traumatic events but rather by 'ongoing patterns of everyday noxious experiences with family members and peers which cumulatively strengthen the schema' (Young 1990: 11). Lesbian, bisexual and gay people often experience such an ongoing attack and erosion of self-worth, linked to their growing awareness of belonging to a stigmatised group. A minority will go on to develop negative schema that interfere with their ability to function and enjoy life and, in particular, relationships.

There is no research into the prevalence of EMSs in gay people (or anyone else for that matter). However, Rivers (1995) outlines research showing the link between homophobic bullying and later relationship difficulties and greatly increased suicide behaviour in adolescence. This may support the hypothesis put forward in this chapter that many gay and lesbian people presenting for treatment show evidence of strong negative schema. With such clients the usual CBT techniques of cognitive restructuring may need to be supplemented with the prolonged efforts more associated with SFCT. In addition to the greater treatment length there is also more of a focus on the therapeutic relationship, as the presence of such schema will impede or prevent the development of a therapeutic alliance. Specific techniques of schema identification and schema change may also be required (Kennerley 1997). The recognition of the importance of interpersonal process has obvious links with other therapeutic orientations (and is most fully developed by Safran and Segal 1990). Additionally, more emphasis is placed on emotions directly (as clients may have difficulties putting their feelings into words) with techniques borrowed from psychodrama and Gestalt therapy integrated within an explicitly CBT formulation.

Clinical use of the CBT model

This section looks at putting the ideas of CBT into practice. Clinical work with lesbian, bisexual and gay clients can be divided into two general areas: one in which problems are related explicitly to sexual orientation (e.g.

distress regarding being gay and internalised homophobia), and the other where sexual orientation interacts with a more general mental health difficulty (e.g. social anxiety that is exacerbated by the nature of the urban gay scene). In other words, whether same-sex sexual orientation is the focus or the context of intervention. Of course an additional possibility is that mental health difficulties are incidental to sexual orientation and it is important to consider carefully within each individual formulation whether there is indeed a link. The following section examines situations where clinical work is aimed at fostering a positive 'gay-affirmative' identity.

Exploring the client's beliefs about sexuality and formulation

An important aspect of the CBT approach is to make explicit the beliefs that clients have regarding their sexuality. These have a major impact on how clients view their sexual orientation and their ability to forge a positive identity. This is hardly unique to CBT but perhaps the unique contribution is that of specific *techniques* for uncovering such beliefs. For example, keeping thought records is a common homework task and this can give excellent insight into the belief system. Clients are taught to notice whenever they experience a strong emotion related to the focus of therapy. They record what triggered this emotion and the 'automatic' thoughts that were going through their mind.

Within sessions, guided discovery and Socratic questioning can do the same. Questions include:

- What was it about that situation that made you feel sad?
- What does it mean to be attracted to someone of the same sex?
- What are the advantages, disadvantages and limitations?
- What are the 'truths' about gay people's lives and relationships?
- Where did this information come from?
- How long have you held this belief?

Another way of accessing such beliefs is through examining attitudes to other people:

- Who are the 'good' gays and what is the 'acceptable face' of lesbianism?

Client and therapist work together to produce an explicit formulation of the current situation that answers the four questions: 'What are the difficulties?'; 'Why did they arise?' (early experiences and triggering events); 'Why was I vulnerable to these events?' (belief system); and 'What is maintaining the problem?' (behaviours, thought processes, physiology, avoidance etc.). The sharing of this formulation can make sense of problems, thereby reducing the stigma, empowering the client and providing hope for the future. Therefore, once the beliefs around sexuality are uncovered, links are made between such thoughts and the difficulties that clients are having.

Particularly important is to include those aspects of the situation that maintain the problem – for example, avoidance, withdrawal, distorted thinking processes, hypervigilance to threat, etc.

Case examples 1 and 2

Ahmed had known he was gay for many years and had never considered that he would possibly be able to develop a positive identity and form a relationship with another man. Thought records showed that whenever he was in proximity to gay people or thought about making contact he would feel a wave of despair. This was related to thoughts such as: 'All gay men are sophisticated urbanites', 'They would never accept me' and 'I will never be able to have a relationship with anyone'. Such beliefs resulted not only in feelings of despair but also in behavioural avoidance of such situations, meaning that the beliefs could never be challenged and the status quo would never change. This formulation was shared explicitly with Ahmed, and it was then possible to begin challenging the beliefs and undermining the avoidance (see below).

Bev found herself getting very angry while socialising with other lesbians. This seemed to be related to a difficulty coping with women who were butch in any way. Such anger made it hard for her to form new relationships and to enjoy a social life. Thought records and guided discovery showed the following: 'They are letting the side down'; 'Why can't they act more normally?' It was particularly distressing for Bev to acknowledge her own intolerant attitudes, but sharing the formulation of where these beliefs may have originated resulted in relief ('It's not surprising that you hold some negative beliefs given the strength of society's negative messages . . .'). In addition, when the beliefs had been made more explicit they could be submitted to challenge, as described below.

Challenging negative thinking and beliefs

In addition to exploring beliefs, one of the most important aspects of CBT is to convey the message that a belief is only one view of the world and that there may be other, more realistic or helpful ways of looking at the 'evidence'. It can be extremely useful for clients to realise that they construct reality and that they therefore can have some power to change this construction. CBT provides a structure for examining beliefs. The client is taught a process of evaluating thoughts and beliefs:

- What is the evidence for and against this?
- What thought distortions are present in my thinking?
- What is the effect of thinking like this?

- How helpful is it?
- What is an alternative view?

Behavioural tests can often be the most powerful way of challenging beliefs. The 'coming out' process can be looked at as potentially the most important behavioural challenge to beliefs such as 'Everyone would reject me if they knew that I was gay' (see Davies 1996a, for a fuller account of coming out). It is important to set up behavioural tests as 'no-lose' situations and to explore what the implications of negative responses may be:

- Is it better that they know this information now or in several years time?
- Is it better to realise that you can never be friends now or later?
- Will the person still be rejecting after their initial shock has subsided?
- What is the worst that can happen if they reject you?
- How will you cope with this?

Where beliefs are seen to have a basis in fact then the person can approach them in a problem solving way, rather than avoiding the issue. It may be necessary for the client to change aspects of their environment. There will almost certainly be some true loss to process, but being able to distinguish which are the 'real' problem issues and which are the unwarranted, unrealistic fears can be powerfully enlightening.

Ahmed was able to challenge his beliefs regarding 'all' gay men by increasing his exposure to other men, both on the scene and in a gay activity group. He was therefore able to see a broader more representative range. The activity group was particularly helpful in that he received very clear messages of approval and acceptance.

Bev was helped by developing thought challenges such as: 'I don't care what people think about my sexuality, why do I care about 'butch' lesbians? Only ignorant people would lump all lesbians together and I don't care what they think'. She was also able to look at her binary view of the world (masculine-feminine, strong-weak, etc.) and realise that this did not reflect her experience, but merely reflected received cultural ideas.

Where the formulation suggests that part of the problem for the client is a general ignorance about gay culture and community, homework tasks can include reading, or watching films with a more balanced gay theme. This exposure to gay literature or film may be extremely helpful in beginning to challenge heterosexist beliefs. The absence of role models and cultural invisibility can greatly hinder the development of a gay affirmative stance. Of course the therapist must have previously read or viewed any such recommended material.

Psychoeducation in CBT

Unlike some psychotherapeutic approaches, the use of didactic and psychoeducational methods are acceptable in CBT and there is no need to maintain the neutral 'blank screen'. Therefore, explicitly gay affirmative practice (see Davies 1996b) is acceptable within the theoretical model. It is perhaps particularly important, given the history of mental health treatment of sexual minority clients, that there is a discussion around the current state of knowledge and theory regarding sexual identity formation – for example, the myth of 'distant fathers and overprotective mothers'. Another useful framework that can be shared and explored with clients is stage models of coming out (see Davies 1996a). Particularly where the stage of 'exploration' (Coleman 1981/2) is chronologically incongruent, there may be fears of being foolish or inappropriate. When this is put into context the experience can be normalised.

Use of specific techniques to help coming out

Where formulation suggests that difficulties may relate to a lack of social skills or the confidence to use them, role-play within sessions can help. This can equip the person with confidence in the necessary behavioural skills to actually begin the (continual) process of coming out. In addition, assertiveness skills training can be extremely helpful and arm the client with techniques such as broken-record (restating the same point repeatedly), using empathy to defuse situations and having patience with other's difficulties and reactions.

Where sexual orientation is the context for CBT work

We now explore areas where sexual orientation is the context for a more general difficulty. This is perhaps best illustrated by the case histories described: social anxiety exacerbated by the gay scene; jealousy in the context of negotiation in a gay male couple; and finally a more schema-focused approach. In the last example it is hypothesised the schema developed from, and was strengthened by, reactions to the sexual orientation of the client. It is not suggested that these provide an exhaustive list but rather show the CBT approach in practice. Importantly within each case an individualised formulation was used to guide individually-tailored treatment plans.

Case example 3: social anxiety

Social anxiety is driven by a 'fear of negative evaluation' and high levels of evaluation take place in many gay bars. In addition there can be an extremely perfectionistic standard within gay male culture and an ever-present current of competition often focused around clothing, lifestyle and body image, which is seldom explicitly acknowledged. In this potentially intimidating atmosphere it is therefore hardly surprising that clients experience anxiety.

Charles had developed anxiety problems following the end of an extremely difficult relationship. Well-adjusted to his sexuality and previously confident, he found it extremely anxiety-provoking socialising on the gay scene and making contact with potential new partners. He additionally found the contrast between his old and new self frightening and incomprehensible. Notable in the formulation of his difficulties were the subtle forms of avoidance he employed, so that while present in a bar he would be looking at the floor or out of the window. He was also constantly scanning his body for signs that his anxiety was visible to onlookers.

In therapy he was particularly helped with the formulation of his difficulties. He had already linked the development of his difficulties with the end of the relationship but now could see that their maintenance was due to the factors outlined above, and therefore more within his power to change. He was taught distraction techniques, thought challenges to the anxious thoughts regarding his attractiveness and then a graded hierarchy for exposure to the pub and club scene without using his subtle avoidance. He quickly progressed along this route and his confidence returned. Once this immediate problem was overcome he used his remaining sessions to begin processing his grief over the loss of the relationship.

Case example 4: 'morbid' jealousy

An additional problem can relate to the flexibility of relationships within gay couples. There is a romanticised heterosexual ideal within 'mainstream' society and this model is held up as the blueprint for all relationships. Within gay communities this may be adopted to varying degrees. Problems can arise when each person in a couple has conflicting rules regarding exclusivity and priority.

David came to treatment with low mood and morbid jealousy. He lived with his partner who was frequently away on business. The rules that had been negotiated permitted threesomes and anonymous, recreational sex. However, David had found it increasingly difficult to control his jealous ruminating, checking and insecurity. This was despite the fact that he felt that this was the type of relationship that he wanted (he had explored this and other relationship styles and had also considered the advantages and disadvantages of each).

Formulation of his difficulties showed beliefs relating to the short-lived nature of gay relationships and feelings of low self-worth. A certain level of jealousy can be seen as inevitable and have positive aspects in any relationship but here it had become out of control due to behaviours such as the ruminating and checking which, although providing short-term relief, actually increase the difficulties in the longer term. Individual work helped David to challenge beliefs regarding his self-worth and his partner's love for him. He was also taught ways to limit the time spent ruminating and checking, using a combination of thought challenge and distraction. Couple therapy helped to affirm their commitment to the relationship and enabled them to experiment with ways of enhancing their communication and negotiation styles.

Case example 5: schema-focused work

The final example relates to the use of schema-focused techniques.

Maya came for treatment as a result of low mood, social isolation and long-standing issues of self-esteem. Over a long period of assessment it became clear that her difficulties were related to a very core feeling that she was unacceptable and that other people would reject her. The origins of this belief were in her relationship with her mother who she felt had neither approved of, nor accepted her. Maya had struggled to achieve a sense of being valued, particularly given the growing realisation that she was bisexual and her mother's outright hostility to her when her sexuality became known.

In order to compensate for such feelings of inadequacy, Maya tried to dominate socially to see herself as superior to the people she came into contact with (schema compensation). It is clear how behaving in such a way made it difficult for other people to accept her. In addition she was extremely sensitive to criticism and would be left feeling suicidal should any criticism arise and she were unable to totally denigrate the person that had made it. A bias operated here, in that any positive feedback was instantly rejected ('They want something from me', or 'They are just being nice') while any negative comment would instantly 'hit home'.

Therapy enabled Maya to make links between her early upbringing and some of the extreme beliefs that made her life difficult: 'Never trust anyone for anything'; 'You must never be vulnerable at any time or people will attack you'. She also became more aware of the repeating patterns of behaviour that maintained her 'unacceptability' and 'rejection' schemas. The schema as prejudice model (Padesky 1994b) was explored and she was able to begin interrupting the process of discounting positive information. She was also able to review her evidence of not being accepted in the past. The therapeutic relationship was used as a model where she could explore her usual reactions to intimacy and drop some of her defensiveness. She gradually began to form alternative views relating to acceptance by self and others.

Guidelines for good practice

This final section outlines some general guidelines for ethical CBT work with lesbian, bisexual and gay clients.

- Therapist beliefs must be explored and submitted to challenge. These obviously include negative beliefs, but also overly positive, compensatory beliefs and those denying any difference between gay and straight experience. Unless a gay affirmative stance can be truthfully offered the therapist should not work with such clients.
- Therapists must educate themselves through widespread reading, training, specialist supervision (see Chapter 4) and consultation with knowledgeable others in order to be able to challenge clients' distorted perceptions regarding sexuality. There is now a wealth of material including as a core text Cabaj and Stein (1996) and, to give a UK perspective, *Pink Therapy* (Davies and Neal 1996).
- Current conceptualisation of sexual identity formation must be known and where appropriate shared with the client.
- Diversity and heterogeneity of clients must be acknowledged both in terms of ethnicity, age, geography, class etc. (Greene 1994).
- It is unacceptable and unethical to offer or agree to attempt a sexual orientation 'conversion', or to refer to organisations offering such treatments. The negative effects of such treatments should be made known to clients (e.g. see Stein 1996a). The message should be: they don't work, and they may well harm you.
- There must be some recognition that binary notions of sexual orientation and identity as fixed and immutable represent a biomedical model and the reality is probably more in line with social constructivist positions regarding fluidity, change and sometimes even choice (see Stein 1996b; Neal 1998).
- The concept of 'sexual addiction' is controversial and any 'treatment' must be carefully considered through consultation and supervision.

Concluding remarks

This chapter has illustrated the CBT approach for working with sexual minority clients. CBT can be a highly effective approach to working therapeutically with the broad range of difficulties faced by such clients. Particular strengths of this way of working include the reliance on an individualised case conceptualisation (reflecting the uniqueness of each client), the collaborative, transparent stance, and the virtual absence of a homophobic or heterosexist history. In addition there is strong empirical support for the effectiveness of CBT for many clinical problems.

Acknowledgements

Thanks are due to many people but in particular Khadija Rouf, Anu Sayal-Bennet, Helen Kennerley, Richard Long and my partner Dick L'Estrange.

References

Bancroft, J. (1974) *Deviant Sexual Behaviour: Modification and Assessment.* Oxford: Clarendon.

Beck, A.T. (1976) *Cognitive Therapy and the Emotional Disorders.* New York: Meridian.

Beck, A.T. (1988) *Love is Never Enough.* Harmondsworth: Penguin.

Beck, A.T., Freeman, A., Pretzer, J., Davis, D.D., Fleming, B., Ottavani, R., Beck, J., Simon, K.M., Padesky, C., Meyer, J. and Trexler, L. (1990) *Cognitive Therapy of Personality Disorders.* New York: Guilford.

Cabaj, R.P. and Stein, T.S. (eds) (1996) *Textbook of Homosexuality and Mental Health.* Washington: American Psychiatric Press.

Campbell, I.M. (1985) The psychology of homosexuality, in A. Ellis. and M.E. Bernard (eds) *Clinical applications of Rational Emotive Therapy.* London: Plenum.

Church, J., Green, J., Vearnals, S., and Keogh, P. (1993) Investigation of motivational and behavioural factors influencing men who have sex with other men in public toilets (cottaging), *AIDS Care*, 5(3): 337–46.

Coleman, E. (1981/2) Development stages of the coming out process, *Journal of Homosexuality*, 7: 31–43.

Davies, D. and Neal, C. (eds) (1996) *Pink Therapy: A Guide for Counsellors and Therapists Working with Lesbian, Gay and Bisexual Clients.* Buckingham: Open University Press.

Davies, D. (1996a) Working with people coming out, in D. Davies and C. Neal (eds) *Pink Therapy: A Guide for Counsellors and Therapists Working with Lesbian, Gay and Bisexual Clients.* Buckingham: Open University Press.

Davies, D. (1996b) Towards a model of gay-affirmative therapy, in D. Davies and C. Neal (eds) *Pink Therapy: A Guide for Counsellors and Therapists Working with Lesbian, Gay and Bisexual Clients.* Buckingham: Open University Press.

Dryden, W. (1996) *Inquiries in Rational Emotive Behaviour Therapy.* London: Sage.

Dryden, W. and Neenan, M. (1995) *Dictionary of Rational Emotive Behaviour Therapy.* London: Whurr.

Ellis, A. (1956) The effectiveness of psychotherapy with individuals who have severe homosexual problems, *Journal of Consulting Psychology*, 20: 191–5.

Ellis, A. (1962) *Reason and Emotion in Psychotherapy.* New York: Lyle Stuart.

Ellis, A. (1965) *Homosexuality: Its Causes and Cure.* New York: Lyle Stuart.

Fennell, M.J.V. (1997) Low self-esteem: a cognitive perspective, *Behavioural and Cognitive Psychotherapy*, 25: 1–25.

George, H. (1993) Sex, love and relationships: issues and problems for gay men in the AIDS era, in J. Ussher and C. Baker (eds) *Psychological Perspectives on Sexual Problems.* London: Routledge.

Greene, B. (1994) Ethnic-minority lesbians and gay men: mental health and treatment issues, *Journal of Consulting and Clinical Psychology*, 62: 243–51.

Haldeman, D.C. (1994) The practice and ethics of sexual orientation conversion therapy, *Journal of Consulting and Clinical Psychology*, 62: 221–7.

Hanson, G. and Hartmann, G. (1996) Latency development in prehomosexual boys, in R.P. Cabaj and T.S. Stein (eds) *Textbook of Homosexuality and Mental Health.* Washington: American Psychiatric Press.

Kennerley, H. (1997) Schema-focused cognitive therapy (*Psychotherapy Section Newsletter*, 22: December). Leicester: British Psychological Society.

Kuehlwein, K.T. (1992) Working with gay men, in A. Freeman and F.M. Dattilio (eds) *Comprehensive Casebook of Cognitive Therapy*. New York: Plenum.

Neal, C. (1998) Queer therapy, past and future. Keynote speech to ALGBP Conference 1997 in *Association of Lesbian, Gay and Bisexual Psychologies Newsletter*: January.

Padesky, C. (1989) Attaining and maintaining positive lesbian self-identity: a cognitive therapy approach, *Women and Therapy*, 8: 145–56.

Padesky, C. (1994a) Schema change processes in cognitive therapy, *Clinical Psychology and Psychotherapy*, 1: 267–78.

Padesky, C. (1994b) Schema as self-prejudice, *International Cognitive Therapy Newsletter*, 5/6: 16–17.

Rivers, I. (1995) Mental health issues amongst lesbians and gay men bullied in school, *Health and Social Care in the Community*, 3: 380–8.

Safran, J. and Segal, Z. (1990) *Interpersonal Processes in Cognitive Therapy*. New York: Basic Books.

Scragg, P. (1996) An initial functional analysis of addiction to 'cottaging' based on five cases, *Clinical Psychology and Psychotherapy*, 3: 277–87.

Silverstein, C. (1996) History of treatment, in R.P. Cabaj and T.S. Stein (eds) *Textbook of Homosexuality and Mental Health*. Washington: American Psychiatric Press.

Stein, T.S. (1996a) A critique of approaches to changing sexual orientation, in R.P. Cabaj and T.S. Stein (eds) *Textbook of Homosexuality and Mental Health*. Washington: American Psychiatric Press.

Stein, T.S. (1996b) The essentialist/social constructionist debate about homosexuality and its relevance for psychotherapy, in R.P. Cabaj and T.S. Stein (eds) *Textbook of Homosexuality and Mental Health*. Washington: American Psychiatric Press.

Ussher, J. (1990) Cognitive-behavioural couples therapy with gay men referred for counselling in an AIDS setting: a pilot study, *AIDS Care*, 2: 43–51.

West, D.J. (1977) *Homosexuality Re-examined*. London: Duckworth.

Wolfe, J.L. (1992) Working with gay women, in A. Freeman and F.M. Dattilio (eds) *Comprehensive Casebook of Cognitive Therapy*. New York: Plenum.

Yankura, J. and Dryden, W. (1994) *Albert Ellis*. London: Sage.

Young, J.E. (1990) *Cognitive Therapy for Personality Disorders: A Schema Focused Approach*. Sarasota, FL: Professional Resource Exchange, Inc.

Existential-phenomenological therapy

Introduction

This chapter outlines the existential-phenomenological* approach to therapy and reviews what existential writers have said on the topic of sexuality in general, and lesbian, gay and bisexual sexuality in particular. Considerations of theory and how this might influence practice follow. The chapter ends with a consideration of some of the issues that require attention in the provision of a lesbian and gay affirmative therapy. The nature of the chapter means that all of these areas are considered in rather a brief way and readers are encouraged to make use of the references to review areas of further interest.

A brief overview of the approach

The origins of existential thinking have been traced back to a Sunday afternoon in 1834 when a young Dane, Søren Kierkegaard, sat in a café musing about his place in the world (Yalom 1980; du Plock 1996: 34). Since then, existential thought has influenced therapeutic practice, yet it has tended to gather less celebrity than the psychoanalytic, the humanistic or the cognitive-behavioural approaches. However, there has been a tremendous increase in, and awareness of, existential approaches to therapy in the last two decades (du Plock 1996).

* For the sake of brevity the term 'existential' is used rather than 'existential-phenomenological'.

Before thinking specifically about the relationship between existential therapy and sexuality in general, and lesbian, gay and bisexual sexuality specifically, it is important to outline some of the central tenets of the approach. Those wanting greater elaboration are referred to 'The existential-phenomenological paradigm' (Spinelli 1996a), *Existential Counselling in Practice* (van Deurzen-Smith 1988) and *Existential Therapy* (van Deurzen-Smith 1995). The term 'existential' is used in the literature in a number of ways, some of which appear to be at odds with the approach described in this chapter. There are many texts in which the term 'existential' is overtly tagged onto the end of 'humanistic' (Clarkson 1995) or seen as a supportive/experiential therapy (Roth and Fonagy 1997). This is a representation that practitioners of the approach would not necessarily recognise due to the fact that it does not acknowledge some of the most significant ways in which these two approaches differ – both in understanding the person and in therapeutic practice (Spinelli 1994). One example might be the view taken of freedom. In the existential approach, a view is taken of freedom that allows us to consider its nature in relation to the limitations intrinsic to it (Ironside 1994), or what has been termed a 'situated freedom' (Spinelli 1994: 296). Thus, the clarification of the client's experience is often characterised by a clarification of the stance that is taken towards the limitations faced. In comparison, with their roots in the human potential movement, humanistic approaches have at times privileged freedom rather than the limits that go hand in hand with freedom. This paints a somewhat different picture of the individual and approaches to practice.

There is no one form of existential therapy, as the existential approach is fundamentally opposed to universalising and categorising. This results in difficulties when attempting to elaborate on 'the' existential theory or technique. Instead there are beliefs held by specific existentialists, such as Sartre, Heidegger or Kierkegaard (Milton *et al.* 1998), and the phenomenological method to guide therapeutic thought. Thus, this is an approach that is as firmly based in philosophy as it is in psychology. Existential thought is first evident in psychological discourse in the formulations and practices of Ludwig Binswanger, a Swiss psychiatrist working in the early part of this century (van Deurzen-Smith 1997).

There are some central tenets that are applicable to understanding existence, thinking about therapy and even particular aspects of being, such as sexuality. The existential paradigm does not consider the person as an individual, but rather as *Dasein*. This term translated means 'Being-in-the-World'. The use of the hyphens highlights a central understanding of this approach, which is that the person is embedded in the world and can only be understood as such. There cannot be an independent *Dasein*. The world comprises physical, social and intimate dimensions as well as the world of values. Thus, this approach would see discussion about inner and outer worlds as inappropriate, as there is no proven object that is an 'inner' or 'outer' self: distinct and separate 'inner' and 'outer' selves are an impossibility. This is distinct from many approaches based on the natural sciences, which are in turn based on the assumption that subject and object are separate. It is through a lived engagement that people experience their world and their world is made up of what they perceive.

Psychological disturbance and health

Central to an existential understanding of human experience and distress is meaning. It is understood that we take a stance towards an experience, and it is this stance, in its emotional, cognitive, behavioural and value dimensions, that shapes the form that is experienced and observed. Thus, different people (or the same people at different points in time) may experience similar phenomena in very different ways.

Psychological distress is thus understood to be a consequence of the particular stance taken towards these experiences. Distress is particularly difficult for people when the stance they take is a sedimented one, where other possible options and interpretations are not available for consideration. 'Sedimentation' is a term meaning the way in which 'human beings become stuck or fixed in certain beliefs and behaviour patterns that deposit themselves deep down in our belief systems' (Strasser and Strasser 1997: 90).

Existential approaches to sexuality

Very little has been written directly on issues of lesbian, gay and bisexual sexuality from an existential position (Spinelli 1996b; Cohn 1997). This is strange for two reasons. First, as noted by Wolf (1997), lesbian and gay sexuality has functioned as the main issue through which ideas and discourses around sexuality have rotated for the last century or so. Second, because of the attention existential philosophy generally gives to the fundamental givens of life, of which an embodied sexuality must be one.

Most of those existential writers who mention sexuality do so in order to highlight the struggles people have with existential issues, rather than to try to develop a theory of sexuality *per se*. Universal theories of development are not a characteristic of a phenomenological stance due to the fact that such theories inevitably move away from phenomena as it is experienced. Where examples of sexual experience are used, some are of heterosexual experience (Frankl 1967; Kruger 1979; Yalom 1980; Sartre 1981) and some are of gay male experience (Laing 1961; Sartre 1981; Strasser and Strasser 1997).

However, lesbian and bisexual experiences are frequently absent. Where these examples are concerned, it is possible (although far from ideal) to substitute gendered identities and/or sexual identities without coming upon theoretical contradictions – for example, when Sartre (1981) talks about 'the homosexual' living in bad faith, this can also be applied to those who hold an identity as a lesbian. Indeed where an identity is held as hetero-sexual or bisexual the theory is also relevant. The existential focus is not that it is being lesbian, gay or bisexual that creates a situation of bad faith, but rather that rigidly identifying oneself with one identity leads to sedi-mentation and an existence of bad faith due to the limitations that are imposed on existential possibilities. Another example is to be found in the writings of Laing. He describes a heterosexual man who cannot bear being the object of another man's attraction, thus illustrating the limitations of that man and again attributing the difficulty to a stance that excludes possibilities for existence (Laing 1961). These positions can be the same regarding any sexual orientation as, in this paradigm, the important aspect is 'orientation' rather than, or just as much as, the 'sexual'. In some ways an existential approach requires therapists to eliminate assumptions based on a sexual identity and to focus on the client's experience of being in the world sexually.

Not only is Binswanger (1963) one of the first writers to incorporate existential ideas into psychological discourse, he is also another important contributor who has written on the issue of sexuality. He has argued that our current understandings of sexuality are insufficient. He criticises psy-choanalysis for ignoring 'the possibility that these biological needs are them-selves enmeshed in a larger meaning-matrix, and therefore, themselves point to something beyond themselves' (1963: 75). He points out that there is a danger in relying too exclusively on particular theoretical constructions of sexuality.

An existential understanding, following on from the notion of *Dasein*, will focus on the relational function that human sexuality has for human existence. The philosopher Macquarrie has clearly noted that 'if sexuality is the bodily foundation of the simplest kind of community (sexual union or marriage); it is also the act that has the potentiality to found the next order of community, the family' (1972: 117).

As mentioned above, Laing is also an existentially-oriented therapist who has written briefly on sexuality. He criticised 'any theory of sexuality which makes the "aim" of the sexual "instinct" the achievement of orgasmic potency alone, while the other, however selectively chosen, is a mere object, a means to this end, ignores the erotic desire to make a difference to the other' (1961: 85). Both authors point to the existential focus on the rela-tional intentionality which is central to an accurate understanding of the experience and of being, and therefore of sexual identity. And again, the dualistic assumptions of psychoanalysis are criticised. May offers us thoughts on why these criticisms are important and notes that 'when we talk of sexuality in terms of sexual objects, as Kinsey did, we may garner interest-ing and useful statistics, but we simply are not talking about human sexual-ity' (1983: 30), at least not as it is experienced. This can easily be tested in our own reflections on our experiences of attraction, desire, love and sexual behaviour and how these vary from superficial statistical representations.

Thus, while the existential literature on sexuality is not voluminous, particularly in comparison to the psychoanalytic literature, it must be noted that a focus on homosexuality is nonetheless present. Many traditional views and understandings of sexuality are 'significantly challenged by existential-phenomenological theory and . . . via this challenge, [are] a novel means to examine and understand the sexual concerns that our clients bring to therapy, or which we ourselves may be experiencing' (Spinelli 1996b: 5).

Of the limited writing on sexuality, Merleau-Ponty (1962) has discussed its nature most directly. In doing so he 'is not interested in the issues of male or female sexuality, sexual orientation, or the socio-political dimensions of sexuality. His is an investigation aimed towards the clarification of sexuality as it is revealed in its intentional dimension' (Spinelli 1996b: 7). Thus, as with many issues, while the existential approach acknowledges both the personal and the constructional aspects of experience, it attempts to go back to the things themselves (Husserl 1977). When writing on sexuality, Merleau-Ponty notes that 'we are concerned, not with a peripheral involuntary action, but with an intentionality which follows the general flow of existence and yields to its movements . . . sexuality is not an autonomous cycle' (1962: 157). Thus, he argues clearly that sexuality is more than a physical or biological phenomenon, but rather is an aspect of life created and manipulated through intentionality.

In a recent paper, Spinelli (1996b: 6) shows us how:

> With regard to sexuality, it is evident that, unlike virtually every other creature, our desire to engage in sexual activities is not solely, nor primarily, dictated by biological 'cycles' linked to the reproduction of the species. We do not engage in sexual relations with the principal aim that such will lead to the birth of our offspring. Rather our most common sexual activities seek to ensure that just such an outcome is avoided.

Literature on lesbian, gay and bisexual sexuality

In the existential literature that does exist, lesbian and bisexual sexuality is often not explicit and the term 'homosexual' is used, rather than lesbian, gay or bisexual. Only a few writers have discussed lesbian or gay male sexuality directly from an existential perspective. Of those who have, Boss (1949) discussed it in some detail. Boss views homosexuality as a perversion: he clearly positions human sexuality in a bio-reproductive framework with heterosexuality as the healthy norm. He has been accused of having moved away from the phenomenological position he espoused (Cohn 1997), to one that is decidedly more Freudian than Freud – in that it is based in a normative and medical framework, rather than an existential understanding based in intersubjectivity. Cohn suggests that, in using the term perversion, 'Boss does not imply dismissal or condemnation, he sees the various sexual "perversions" as attempts to achieve loving relationships in situations where the capacity to realise them fully is inhibited or crippled' (1997: 95).

While Boss attempts to recognise the relational possibility inherent in all forms of sexuality, his view implies that heterosexuality is a definite default position, the benchmark for sexual maturity. Thus, as in much traditional psychoanalytic writing, Boss felt that homosexuality was an arrest of development. Cohn finds this unacceptable from an existential position and suggests that any 'view [which] proposes unilinear causal connections between our anatomy and physiology and our way of being . . . entirely ignores context and history. It is, therefore, unphenomenological' (1997: 90).

Homosexuality is also addressed in contemporary existential writings. Cohn has highlighted that 'for the existential psychotherapist, homosexuality is not a "condition" brought about by specific factors, but a way of being in which whatever is "given" is most delicately intertwined with our responses' (1997: 95). 'Phenomenologically, the attempt to find a particular "cause" to explain an imprecisely defined area on the wide spectrum of sexuality is quite meaningless' (1997: 94). In fact, from an existential perspective, lesbian, gay and bisexual sexuality cannot be developmental arrest, nor can it be a pathology that needs to be 'cured'. This is because, for a form of sexuality to be viewed in this way, essentialist interpretations of the 'truth' must be accepted.

The existential view is that sexuality and the experience of sexual identity must be constructed phenomena. We 'identify ourselves as homosexual, heterosexual or any-kind-of-sexual, not because of past circumstances or biological dictates, but because it is who we say we are' (Spinelli 1996b: 18–19). This highlights the interpretive aspect of experience and allows for the experiences of people to be foregrounded. In holding this view the existential approach challenges both the homophobe and lesbian, gay and bisexual affirmative therapist alike. Spinelli notes that 'to distinguish this particular means of disclosure as inherently different, unique, problematic or perverse has no basis – other than at the level of an interpretive bias that must be challenged rather than condoned' (1996b: 13). Spinelli has suggested that an existential perspective must accept that 'homosexual relations express the very same intersubjective desires to be with others as can be ascertained in all other sexual manifestations' (1996b: 13). This is particularly important when helping the client consider his or her own experience.

An existential understanding of sexuality subverts the biological assumptions and Cartesian/dualistic thinking that underpins much of our day-today (as well as psychoanalytic) thinking on sexuality: e.g. right and wrong, normal and perverse, moral and immoral. These are flawed and Spinelli notes that it is only possible to label lesbian, gay and bisexual sexuality 'as "unnatural" if contextualised within reductive assumptions of "reproductively directed sexual impulses gone awry"' (Spinelli 1996b: 13). Once this assumption is questioned and dismissed as being inadequate, we must attempt to develop our understandings of sexuality further.

In existential theory, the context is seen as intrinsic to our existence and an important aspect to consider in any therapy. It should be noted that in political and social terms, the experience of a lesbian, gay and bisexual identity is constructed in very different ways to heterosexual identities. Because of the current and historical hostility directed at lesbian, gay and bisexual behaviour, Cohn has noted that 'homosexual people are, of course, especially vulnerable in a situation in which they are targets of persecution' (1997: 89).

Theoretical contributions

Existential theory challenges many contemporary understandings of sexual identities, particularly those of an essentialist nature. An existential understanding requires us to consider the constructive, interpretive aspect of identity. While not denying that there are some aspects of our sexuality that are 'given' (for example, the fact that our sexuality is an embodied experience), an existential approach recognises that there is a difference between the fact of lesbian, gay or bisexual desire and behaviour and the consciousness of oneself as lesbian, gay or bisexual. This consciousness is open to variations in meaning and it is herein that choices are made. This does not necessitate simplistic, causal or easy choices, as when involved in a sexual situation we may have no sense of the fact that we constitute our world, nor that we have choices in this experience (Yalom 1980; du Plock 1997). This paradigm acknowledges that our responses to such givens vary enormously (Spinelli 1989; Cohn 1997), and therefore assumptions about a universal truth are simplistic. In this view then, it is not the particular acts that are of major significance, but 'rather the particular personal and sociocultural meanings associated with them that are of importance to the current debate on human sexuality' (Spinelli 1997: 16).

The implications are of a recognition that there is no single experience of being a lesbian, of being a gay man, of being bisexual or of being heterosexual. However, there are 'infinite ways of "being-in-the-world homosexually"' (Cohn 1997: 95), or even sexually. An existential view of sexuality cannot accept a 'normative' view of people's experience, whether this concerns norms about gender roles, sexual identity, or any other characteristic that is prone to categorisation (Spinelli 1989; Milton 1996; Cohn

1997). If we were to accept these assumptions, difficulties are immediately evident. Cohn, using gender as his example, shows that these assumptions imply 'that there [are] definite masculine and feminine potentialities and that we know how to define them. Also it takes for granted that whatever we call "masculine" is present only in men . . . [this] seems to be neither phenomenological nor existential' (1997: 95). These norms are not useful: 'we are all sexual beings and our sexuality, like all existence, has "given" aspects. It is our responses . . . which vary' (Cohn 1997: 89). This approach requires us 'to explore what these "givens" are and the ways in which we respond' (Cohn 1997: 89).

The existential literature has addressed a concern about foregrounding 'sexuality' over 'orientation' (Binswanger 1963; Foucault 1978; Sartre 1981; du Plock 1997). Sartre has written that to live as 'a homosexual' is to live in bad faith, as to take on one identity is an inauthentic description of ourselves. We must acknowledge the range of possible ways of being that we all negotiate. It is by speaking of 'I' that we identify ourselves and give meaning to our existence (Milton *et al.* 1998). Du Plock (1997: 69) has suggested that in an existential model:

> a sexual orientation . . . becomes . . . an orientation, a choice regarding being-in-the-world, just as sexual relationship is a choice regarding how to relate in the world. We pay too little attention to this 'orientation' of sexual orientation, falling into the trap . . . of foregrounding sex to the detriment of any other analysis of the surrounding culture and the power relations in this culture.

Again, the recognition of an aspect of choice in experience must not be taken simplistically to suggest that we have unlimited choices, but rather that we have a freedom to be within the givens that exist. We have situated choices: as lesbians, gay men and bisexual people, we have choices in how we experience and live with our sexualities to some degree. The existential approach thus requires 'an understanding of sexuality which neither pathologises it, nor treats it as a thing in itself separate from the individual's project of being or their lived situation in their culture and society' (du Plock 1997: 70). This does not imply a woolly liberal view that 'everyone is the same', as the existential approach considers 'context' a crucial issue. This view attends to complex interrelationships and allows the therapist to challenge sedimented assumptions about the 'reality' of any one identity, or the denial of the freedom that we all have. However, the focus of the context requires the therapist to note the fact that lesbians, gay men and bisexuals exist in a society rife with prejudice and therefore are vulnerable to a range of hostilities. Thus sexual identities and sexual activities 'become problematic for clients because they feel they are "not normal" by the rules of their sociocultural context – even though they are in fact quite happy with the way they experience sexual satisfaction' (Cohn 1997: 98).

Case example I

This point is evident in work I have written about elsewhere. A client of mine, Roberto, described a number of dreams to me. These dreams clearly illustrated that while experiencing his sexuality in a very meaningful manner in his sexual relationships with other men, there were times when Roberto experienced his sexuality as much more problematic. This tended to occur in social contexts where Roberto was most vulnerable to anti-gay prejudice (Milton 1997).

Therapeutic technique

As so little has been theorised about sexuality from an existential perspective, it must be noted that existential therapeutic practice is influenced by the central tenets of the approach. This approach is known for not attempting to provide answers for clients, and for challenging the attempts by therapists to 'cure' people. In fact 'perhaps, more than the psychoanalytic approach [the existential approach] eschews dogma, so has not taken the form of a specific creed or orthodoxy' (du Plock 1996: 30). The role of the existential therapist is thus to assist people in their efforts to clarify their worlds (the limitations and constraints over which they have no control) and their experiences, and to find meaning in their existence. As Kruger puts it (from a male perspective) 'the spatiality of closeness and distance, the glance, the touch, smell and taste are just as much involved in sexuality as the hardening of the penis' (1979: 215). So while some discourses isolate the sexual organs or particular sexual activities, an existential perspective requires the meaning of the greater context to be given credence. In essence, the physical should not be privileged above the relational, the sexual over the erotic. This stance is based on the understanding that one person can never fully know the experience of another, and it is therefore impossible to clarify the experience for them. In addition, it is thought that the most powerful experiences from which we learn are the ones in which we are most fully engaged.

The 'technique' that is generally seen as central to this approach is the phenomenological method, which is an attempt to return to the things themselves (Husserl 1977). To do this, the phenomenologist attempts to follow three basic principles. First, to 'bracket' his or her own assumptions and agendas. This is not an unconsidered shutting out of the therapist. On the contrary, the presence of the therapist, in a variety of different ways, is seen as crucial to the therapeutic process. The therapist must develop a high degree of self-awareness in order to be informed of their own experience in the room with the client, as well as developing the ability to put aside such personal experiences, if only temporarily and in a limited fashion. Bracketing allows the therapy and the interventions to take a descriptive and challenging stance, whereby the therapist and client attempt to fully describe the client's experience.

The second principle requires the therapist to encourage (at least initially) a full description of as much of the situation as is possible. The third principle requires that significance be withheld for at least the initial period of description.

These steps have been described as the rules of bracketing, description and horizontalisation (Spinelli 1989). When writing about therapeutic method, Spinelli (1995: 49) notes that an existential approach:

> demands that the therapist remain at the level of 'descriptive challenge' so that the interventions made are invitations to explore and clarify the meanings of client statements as perceived and understood by the client . . . a willingness on the part of the therapist to both confront and seek to set aside, or 'bracket', the plethora of personally held views, opinions and meaning biases concerning the issue being disclosed and explored by the client.

When taking this approach with clients, van Deurzen-Smith offers an insight to the process. She writes of a lesbian client who, after a period of anxiety about her sexual identity and concern about the response she would receive from others, 'came to the conclusion that she was no longer afraid of people thinking her a lesbian as she probably was and should be proud of it' (van Deurzen-Smith 1988: 182).

Case example 2

I have written elsewhere about my own work with a client, Sean. Sean was a young gay man who came to therapy at a time in his life when he was trying to come out in familial and work contexts. For many of us, this process is accompanied by anxiety: anxieties about the responses we will receive from those around us, anxieties about the meaning of a change in our self-construct and, of course, anxieties related to the uncertainties we face during this process. As a therapist many of my interventions were focused on a descriptive exploration about the meanings that being a gay man might have for Sean, for his friends, family members and colleagues. While this exploration highlighted a number of assumptions that were quite frightening to Sean, the process had the effect of allowing a multiplicity of meanings associated with sexual identity to emerge. This appears to have been an important factor in Sean's movement 'from feeling he had to find a label, (i.e. I am gay or I am straight), to something akin to "I can be whoever I am, I have a choice in whether I use a label or not"' (Milton 1996: 30) – an example of a move to increased authenticity for Sean.

This changing perspective allowed a lessening of anxiety and a greater ability to consider the nature of his sexuality as it was, rather than what it should or shouldn't be according to historical and cultural norms that threaten to stand in the way of being. It also allowed Sean to become aware of the role he might take in a co-constructed identity.

Unhelpful aspects of theory

When any therapy becomes focused on theory there are likely to be problems, regardless of the theoretical orientation that one adheres to. This would appear to apply equally to an existential approach as to any other and this criticism has been applied to Boss' view of homosexuality as discussed above.

With the focus on individual freedom and limitations, with its recognition that there are limits to what one person can achieve for another, this approach can offer the potential for clients to find their own way and to find a different way of being-in-relationship. Despite this there are some clients who may not find this approach useful – for example, a phenomenological approach might be quite frustrating for those who accept a medicalised view of their difficulties. This is not to say that the existential therapist denies what others might construct as 'pathology'. The existential therapist recognises the phenomena and the experience of deep distress, but conceptualises it as a stance taken towards particular issues and experiences. This may not be the best approach for those who cannot risk seeking the answers in themselves rather than through the actions of another. Where the client and the therapist are working from widely different perspectives this approach to therapy may not be helpful. However, this is true of all therapeutic relationships.

A criticism, which can be made of the existential literature, is that much of the older literature reads with a predominantly male tone. As with many psychotherapeutic schools those writing throughout the development of the literature were men, using men in their descriptions or using male constructions of women's experiences. In doing so, existential literature, like other schools of therapy, has been primarily shaped by a heterosexual male perspective with the agendas and the experiences of other groups (for example, lesbian and heterosexual women, gay men and bisexual people) being silenced or pathologised. This highlights the limitations of writers' and practitioners' abilities to bracket themselves and their contextual assumptions. There are examples in the theories of such writers as Merleau-Ponty and Sartre that can equally well lead us to consider the experience of men and women, heterosexuals, lesbians, gay men and bisexuals without compromising the argument.

Existential therapists are inevitably embedded in the times and culture they live in. Examples of this might be popularly-held liberal views that 'We are all the same'. It is important critically to consider such assumptions and have an attitude of continual reflection in order to monitor one's practice, to encourage the ability to 'bracket', and to consider ways in which we can be open to the widest range of meanings available. These limitations to bracketing may be countered to some degree through therapists' willingness to reflect on their own life experiences and on those of others. It is also important that the existential therapist has been immersed in society from a number of positions and has experienced and come through their own existential crises.

The development of a flexible approach to therapeutic work as well as a thorough knowledge of theoretical models of therapeutic practice can all encourage flexibility of mind and of being, and of being-in-the-world-with-another.

Issues to be addressed when working affirmatively

There is an important issue concerning whether existential therapy can be lesbian, gay and bisexual affirmative, and for the existential perspective this is, unsurprisingly, an issue of meaning. In the lesbian and gay affirmative literature there are various positions taken. Some appear to take an essentialist position and suggest that lesbian and gay affirmative work is a model with prescribed practices and views that are taken towards therapeutic work (Clark 1987). Others appear to see lesbian and gay affirmative work as an issue of attitude that runs through practice.

If lesbian, gay and bisexual affirmative therapy is assumed to be a model with particular views and practices, an existential position cannot take up the notion of being 'lesbian, gay and bisexual affirmative' without losing the central tenets of the approach. Du Plock (1997) has considered this. In discussing *Pink Therapy* (Davies and Neal 1996), he critiques the essentialist interpretations that are possible and raises a number of questions. His clearest concerns are about the term 'affirmative' (which can be taken to mean promoting), and Clark's (1987) 'Twelve Guidelines for Retraining and Ground Rules for Helping'. Du Plock points out that 'the existential-phenomenological therapist who wishes to be gay affirmative (or anything affirmative) is going to have a problem here, since the gay affirmative approach calls upon us to desist from bracketing . . . to desist from the entire phenomenological method' (1997: 56) – and to take a more traditionally patriarchal, technological and inauthentic stance towards being-with-others.

If lesbian, gay and bisexual affirmative therapy is actually lesbian, gay and bisexual 'promoting' therapy, a clear stance must be taken. Sexuality has to be foregrounded and certain possibilities of identity are privileged over others. Assumptions must be made about an identity that is lesbian, gay or bisexual. By foregrounding sexuality, we lose the ability to create the space needed to consider, describe and challenge the variety of experiences of sexuality and accept the developing experience that is most authentic. This is not phenomenological. Du Plock notes that 'rather than, even temporarily, adopting the position of a positive authority figure I would suggest that we might want to explore the client's experience . . . There is a danger . . . in any sort of affirmative therapy . . . of the therapist becoming the very "expert" we all agree we do not want to be' (1997: 59). When we attempt to affirm or promote anything, we risk prescribing, overtly or covertly, particular ways of being or identities and this threatens our ability to value, embrace and engage with difference.

Despite this, it seems entirely possible to provide a non-pathologising, contextually aware, sensitive therapy to clients, which will be experienced as affirming of lesbians, gay men and bisexual people in their entirety. If we rethink what 'affirmative' might mean we have to consider whether it should mean being open to and accepting of lesbian, gay and bisexual sexuality. To accept the other in their 'otherness' includes, and goes beyond, particular social identities: it is a moment of justice in relationship, where we are seen, heard and taken seriously and valued for who we are. If this is what is meant by 'affirmative' then existential therapy will have no difficulty in being so.

The cornerstones of phenomenological practice provide a fertile ground for such an affirmative therapy. The rule of description assists in developing a full and rich description of the client's world and experience and the elaboration of possible modes of existence. With lesbian, gay and bisexual clients this may include a description of living as 'the Other' in a heterosexist world. The rule of horizontalisation assists the clarification of meanings specific to the client and their different worlds rather than any prescribed ones.

This will allow space to identify socially specific phenomena that impede the development of authentic sexual identities. The rule of bracketing assists by aiding therapists' awareness of their own feelings and thoughts and the use that is made thereof. Thus, du Plock's interpretation of lesbian and gay affirmative therapy may not be the interpretation desired by some. However, it is important to recognise that texts can be viewed in a number of ways and therefore we must take care when describing ways of engaging in therapy. It is important for an existential approach to therapy to foreground its phenomenological focus as this is a primary way of engaging with clients in their own worlds rather than subjecting our clients to being mere objects.

Guidelines for good practice

- An existential approach makes a particular call to be aware of the context in which people live, while continually challenging the beliefs and understandings of both the individual and socially accepted views of reality – both the possibilities and the limitations.

- Due to the importance of the interpersonal encounter, therapists need to be clear on their own experience of sexuality.
- A pathologising view of clients' experiences cannot claim to be phenomenological.
- The therapist must be mindful to explore the meanings and experiences of the client, without imposing a particular view on any states of being.
- When thinking of sexual orientation, 'sexuality' should not be fore-grounded at the expense of 'orientation'.

Acknowledgements

These ideas have been increasingly clarified through review, discussion and challenging debate with my colleagues Maureen Taylor and Dale Judd.

References

Binswanger, L. (1963) *Being-in-the-World: Selected Papers of Ludwig Binswanger*. New York: Harper Torchbooks.

Boss, M. (1949) *Meaning and Content of Sexual Perversions*. New York: Grune & Stratton.

Clark, D. (1987) *The New Loving Someone Gay*. Berkeley, CA: Celestial Arts.

Clarkson, P. (1995) *The Therapeutic Relationship: In Psychoanalysis, Counselling Psychology and Psychotherapy*. London: Whurr Publishers.

Cohn, H. (1997) *Existential Thought and Therapeutic Practice: An Introduction to Existential Psychotherapy*. London: Sage.

Davies, D. (1996) Working with people coming out, in D. Davies and C. Neal (eds) *Pink Therapy: A Guide for Counsellors and Therapists Working with Lesbian, Gay and Bisexual Clients*. Buckingham: Open University Press.

Davies, D. and Neal, C. (eds) (1996) *Pink Therapy: A Guide for Counsellors and Therapists Working with Lesbian, Gay and Bisexual Clients*. Buckingham: Open University Press.

du Plock, S. (1996) The existential-phenomenological movement, 1834–1995, in W. Dryden (ed.) *Developments in Psychotherapy: Historical Perspectives*. London: Sage.

du Plock, S. (1997) Sexual misconceptions: a critique of gay affirmative therapy and some thoughts on an existential-phenomenological theory of sexual orientation, *Journal of the Society for Existential Analysis*, 8(2): 56–71.

Foucault, M. (1978) *The History of Sexuality – Volume One: An Introduction*. Harmondsworth: Penguin.

Frankl, V. (1967) *Psychotherapy and Existentialism: Selected Papers on Logotherapy*. Harmondsworth: Penguin.

Husserl, E. (1977) *Phenomenological Psychology*. The Hague: Nijhoff.

Ironside, K. (1994) 'Freedom and limitations within the therapeutic interaction', unpublished MA dissertation. School of Psychotherapy and Counselling at Regents College.

Kruger, D. (1979) *An Introduction to Phenomenological Psychology*. Kenwyn: Juta and Co.

Laing, R.D. (1961) *Self and Others*. Harmondsworth: Penguin.

Macquarrie, J. (1972) *Existentialism: An Introduction, Guide and Assessment*. Harmondsworth: Penguin.

May, R. (1983) *The Discovery of Being: Writings in Existential Psychology*. New York: W.W. Norton & Co.

Merleau-Ponty, M. (1962) *Phenomenology of Perception*. London: Routledge and Kegan Paul.

Milton, M. (1996) Coming out in therapy, *Counselling Psychology Review*, 11(3): 26–32.

Milton, M. (1997) The case of Roberto: issues of meaning in HIV-related psychotherapy, in S. du Plock, (ed.) *Case Studies in Existential Psychotherapy and Counselling*. Chichester: Wiley.

Milton, M., Taylor, M. and Gaist, B. (1998) Professional identities in the NHS: existential perspectives, *Journal of the Society for Existential Analysis*, 9(1): 114–28.

Roth, A. and Fonagy, P. (1997) *What Works for Whom? A Critical Review of Psychotherapy Research*. London: Guilford Press.

Sartre, J.P. (1981) *Existential Psychoanalysis*. Washington, DC: Gateway Editions.

Spinelli, E. (1989) *The Interpreted World: An Introduction to Phenomenological Psychology*. London: Sage.

Spinelli, E. (1994) *Demystifying Therapy*. London: Constable.

Spinelli, E. (1996a) The existential-phenomenological paradigm, in R. Woolfe and W. Dryden (eds) *Handbook of Counselling Psychology*. London: Sage.

Spinelli, E. (1996b) Some hurried notes expressing outline ideas that someone might someday utilise as signposts towards a sketch of an existential-phenomenological theory of human sexuality, *Journal of the Society for Existential Analysis*, 8(1): 2–20.

Spinelli, E. (1997) Human sexuality and existential phenomenological inquiry, *Counselling Psychology Review*, 12(4): 170–8.

Strasser, F. and Strasser, A. (1997) *Existential Time-Limited Therapy: The Wheel of Existence*. Chichester: Wiley.

van Deurzen-Smith, E. (1988) *Existential Counselling in Practice*. London: Sage.

van Deurzen-Smith, E. (1995) *Existential Therapy*. London: Society for Existential Analysis.

van Deurzen-Smith, E. (1997) *Everyday Mysteries: Existential Dimensions of Psychotherapy*. London: Routledge.

Wolf, D. (1997) Making sense of homosexuality, *British Journal of Psychotherapy*, 13(3): 351–7.

Yalom, I.D. (1980) *Existential Psychotherapy*. New York: Basic Books.

Gay, lesbian and bisexual therapy and its supervision

Introduction

This chapter examines some of the implications of providing supervision to therapists working with lesbians, gay men and bisexual people, as well as to therapists who are themselves lesbian, gay or bisexual. It reviews recent work in developing gay affirmative therapy and endeavours to draw out ideas and principles that may be useful and applicable to supervision. Supervision in this context follows the British Association for Counselling's (BAC) 1998 definition (BAC 1998, para. B.6.3).

Historical perspective

Historically those approaches to psychology and therapeutic practice that have pathologised homosexuality have brought the same constrictions to supervision. In supervision literature homosexuality and bisexuality appeared only as evidence of the client's pathology and were treated as such. In most cases there was no question of the supervisor being lesbian, gay or bisexual because these were barred from training in many training institutions (O'Connor and Ryan 1993; Ellis 1994), and even if they did train they found difficulty in advancement. However, homophobic attitudes may have retained their hegemony longer in supervision than in therapy generally: it has taken time for lesbians and gay men to train as therapists and develop supervisory skills, just as it has taken time for heterosexual therapists to receive non-discriminary training as some institutions have developed more enlightened attitudes and programmes.

As a result of the development of humanistic approaches to therapy working from a variety of theoretical bases, the declassification of homosexuality as a mental illness by the American Psychiatric Association in 1973, the removal of homosexuality from the *Diagnostic and Statistical Manual* (1980), and more recently the declassification of homosexuality by the World Health Organization (WHO 1992), more accepting attitudes have developed and have influenced therapy and subsequently supervision.

In spite of this, however, the experience of most lesbian, gay and bisexual therapists and supervisors has been far from easy. In the UK, few therapy training courses (and even fewer supervision courses) include sessions on working with lesbian, gay and bisexual clients, and those that do often group the work together with that on other marginalised groups under a broad equal opportunities heading. Graham *et al.* (1983) suggest that practitioners have been left to themselves to adapt their attitudes and behaviour away from the abandoned pathology model and have had to develop more supportive work on their own. Rudolph (1988) found that one in three therapists still expressed negative attitudes. It is hardly surprising therefore that the surveys and anecdotal evidence he cites also show that clients were dissatisfied with their therapists' negative and prejudiced attitudes and their lack of understanding of homosexuality. Mann's (1994) survey of a small number of counsellors showed that all had experience of working with lesbian and gay clients but that none had received any specific training. Nevertheless half of those interviewed thought they would have no difficulty in working with lesbian and gay clients.

The experience of lesbian and gay clients has been recorded only indirectly in the literature, which focuses on therapists and how they work rather than how clients experience the therapeutic relationship (Silverstein 1991), though Young (1995) starts to redress the balance.

Records of the experience of lesbian, gay and bisexual therapists are even rarer. A workshop held at the 1996 annual conference of the Association for Lesbian, Gay and Bisexual Psychologies UK (Pett 1997) which looked at supervision in the context of gay affirmative therapy is believed to be one of the first of its kind in Britain. Seventeen participants discussed their experiences of supervision. Positive experiences in supervision were identified as: being able to tell their own story in their own way and having this respected; the safety of the one-to-one situation; and the fact that issues of race, gender, class and sexuality were included and asked about in the supervision process. Negative experiences identified were supervisees having to raise the broader context themselves in supervision, and feeling less safe in group supervision.

In the last few years there has been a growth in training courses for supervisors. Again these tend to ignore the issues and needs of lesbian, gay and bisexual trainees and clients. In the author's experience, work on equality was not seen by course participants to be essential and, on the one occasion some equalities work was introduced, many participants had difficulty in dealing with the material, but still maintained they were able to supervise the work of lesbian, gay and bisexual therapists and handle the material of lesbian, gay and bisexual clients adequately.

Gay affirmative supervision: learning from gay affirmative therapy

Gay affirmative supervision as a parallel to gay affirmative therapy has yet to develop. One way of reflecting how it might do so is to look at the key ideas in gay affirmative therapy and to consider how they might be applicable to supervision.

Gay affirmative therapy is now recognised in the UK. In recent years a number of seminal texts have appeared, research is being undertaken, and a number of critiques have appeared which have helped to clarify and develop the concept. Davies presents a model 'for working with clients who identify as lesbian, gay or bisexual which does not pathologize or discriminate against such clients' (1996a: 24). He argues that a gay affirmative approach to therapy is not a new independent system of therapy but is nonetheless more than the sound application of Rogerian core conditions or psychodynamic or cognitive behavioural principles. The gay affirmative approach goes beyond current therapeutic practice and spans the range of theoretical schools. Davies accepts the term 'gay affirmative' as it is already in common usage and uses it in the sense that 'the gay affirmative therapist affirms a lesbian, gay or bisexual identity as an equally positive human experience and expression to heterosexual identity' (1996a: 25).

Maylon (1982: 69) describes gay affirmative therapy as challenging the view that homosexual desire and fixed homosexual orientations are pathological and regards homophobia rather than homosexuality as a major pathological factor. Clark (1987) and Isay (1989) both believe that neutrality on this point is not possible as everyone has been exposed to negative attitudes and beliefs about same-sex relations. Davies (1996a: 25) develops Isay's emphasis on 'the importance of the undeviatingly uncritical, accepting attitude in which the therapist's thoughtfulness, caring and regard for the patient are essential' (Isay 1989: 122) into what he calls the 'core condition' of *respect*: respect for the client's sexual orientation, for personal integrity, for lifestyle and culture, together with respectful attitudes and beliefs on the therapist's own part. This respect Davies relates to Clark's (1987) 'Ground Rules for Helping' and 'Twelve Guidelines for Retraining'. However, Clark takes a much stronger position: his understanding of 'respect' is more interventionist, with the therapist taking almost a normative role, providing the client with a model of how to be gay, and arguing that the rules and guidelines should take precedence when they conflict with

existing therapeutic practice. Many supporters of the notion of gay affirmative therapy would consider a number of Clark's rules and guidelines
inappropriate to therapy. Nevertheless Davies finds important elements in
each, particularly for training or retraining therapists.

Davies identifies other aspects of gay affirmative therapy that are relevant
to our discussion. One of these is the role of the therapist as an educator,
by providing clients with information – for example, on the coming out
process. He argues that:

> This educative function can:
> 1 provide reassurance that the client is going through a normative
>   experience;
> 2 help make sense of some of their feelings, and inspire hope in a
>   resolution;
> 3 delineate some of the developmental tasks necessary for a healthy
>   integration of sexual identity into the wider personality structure.
>
> (Davies 1996a: 35)

In discussing the third of these points, Davies explicitly refers to the role of
supervision and personal therapy for practitioners 'to monitor their own
responses to sexual diversity' (1996a: 40).

In summary, Davies proposes a model of gay affirmative therapy in which:

- homosexuality and bisexuality are accepted as equally valid expressions
  of human sexuality and homophobia is perceived to be pathological;
- clients are respected for their sexuality, choices and lifestyle;
- therapists examine their own beliefs, attitudes and feelings towards
  homosexuality and bisexuality, understand how homophobia and
  biphobia operate, and are aware of the coming out process and other
  related aspects of the lives of lesbian, gay and bisexual people;
- therapists are aware of their own power to reinforce disapproving social
  norms and reflect on using this power in client-affirming ways akin to
  re-parenting negative psycho-social experiences;
- therapists have an educative role, both with clients and within wider
  communities.

In a workshop given at the Third BAC Research Conference Harrison
(1997 and personal communication) offered a critical analysis of the literature of gay affirmative therapy. Using a new research paradigm in which
knowledge is viewed as socially constructed he surveyed 33 journal articles
and summaries of conference papers from 1982–95. From these he identified 15 themes, which he has developed into an integrated model of gay
affirmative therapy (Harrison forthcoming). His model includes the following
points:

- therapists' self-awareness and awareness of personal bias;
- development of specialist knowledge and skills for work with gay clients;

- a non-pathological view of homosexuality;
- challenging oppression using a variety of strategies;
- familiarity with the types of problems presented by gay clients;
- appropriate interventions selected by the 'users of the model';
- a range of therapeutic interventions and skills used according to the client's needs;
- an integrative approach using a range of counselling orientations.

Harrison also identifies three domains of gay affirmative therapy: work with clients to resolve conflicts; a non-pathological approach adopted by organisations; and a proactive social movement fighting for gay civil rights.

As can be seen, gay affirmative therapy has a clear outline but, in Harrison's words, still appears 'fragmented and difficult to describe' (1997: 188). The reader will have also identified a number of elements that seem at odds with traditional therapy boundaries and accepted 'standard' practice, as well as a number of internal inconsistencies.

Critiquing gay affirmative therapy

In a critique of gay affirmative therapy from an existential-phenomenological perspective du Plock (1997) discusses a number of points already identified, in particular Clark's (1987) formulation. While all du Plock's points are of interest and provide a tentative alternative way of working with lesbian and gay clients, the following are of immediate relevance to the present argument.

First, du Plock takes issue with the notion of *affirmative*. On the face of it the idea is 'wholly admirable: a respectful way of working with a group which, historically, has been much abused in the name of "treatment"' (du Plock 1997: 56). However, he believes a gay affirmative approach is prescriptive because, he argues, 'affirmative' means we are in favour of something and wish to promote it. For him the alternative to 'gay affirmative' is not 'gay negative': rather he seems to argue in favour of a gay-neutral approach. This is claimed in the name of the phenomenological principle of 'bracketing', the setting aside of the therapist's world view to enter that of the client. But as Spinelli (1989) points out more than once, this is ultimately impossible. Existential therapists are not blank screens on which the client appears, but people who bring to the therapeutic encounter the very thoughts, experiences and judgements which they bracket. These may indeed be bracketed to a greater or lesser degree, but they do not disappear. Du Plock argues in favour of therapists having no view of homosexuality (which seems somewhat naive). The alternative is not whether the therapist is for or against homosexuality, but whether they accept homosexuality as a part of the normal spectrum of human sexuality. It is interesting to note that du Plock does not argue that therapists should bracket all their thinking about heterosexuality, or adopt a heterosexual-neutral position (see Chapters 3 and 7).

The term 'affirmative' often seems to slip from its original meaning of 'accepting' to one of 'promoting'. This is seen in du Plock's understanding of Clark's 'Twelve Guidelines for Retraining' and 'Ground Rules for Helping'. While some of these may be seen as 'encouraging', encouraging cannot be equated (as du Plock does) with being prescriptive. He appears to confuse Clark's original formulations and the purpose Davies (1996a) makes of them: namely, to discuss aspects of working therapeutically with lesbian and gay clients. Up to this point what he challenges is not gay affirmative therapy but Clark and others' formulation of it.

Du Plock's second challenge to the notion of 'affirmative' in the models of Clark and Davies is that he sees it as inevitably linked to information-giving and the authority role of the therapist. For him 'Practical suggestions should probably be the exception rather than the rule in therapy. In gay-affirmative therapy they seem to be an integral part of the work' (1997: 61). Most therapists would probably agree, though it is a moot point whether information-giving has to be an integral part of gay affirmative therapy. When it comes to supervision however, information-giving may have a larger role to play, and in the supervision of new and inexperienced counsellors it can be essential.

Third, du Plock concedes that knowledge of the coming out process is useful but reminds us that it is not a normative process that the client must be guided through by the therapist but is 'very varied and complex and not a discrete linear progression' (1997: 62), a point also made by Davies (1996b). Where du Plock and Davies appear to differ is that Davies (personal communication) sees coming out as normative in that everyone has to do it in some way, while du Plock stresses the individual nature of the process so that it cannot be seen as normative, or the same for all. What is important is that the client finds his or her own way of being gay or lesbian: 'Much of the value of the concept of being gay is the way in which it provides a space which each individual can invest with a different meaning. One of the joys (and challenges) of being gay is the opportunity such an identification provides for inventing oneself' (du Plock 1997: 62–3).

Du Plock goes on to reiterate existential criticism of humanistic theory (Spinelli 1994) and apply it to Davies' model of gay affirmative therapy. It is relevant here inasmuch as it highlights how limited our understanding of sexuality still is. Du Plock argues in favour of seeing homosexuality as part of what existential-phenomenological theory calls the 'self construct' (Spinelli 1996), and that *being* gay is the construct rather than *how* one is gay. He seems to suggest that a person's sexuality is not part of their 'thrown-ness' or 'being-in-the-world' but only a choice about *how* to be-in-the-world. He does not suggest how or why people choose to be, heterosexually, homosexually, or bisexually. And yet lesbians, gay men and bisexual people do experience their sexuality not just as choice or preference for people of the same gender, as Spinelli and du Plock suggest, but also as a 'given' of existence (Cohn 1997). The choice alone position nicely does away with the grounds for homophobia but it does not fully describe people's experience of their sexuality (for a fuller discussion of this, see Chapter 3).

To conclude this discussion, I believe we can identify a number of key ideas which have implications for supervision. These relate to therapists' understanding of homosexuality and knowledge of matters related to it, to their understanding of themselves and their responses to their client's way of being, and to what they do or do not see as appropriate to the therapeutic situation.

Approaches to supervision for gay affirmative therapy

The BAC definition of supervision is very broad. Indeed it needs to be, for not only does it have to cover the supervision of a wide spectrum of theoretical models of therapy, it also has to cope with a number of theoretical models of supervision. The *Code of Ethics and Practice for the Supervision of Counsellors* (BAC 1988) lists six key elements. These state: the purpose of supervision as meeting the needs of the client; the formal collaborative nature of the process; the monitoring and clarifying of the relationships involved; what supervision is not concerned with; confidentiality; and the need for regular supervision.

Supervision in the UK has distinguished itself from that common in the USA in that in Britain, supervision is used by therapists as a consultation to guarantee their work and support them in it, whereas in the USA it is generally seen in the context of training. Thus one of the most popular models in the USA has been the Developmental Model of Stoltenberg and Delworth (1987) which provides a sequence of developmental stages for supervisees to move through as they gain experience. British approaches however have developed more from the theoretical schools of therapy in an attempt to provide supervision that is theoretically appropriate to the working of the therapist. Thus there have developed models of person-centred supervision (Mearns 1991; Frankland 1993), models derived from psychodynamic theory (Mattinson 1977; Casement 1985), behavioural approaches (Bradley 1989), tentative existential approaches (Pett 1995; Wright 1996) as well as more integrative models (Hawkins and Shohet 1989; Page and Wosket 1994). In general, person-centred supervision will focus on the core conditions, psychodynamic supervision on transference, countertransference and parallel process, and behavioural supervision on skill analysis, the construction and implementation of strategies and goal accomplishment.

In addition to these theoretical considerations, supervision must encompass what I have called 'dimensions' (Pett 1995: 119). These include the interpersonal relationship, the social context in which the encounter takes place, the managerial dimension and the developmental dimension. It is in the first two of these that consideration of gay affirmative supervision may be best situated.

In the interpersonal dimension the supervisor will consider the relationship with the therapist and the therapist's relationship with clients. By making explicit the aspects of gay affirmative therapy discussed above, respect and trust will be built up between supervisor and therapist. The supervisor will develop an understanding both of the therapist's personal symbols and meanings and, through the therapist, of the clients' views of their worlds.

The social dimension of supervision explores how the social context influences what happens between supervisor and supervisee, and between supervisor, therapist and client. This is a dimension that is little explored in the literature. The roles of gender and race in the relationship are discussed by Kadushin (1985) and those of the organisation, family and community by Ekstein and Wallerstein (1958) and Szecsody (1990). The social dimension can include all aspects of difference, particularly those implying social disadvantage. Here it would be appropriate to understand the context in which the lesbian, gay or bisexual therapist lives and works, as well as the social contexts of clients' lives. This will include the way the therapist is 'out' in both personal and professional life, as well as the broader context of homophobia in which supervisor, therapist and clients live.

Any form of supervision not only needs to take into account therapists' theoretical approach but also therapists' needs and the needs of their clients. Supervision will therefore reflect: the therapist's level of development; the supervisor's relationship with the therapist's employing organisation, if there is one; the therapist's style and way of working; and the client's aims for therapy.

Earlier in this chapter mention was made of the factors lesbian, gay and bisexual therapists identified as important to them. The therapists wanted to be accepted in supervision and respected for who they were, in the way they presented themselves without the mediation of any norm, particularly any norm that stereotyped or defined their identities for them. Linked to this was the need for a sense of safety, which was expressed as caretaking by their supervisor and was further supported by having supervision in a one-to-one rather than a group context. However no one mentioned the possibility of gay group supervision: perhaps this might be difficult to organise outside large cities. The therapists expected the supervisor to set a context in which issues of race, gender, class and sexuality were not only included but also raised and talked about by the supervisor in the session. The therapists had found it burdensome when they were the only ones to raise such issues, particularly in group settings. Lastly, the therapists characterised a successful supervisory relationship as one in which there was both transparency and mutuality.

Implicit in these therapists' approaches to their supervision is a basic understanding on the part of the supervisor of homosexualities and associated lifestyles and cultures so that they are not only able to understand the material presented but also to respond respectfully and meaningfully with their lesbian, gay and bisexual supervisees.

In terms of gay affirmative attitudes, therefore, it seems that lesbian, gay and bisexual therapists seek from their supervisors much the same attitudes as do lesbian, gay and bisexual clients from their therapists. I therefore suggest that any supervision which respects supervisees will be one which accepts homosexuality and bisexuality as equally valid expressions of human sexuality and perceives homophobia to be pathological, and in which:

- supervisors examine their own beliefs, attitudes and feelings towards homosexuality and bisexuality;
- supervisees are respected for their sexuality, choices and lifestyles;
- supervisors understand how homophobia operates and are aware of the coming out process and other related aspects of the lives of lesbian, gay and bisexual people;
- supervisors may, when appropriate, use supervision in an educative or informative way, which may include both the challenging of negative stereotypes and the giving of information.

Some suggestions towards a model of gay affirmative supervision

In many ways any gay supportive or affirmative supervision will differ little from what could be described as 'good' supervision, just as gay affirmative therapy differs little from generally good therapy. However, what has traditionally been termed 'good' supervision cannot be considered 'gay affirmative' (or for that matter truly 'good') until it proves itself to be such. In this final section we examine some of the characteristics that supervisors have to exhibit to be considered 'gay affirmative'. These will be useful criteria for therapists in search of a gay affirmative supervisor because they are lesbian, gay or bisexual, or because they work with lesbian, gay and bisexual clients. Indeed, they are the criteria all supervisors and therapists should exhibit, and be given a grounding in as part of their basic training.

To this end I believe the BAC definition of supervision needs modification. While it is unrealistic to expect every therapist to be able to work with every client, and every supervisor to be able to work with every therapist, it should be a basic requirement of all therapists and supervisors that they are able to work effectively, at least initially and in non-specialist areas, with clients despite differences of gender, age, ethnicity, disability and sexuality, as well as know how to make appropriate supportive referrals. Work on National Vocational Qualifications (NVQs) and other competence measures for training and practice (Young 1995: 13–18) seems to be moving in this direction.

In this context I would want to redefine my own working definition of supervision (Pett 1995: 120–1). For me, supervision, if it is gay affirmative, is a mutually agreed and boundaried interpersonal working relationship between a supervisor and supervisee/s which provides support to the latter to assure competent and increasingly good quality counselling for the benefit of clients. This relationship is further characterised by interpersonal, social, developmental and process dimensions, which include respect for, and an acceptance and understanding of, lesbian, gay and bisexual sexuality, culture and lifestyle. We can now consider these characteristics in more detail and suggest some ways in which they may be applied in supervision.

For each characteristic some practical suggestions are provided. They should be considered as far as they are appropriate to the supervisor's theoretical orientation and personal style. If they are not appropriate the supervisor should consider what alternatives would be appropriate for them. If supervisors cannot provide alternatives they should consider whether their orientation and style are hindering them from adopting the broadly defined gay affirmative approach to supervision proposed in this chapter and whether they should refrain from supervising lesbian, gay and bisexual therapists and those working with lesbian, gay and bisexual clients.

Characteristic 1: gay affirmative supervision accepts homosexuality and bisexuality as valid expressions of human sexuality and homophobia is perceived to be pathological

This will be the key element of gay affirmative supervision as it both defines such supervision and permeates it. Supervisors not only understand homosexuality and bisexuality as equally valid forms of human sexuality but this understanding informs their work. This knowledge is reviewed and regularly updated as new insights and developments are published and are supplemented by an increasing familiarity with lesbian, gay and bisexual lifestyles and culture.

This understanding allows supervisors to comprehend the material their supervisees bring to them and provides a framework in which to discuss it. It enables them to talk informatively about sexuality with their supervisees and to pass on their knowledge and understanding as appropriate and when required.

Supervisors can check their practice against the following questions:

- How did I acquire my knowledge of sexuality? From whom?
- What were the messages I received about homosexuality and bisexuality?

- How do my current ideas differ from those I received?
- What elements in my training as a therapist and as a supervisor helped develop my understanding of sexuality?
- When was the last time I read an article or undertook some form of study or training which dealt with lesbian, gay and bisexual issues?
- What experience have I had as a therapist in working with lesbian, gay and bisexual clients and supervisees? How successful was this work?
- What do I understand by 'homophobia'? How does it work? How could I explain it to my supervisees?
- What do I understand by 'coming out'? What is involved? Is it necessary?

Some follow-up activities could include:

- planning further reading;
- attending a workshop on lesbian, gay and bisexual issues at a conference;
- attending a short course or seminar on lesbian, gay and bisexual issues.

Characteristic 2: supervisors examine their own beliefs, attitudes and feelings towards homosexuality and bisexuality

This characteristic follows from the previous one and is its implementation. Theoretical knowledge is not sufficient. Supervisors have to access their own beliefs, feelings and attitudes honestly and to challenge themselves. This self-awareness will enable supervisors to be aware of their strengths and limitations, and help supervisees explore their own knowledge, beliefs, understandings and feelings, as well as facilitate their supervisees' understanding of their clients' own beliefs, attitudes and feelings about their sexuality.

For supervisors to develop this openness, lesbian, gay and bisexual awareness (and sexuality in general) need to be an essential part of the curriculum for supervisor training. If such awareness is not seen to be important enough to appear in the curriculum it is unlikely to be important to supervisors in their careers. It may not be until they find themselves out of their depth with supervisees that they think about developing their understanding. The supervisor will be then learning at the expense of the supervisee.

Supervisors cannot work effectively on issues of sexuality unless they have explored, come to terms with and become comfortable with their own. They should regularly explore their attitudes and feelings in their own therapy and in the supervision of their own supervisory work. Regular reading, study groups, workshops at conferences and so on can also play a part in this continuing development.

Supervisors can check their practice against the following questions:

- What experience have I had as a therapist in working with lesbian, gay and bisexual clients and supervisees? How successful was this work?
- When dealing with such clients what makes me uneasy or uncomfortable? Why am I uncomfortable?

- What aspects of lesbian, gay and bisexual lifestyles am I uncomfortable with? Why am I uncomfortable?
- What support do I have as a supervisor to discuss my own concerns about sexuality and working with lesbian, gay and bisexual clients and supervisees?
- Have I explained my own understanding of and position on sexualities to my current supervisees? If not, why not?
- How have my lesbian, gay and bisexual clients and supervisees challenged me in the past? What have I learnt from these challenges?
- How do I explain my own understanding of and position on sexualities to my prospective supervisees?
- What kind of mutual understanding and agreement on sexuality do I need with prospective supervisees before agreeing to become their supervisor?
- How do I define my work as gay affirmative? How does this square with my theoretical orientation?

Some follow-up activities could include:

- supervisors using some of their own supervision or therapy time to explore their thoughts, beliefs, feelings and attitudes;
- spending some time to think through and write down their position;
- thinking about how they would raise these issues with their clients and supervisees;
- developing some key questions for discussion with prospective supervisees.

Characteristic 3: supervisees are respected for their sexuality, choices and lifestyle

Lesbian, gay and bisexual therapists cannot operate optimally if they do not feel safe with their supervisors or if they feel they have to dissimulate and hide parts of their work or themselves. They expect supervisors to respect them, and this respect will include respect for their sexuality, choices and lifestyle, however different these may be from those of the supervisor. It is not enough for supervisors to say that they respect their supervisees. Respect needs to be demonstrated in word and action.

In work with lesbian, gay and bisexual supervisees this respect will show itself in a number of ways. First and foremost will be an acknowledgement of difference, a willingness to listen to the supervisee, and an acknowledgement that the supervisee may know more about these matters than the supervisor. Many lesbian, gay and bisexual therapists experience the lack of open acknowledgement of difference and the failure to bring issues related to it into the open as an inability on the supervisor's part to handle the issue comfortably. This suggests to them that the supervisor is personally uncomfortable with the topic and unable to deal with it, and consequently unable to cope appropriately with the clients' material when this is presented in supervision sessions. Supervisors therefore need to be the first to raise issues and show an appropriate willingness to talk about them without prying or displaying a prurient interest. In particular supervisors need to address sensitively and frankly issues of difference in sexuality between supervisor and supervisee, and between supervisee and client, without on the one hand trivialising such differences or reducing them to stereotypes or clichés, or on the other hand blowing them up out of proportion.

Supervisors also need to be aware that the supervisees' experience is equally valid. Supervisors must not misuse the power of the supervisory role but show humility in acknowledging the supervisees' greater knowledge of matters of lesbian, gay and bisexual sexuality when this is the case. They should also not 'normalise' lesbian, gay and bisexual experience as if there were clear-cut ways or models of being lesbian, gay or bisexual.

It is not only the heterosexual supervisor of lesbian, gay and bisexual therapists who needs to demonstrate this understanding and respect. Lesbian, gay and bisexual supervisors also need to demonstrate to their supervisees that, while they may have appropriate levels of knowledge and understanding, they are able to listen to and acknowledge the different experience of their individual supervisees. Asking therapists how they experience their clients' sexuality, or how their clients experience their own sexuality is more important than any statement which shows that the supervisor is 'on the right side'. Having a lesbian, gay or bisexual supervisor is not enough for lesbian, gay and bisexual therapists, just as having a lesbian, gay or bisexual therapist is not enough for lesbian, gay and bisexual clients.

In achieving this respect and establishing the appropriate supportive open supervisory relationship, supervisors will be modelling for their supervisees how to provide the same respect for their clients and will be helping them work with the individual differences of their clients.

Supervisors can check their practice against the following questions:

- How forthcoming have my clients and supervisees been in discussing lesbian, gay and bisexual matters with me? Why is this?
- How do I deal with any discomfort I have about lifestyles when working with my clients and supervisees?
- Am I able to discuss this appropriately with my clients and supervisees? What does 'appropriately' mean for me in this context? Does it vary for work with clients and work with supervisees?
- How do I discuss difference with my supervisees?
- How do I build and show respect for my supervisees?
- Am I the first to raise issues of difference and sexuality or do I wait until my supervisees raise them?
- What support do I have as a supervisor to discuss my own concerns about sexuality and working with lesbian, gay and bisexual clients and supervisees?

Some follow-up activities could include:

- having a review session asking supervisees how they perceive their supervisor's attitudes to their sexuality, choices and lifestyle or to those of their clients;
- supervisors spending some time in their own therapy or supervision reviewing their attitudes and responses to their clients' and supervisees' sexuality, choices and lifestyles, and how they show their respect.

Characteristic 4: supervisors understand how homophobia operates, are aware of the coming out process and other related aspects of the lives of lesbian, gay and bisexual people

Coming out is a key developmental, emotional, social (Minton and McDonald 1985; Babuscio 1988; Greene 1994; Davies 1996b) and spiritual (Whitehead and Whitehead 1986; Woods 1988; Heyward 1989; Thompson 1995) process in the lives of lesbians, gay men and bisexual people. It is also an intensely personal one, linked to other stages of development. Any supervisor or therapist working with lesbians, gay men and bisexuals needs to understand the process in general as well as be open to individual difference (Davies 1996b).

Coming out is of course related to, even a product of, homophobia (Smith 1971; Forstein 1988; Shidlo 1994; Davies 1996c). Many lesbians, gay men and bisexual people do not understand how homophobia functions to marginalise and oppress them. It is essential therefore that both therapist and supervisor understand how homophobia operates so that they are able to help clients develop an understanding of how it is operating in their own lives and how they can respond to it. This understanding will need to be realistic, avoiding the extremes of accepting it as one's unfortunate lot and pretending that it does not exist. Most lesbians, gay men and bisexual people have to live a continual balancing act between being open about who they are and being careful to avoid exposing themselves to dangerous expressions of homophobia. They do not always and everywhere feel able or willing to challenge homophobia, and this needs to be acknowledged in a supportive way.

Supervisors can check their practice against the following questions:

- What do I understand by 'homophobia'? How does it work?
- How do I challenge homophobia when I come across it in my own life?
- How could I explain homophobia to my supervisees?
- What do I understand by 'coming out'? What is involved? Is it necessary? What are the risks involved?
- How could I explain the coming out process to my supervisees in a way that allows for individual differences?

- What are the main characteristics of the process and how do they link with other developmental processes? What are the implications for clients' emotional, social and spiritual development?

Some follow-up activities could include:

- supervisors working out their own definitions of homophobia and coming out;
- considering how homophobia affects their own life whatever their sexuality;
- reviewing their own coming out process if they are lesbian, gay or bisexual.

(See also Davies 1998 for further practical suggestions for supervisors challenging their own internalised homophobia.)

Characteristic 5: supervisors may, when appropriate, use supervision in an educative or informative way, which may include both the challenge of negative stereotypes and the giving of information

How far supervision is educative will vary according to the model of supervision used, the personal style of the supervisor and the needs of the supervisee. Many therapists, particularly those with little or no training in this work, who start working with lesbian, gay and bisexual clients or with clients exploring their sexuality, will need particular support and an opportunity to learn from their supervisor. They will need to feel safe enough to ask questions and learn, rather than fear showing their lack of knowledge and skill. Such a supportive learning climate will facilitate challenge of negative stereotypes as well as provide a safe place for them to explore their own beliefs, feelings and internalised homophobia.

Informed supervisors can share their knowledge with clients, are able to discuss various models of understanding sexuality, can distinguish between what is gay affirmative and what is not and why, and are able to help their supervisees work through theoretical issues for themselves. Informed supervisors can also suggest appropriate reading and other resources. They are also skilled at discerning what is their own, and what is the supervisees' material and are hence able to model for their supervisees how to do the same with their material and that of their clients.

Supervisors can check their practice against the following questions:

- From my own theoretical orientation how do I see the educative and informative roles of supervision?
- How do I develop the kind of supervisory relationship where supervisees can ask for information without becoming dependent?
- When would I give supervisees information? How would I do this?
- How do I support supervisees who are new to working with lesbian, gay and bisexual clients?

- How do I challenge negative stereotypes? How do I do this with my own clients?
- How do I challenge negative stereotypes in my supervisees? How do I support them in challenging their clients' stereotypes, and their own?
- How can I explain gay affirmative approaches to therapy to my supervisees within their own theoretical framework?
- What reading can I recommend to my supervisees?
- How do I model a gay affirmative approach to therapy in my own supervisory work?

Some follow-up activities could include:

- supervisors could review their own approach to gay affirmative work in relation to their theoretical orientation, perhaps with colleagues;
- think through their own boundaries on giving information in supervision;
- draw up a short introductory bibliography of books and articles they can recommend.

Conclusion

At a time when gay affirmative therapy is defining what therapists need in order to work effectively and respectfully with lesbian, gay and bisexual clients, it is also challenging what until now has been considered 'good' therapy. In time it is hoped it will redefine what is considered 'adequate' or 'good enough' therapy. These developments will have repercussions for supervision. Therapists themselves will demand supervision that is in keeping with the insights and skills they have developed.

As yet the notion of gay affirmative supervision is in its infancy, and some might say it is only just born. This chapter has attempted to show some of the parallels with gay affirmative therapy. While someday 'good' supervision or even 'good enough' supervision will be defined with the needs of lesbian, gay and bisexual therapists and clients in mind, working with these therapists and clients is still seen as a specialist field. It is specialist because many supervisors have not understood what is required of them to provide appropriate supervision. It is hoped that this chapter will help them think about what they need to do to develop the necessary knowledge, skills and attitudes. At the same time it is hoped that this initial attempt to draw out the characteristics of gay affirmative supervision will challenge training institutions to think more carefully about the needs of their trainees, and challenge those that provide training in supervision to consider how they might go about training a new generation of supervisors who can respond professionally to the needs of their lesbian, gay and bisexual supervisees, and to all who work with lesbian, gay and bisexual clients.

References

American Psychiatric Association (1980) *Diagnostic and Statistical Manual of Mental Disorders*, 3rd edn. Washington, DC: American Psychiatric Association.

Babuscio, J. (1988) *We Speak for Ourselves: The Experiences of Gay Men and Lesbians*, 2nd edn. London: SPCK.

BAC (British Association for Counselling) (1988) *Code of Ethics and Practice for the Supervision of Counsellors*. Rugby: BAC.

BAC (British Association for Counselling) (1998) *Code of Ethics and Practice for Counsellors*. Rugby: BAC.

Bradley, L. (1989) *Counselor Supervision: Principles, Process and Practice*. Muncie, IN: Accelerated Development Inc.

Casement, P. (1985) *On Learning from the Patient*. London: Routledge.

Clark, D. (1987) *The New Loving Someone Gay*. Berkeley, CA: Celestial Arts.

Cohn, H.W. (1997) *Existential Thought and Therapeutic Practice: An Introduction to Existential Psychotherapy*. London: Sage.

Davies, D. (1996a) Towards a model of gay affirmative therapy, in D. Davies and C. Neal (eds) *Pink Therapy: A Guide for Counsellors and Therapists Working with Lesbian, Gay and Bisexual Clients*. Buckingham: Open University Press.

Davies, D. (1996b) Working with people coming out, in D. Davies and C. Neal (eds) *Pink Therapy: A Guide for Counsellors and Therapists Working with Lesbian, Gay and Bisexual Clients*. Buckingham: Open University Press.

Davies, D. (1996c) Homophobia and heterosexism, in D. Davies and C. Neal (eds) *Pink Therapy: A Guide for Counsellors and Therapists Working with Lesbian, Gay and Bisexual Clients*. Buckingham: Open University Press.

Davies, D. (1998) The six necessary and sufficient conditions applied to working with lesbian, gay, and bisexual clients, *The Person-Centered Journal*, 5(2): 111–24.

du Plock, S. (1997) Sexual misconceptions: a critique of gay affirmative therapy and some thoughts on an existential-phenomenological theory of sexual orientation, *Journal of the Society for Existential Analysis*, 8(2): 56–71.

Ekstein, R. and Wallerstein, R. (1958) *The Teaching and Learning of Psychotherapy*. New York: International University Press.

Ellis, M.L. (1994) Lesbians, gay men and psychoanalytic training, *Free Associations*, 4(4): 501–17.

Frankland, A. (1993) 'A Person Centred Model of Supervision', unpublished MS. Nottingham Trent University.

Forstein, M. (1988) Homophobia: an overview, *Psychiatric Annals*, 18: 33–6.

Graham, D.L.R., Rawlings, E.I., Halpern, H.S. and Hermes, J. (1983) Therapists' needs for training in counseling lesbians and gay men, *Professional Psychology: Research and Practice*, 15(4): 482–96.

Greene, B. (1994) Lesbian and gay sexual orientations: implications for clinical training, practice, and research, in B. Greene and G.M. Herek (eds) *Psychological Perspectives on Lesbian and Gay Issues, Vol. 1, Lesbian and Gay Psychology: Theory, Research and Clinical Applications*. Thousand Oaks, CA: Sage.

Harrison, N. (1997) Gay affirmative therapy: a critical analysis of the literature, *Counselling: The Journal of the British Association for Counselling*, 8(3): 187–8.

Harrison, N. (1998) Gay affirmative therapy: a micro-macro level continuum. Paper Presented at Fourth BAC Research Conference, University of Birmingham, 21 March.

Harrison, N. (forthcoming) Gay affirmative therapy: a critical analysis of the literature, *British Journal of Guidance and Counselling*.

Hawkins, P. and Shohet, R. (1989) *Supervision in the Helping Professions*. Milton Keynes: Open University Press.

Heyward, C. (1989) *Touching our Strength: The Erotic as Power and the Love of God*. San Francisco: Harper & Row.

Isay, R.A. (1989) *Being Homosexual: Gay Men and Their Development*. New York: Avon Books.

Kadushin, A. (1985) *Supervision in Social Work*, 2nd edn. New York: Columbia University Press.

Mann, L. (1994) Working with lesbian and gay clients, *Counselling*, 5(1): 26.

Mattinson, J. (1977) *The Reflection Process in Casework Supervision*. London: Institute of Marital Studies, Tavistock Institute of Human Relations.

Maylon, A. (1982) Psychotherapeutic implications of internalized homophobia in gay men, in J. Gonsiorek (ed.) *Homosexuality and Psychotherapy*. New York: Haworth Press.

Mearns, D. (1991) On being a supervisor, in W. Dryden and B. Thorne (eds) *Training and Supervision for Counselling in Action*. London: Sage.

Minton, H.L. and McDonald, G.J. (1985) Homosexuality identity formation as a developmental process, in J.P. De Cecco and M.G. Shively (eds) *Origins of Sexuality and Homosexuality*. New York: Harrington Park Press.

O'Connor, N. and Ryan, J. (1993) *Wild Desires and Mistaken Identities: Lesbianism and Psychoanalysis*. London: Virago.

Page, S. and Wosket, V. (1994) *Supervising the Counsellor: A Cyclical Model*. London: Routledge.

Pett, J. (1995) A personal approach to existential supervision, *Journal of the Society for Existential Analysis*, 6(2): 117–26.

Pett, J. (1997) Are we being served? A workshop report, *Bulletin of the Association for Lesbian, Gay and Bisexual Psychologies UK*, February.

Rudolph, J. (1988) Counselors' attitudes towards homosexuality: a selective review of the literature, *Journal of Counseling and Development*, 67: 165–8.

Shidlo, A. (1994) Internalized homophobia: conceptual and empirical issues in measurement, in B. Greene and G.M. Herek (eds) *Psychological Perspectives on Lesbian and Gay Issues, Vol. 1, Lesbian and Gay Psychology: Theory, Research, and Clinical Applications*. Thousand Oaks, CA: Sage.

Silverstein, C. (1991) *Gays, Lesbians, and Their Therapists*. New York: Norton.

Smith, K.T. (1971) Homophobia: a tentative personality profile, *Psychological Reports*, 29: 1091–4.

Spinelli, E. (1989) *The Interpreted World: An Introduction to Phenomenological Psychology*. London: Sage.

Spinelli, E. (1994) *Demystifying Therapy*. London: Constable.

Spinelli, E. (1996) Some hurried notes expressing outline ideas that someone might someday utilise as signposts towards a sketch of an existential-phenomenological theory of human sexuality, *Journal of the Society for Existential Analysis*, 8(1): 2–20.

Stoltenberg, C. and Delworth, U. (1987) *Supervising Counsellors and Therapists: A Developmental Approach*. San Francisco: Jossey-Bass.

Szecsody, I. (1990) Supervision: a didactic or mutative situation, *Psychoanalytic Psychotherapy*, 4(3): 245–61.

Thompson, M. (ed.) (1995) *Gay Soul: Finding the Heart of Gay Spirit and Nature*. London: Harper Collins.

Whitehead, J.D. and Whitehead, E.E. (1986) Three passages of maturity, in R. Nugent (ed.) *A Challenge to Love: Gay and Lesbian Catholics in the Church*. New York: Crossroad.

WHO (World Health Organization) (1992) *International Statistical Classification of Diseases and Related Health Problems (ICD)*, 10th revision. Geneva: WHO.

Woods, R. (1988) *Another Kind of Love: Homosexuality and Spirituality*, 3rd edn. Fort Wayne, IN: Knoll Publishing.

Wright, R. (1996) Another personal approach to existential supervision, *Journal of the Society for Existential Analysis*, 7(1): 149–58.

Young, V. (1995) *The Equality Complex: Lesbians in Therapy – A Guide to Anti-Oppressive Practice*. London: Cassell.

DENIS BRIDOUX AND
        MARTIN WEAVER

Neuro-linguistic psychotherapy

> No two human beings have exactly the same experiences. The model that we create to guide us in the world is based in part upon our experiences. Each of us may, then, create a different model of the world we share and thus come to live in a somewhat different reality.
>
> (Bandler and Grinder 1975: 7)

A flat in Chiswick

'Hi Denis, glad you could come over.'

'Well, I thought that a real meeting would be a good starting point for collaborating on Dominic and Charles' book.'

'Indeed. As two out gay men working as therapists and trainers in NLP, we'll be able to put the ideas across. What do you think?'

'I agree. Together we have plenty of experience to do this well and the advantage with NLP, of course, is that lesbians and bisexual people will also recognise, appreciate and apply the approach we present.'

'Precisely. It will be good to work together again after the NLP training we attended a few years ago where sexuality was never really mentioned, although you and I, with three other gay participants, took the opportunity to relate NLP to our gay identity.'

'I remember you defined your own mission statement [see Appendix A] for your work with the gay community as a result of our talks!'

'That's right, and it still applies. Unfortunately, an article on NLP and gay issues [Bridoux 1997], trying to create a network, didn't get much feedback. My similar rallying calls on relevant Internet newsgroups haven't had much of a response either.'

'So an assertive gay presence hasn't really developed?'

'Not officially yet. I see this chapter as an opportunity to do some outreach and to begin creating an explicit gay context for NLP.'

'NLP can work so well with gay issues. We must focus on the core aspects and on how to relate these to living in a gay, lesbian and bisexual culture which is itself developing.'

'So, how are we going to get started?'

'Why not by telling them what the initials stand for [see Box 5.1] and what Bandler and Grinder, the co-developers of NLP, called the "meta-model" [1975: 24]. After all, that's how it all began.'

Box 5.1   What does NLP stand for?

NEURO-   This refers to our physical nervous system, the neurones and their environment and functioning, and the all-important interconnection and interdependence of mind and body. Mind and body communicate by electrical impulses and chemical reactions, operating as a single system.

LINGUISTIC   This refers to language in its widest sense: not just the words that we use but how we use them. After all, our tonality is very important to meaning and the effect that words have on us – both rhythm and tone – is important. It also refers to our body language and how we use it to emphasise our communications.

PROGRAMMING   This simply refers to the repeated behaviours that we have learned and continue to express, and the way we can change these to achieve what we want.

'OK. As each of us grows up, we construct a model within us of how the world works. After a period of time this internal model becomes the "real" world. On this basis we generate all our beliefs, decisions and behaviours. NLP is ultimately a philosophy, an *attitude*, supported by a rigorous *methodology* and a *technology* to work with this internal model, so that each of us achieves our fullest potential.'

'So, what attitude does NLP represent to us?'

'To quote Richard Bandler: "It's a mindset, characterised by a passionate, omnivorously insatiable sense of curiosity and adventure, motivated by a resolute commitment to succeed, a commitment to seize any opportunity to learn and make the most of life, and a wanton willingness and drive to experiment with the necessary flexibility to achieve and influence" [Bandler 1995: 1].'

'It is thanks to this, coupled with the methodology hinted at above, that we are able to study, model, learn, teach, replicate and alter the structure of our subjective experience, of our internal maps, to tailor them to our requirements; and the tools we use are our perceptual, language and cognitive skills. Unfortunately, there isn't the space to go into fine details about the "technology", such as anchoring, submodalities or perceptual positions.'

'One issue that I'd like to consider is whether this book is asking the right question? For me what is ultimately important is how well the therapist relates to the client, irrespective of their own sexual identity, because, in a sense, whatever approach a therapist takes is irrelevant if their own issues or views on the world cloud their work with a client. After all, even if NLP were the most perfect of philosophies, it is still dependent on the practitioner. Even an NLP therapist can be homophobic or heterosexist.'

'Indeed. As a starting point, we need to identify our well-formed outcome [Cameron-Bandler 1985] [see Box 5.2], practising what we preach and applying to ourselves what we ask others to do.'

'I see our own outcome for this chapter to be about identifying ways of regaining power and control in our lives and of finding happiness, and how NLP can enable gay men, lesbians and bisexual people to do that. I'd like to enable people to move from "effect" to "cause", because that's ultimately what we do. In other words, I'd like people to enjoy living by realising they are in charge of their lives, by regaining a greater degree of control. You should be the one causing events to occur in your life, rather than letting life do things to you.'

'You are referring here to the two main ways we have of responding to events in life: either we address them and interact with the event, being in control, at "cause", or we flee from them, because we believe we cannot deal with them, being out of control, at "effect". Some people call this "the fight or flight response".'

'I personally prefer the word "face" instead of "fight", because who says life has to be a fight? The labels we give things condition our responses towards them: diagnoses are such labels. In NLP we work towards the outcome a person wants, their desired state [Dilts *et al.* 1980], because looking back on the problem from the perspective of the solution enables you to begin thinking of the steps to achieve it. After all, NLP is solutions-oriented. If you want to achieve confidence and self-esteem, why repeat past problems and continually relive unpleasantnesses?'

'I'm still thinking about the idea of being in control. I personally like to use the metaphor of a boat on an ocean. If you compare life to this boat, you're "at effect" when the currents and winds drive you hither and yon. However, if you use a rudder, you can successfully steer yourself, irrespective of the swells and obstacles that may crop up, so that you get to go where you choose to go. We all have this rudder within, but either don't know we've got it or don't know how to use it. I see my job as enabling my clients or course participants to find their own rudder and use it to their advantage.'

'But how do we find where we are on this ocean?'

'Well, nobody can have an absolute awareness of "reality" or "the world out there", because we're limited by our senses. The most we can have is a re-presentation of this reality. And I believe that NLP is about finding out how we build and structure that re-presentation within ourselves.'

Box 5.2   Well-formed outcomes

An outcome stands a far greater chance of being achieved if you:

1 *State it in the positive*
   What do you want? (Use short specific sentences.)

2 *Place it in its appropriate context*
   Where, when, with whom (if any) and by when do you want this outcome?

3 *Express it in sensory-specific terms*
   Imagine you already have it (state this in the present tense throughout, as if you've already got it). What do you:
   ● see
   ● hear (including what you may say to yourself)
   ● feel
   ● smell
   ● taste
   when you achieve this outcome, so that you know when you have it?

4 *Initiate and maintain it by yourself*
   Is there anything in this world that is in the way of you getting your goal? Are you in charge of the changes required? (If not, rephrase your outcome so that you are in charge of the changes. Put yourself at 'cause' in your life, instead of at 'effect'.)

5 *Make sure it preserves all the positive aspects of your current state*
   Will you lose anything that you now have by gaining that goal? (Make sure your outcome is at least as good as what you already have.)

6 *Perceive it as worthwhile*
   Is the outcome worth what it will take to get it? (If not, why bother in the first place?) Is the outcome representative of who you are and who you want to be? (If not, who will you become if you go for it?)

7 *Are you satisfied with all its consequences and implications?*
   What are the consequences of you achieving your goal, for yourself and others involved? Could you live with these consequences? How will it affect other aspects of your life (sexual, personal, professional, spiritual, personal development, health, other), other people around you and, ultimately, your community and the planet (if relevant)? How will your life be different? Is that what you really want?

'Why the hyphen?'

'We receive input through our senses on a continuing basis. Until I mention it, you may not be directly conscious of the typeface we're using, or the weight of the book in your hands, or the quality of the light on the page, or the smell of the paper and glue, etc. [see Box 5.3]. In NLP, we identify three processes: *deletions*, where we unconsciously ignore or cut out certain parts

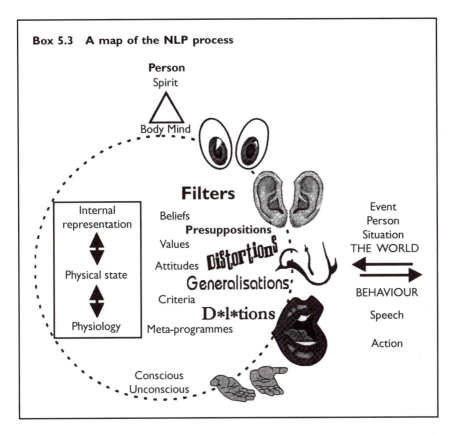

Box 5.3   A map of the NLP process

of the data we receive; *generalisations*, because it is easy to take a single event or piece of knowledge and apply this throughout our lives; and *distortions*, where we create our own understanding of the world – a personal map. All experience is therefore adapted to fit this map.

'Although we perceive all these and more, we're only aware of a minute fraction or selection of them at any one time. We process this input in a variety of different ways, depending on our personality, as it goes through a series of cognitive filters, some of which are: language, memories, decisions, beliefs, values, attitudes and meta-programmes.[1] These constantly *delete*, *generalise* and *distort* our experience of reality, in order to manage in everyday life.

'These deletions, generalisations and distortions can and do occur at *every* level of our experience of reality – and they need to, otherwise we'd be overwhelmed! We create our view of the world from what remains of that information. It is through the interaction of our perceptual and cognitive filters that we develop our internal map of the "external territory" which is the world, our "meta-model". We create this map with our beliefs, values and meta-programmes, behaving and making decisions according to what our internal map tells us.

'Of course, NLP also reminds us that "the menu is not the meal" or "the map is not the territory" [Korzybski 1933: 58], otherwise it would need to be the size of the world! So, it's this map, this "meta-model" which we construct, develop and upgrade throughout our lives, which we consult to extract meaning and how to react to the world around us, and which we operate on, enabling our clients to modify their perceptual and cognitive filters. This enables them to "upgrade" their internal maps, so that they are more aware of the choices they have. So we seek to increase awareness of choices from the outset. "If you always do what you've always done, you'll always get what you've always got: so, if what you do is not working, do anything else at all!" goes an NLP saying.'

' "If you have no choice, you're dead! If you only have one choice, you're stuck. If you have two choices, you're in a quandary. If you have three choices, now you're up to choice! Choose to have at least five choices!" goes another. I love those NLP sayings, those ditties and proverbs which motivate us so much. You know that one "If it works, it's NLP"?'

'That's a generalisation, but I see what you mean: NLP is a model of models, like the Mandelbrot set in mathematics [Capra 1996] and, for that reason, has universal applications far beyond the scope of therapy. Operating from a model of wellness, as opposed to a model of illness, NLP enables you to think of what *you* want for a change.'

'But it's amazing how difficult people find it to identify what they want and the lengths they will go to, in order to tell you what they don't want! If you keep thinking about what you don't want all the time, is it any wonder you keep getting it?'

'That's right! Not processing negatives is one of the ways our unconscious mind operates [James 1995]: in order *not* to think of something, I have to think about it first, so for example, in order *not* to think of my front door I need to think about it first.'

'Before we go any further, I think readers would like to know how it all began [see Box 5.4]. NLP has grown along a different path from other therapeutic processes. Some psychotherapists see themselves as "scientists" in one form or another. Traditionally, science grows because people see a problem, then they seek an explanation in order to develop a theory about what they have seen. Finally they test their theory by experimenting or observing actions. This didn't happen in NLP. Its developers have stated that explicitly in *The Structure of Magic*: "this set of tools is not based upon some pre-existing psychological theory or therapeutic approach" [Bandler and Grinder 1975: 6]. What actually happened was that Bandler and Grinder simply observed what they saw, deconstructed their observations and then recreated them elsewhere. They never really bothered with a theoretical model, they just focused on the outcome. In fact, at the end of

---

Box 5.4   A brief history of NLP

The accepted wisdom is that NLP took shape when Richard Bandler, a mathematics student, met linguist John Grinder at the University of California, Santa Cruz, in 1972. We are told that four specific strands came together in NLP:

- Systems theory, also known as cybernetics, whose pioneer, Gregory Bateson, a personal friend of Bandler's, greatly influenced the work.
- Transformational grammar, discovered by the linguist and thinker Noam Chomsky.
- Neuroscience, a rapidly evolving area of work at the time.
- General semantics developed in the 1930s by Alfred Korzybski.

Bandler and Grinder called their new discipline neuro-linguistic programming because of the systemic way language interacts with our nervous system so as to affect and change our beliefs, habits, skills and behaviours (i.e. programmes).

They also studied outstanding communicators including:

- Carl Rogers, the founder of person-centred therapy;
- Fritz Perls, the father of Gestalt therapy;
- Virginia Satir, developer of family therapy; and
- Milton Erickson, who had regenerated the field of hypnotherapy.

They wanted to know how each of them did what they did to make them excel in their field.

Identifying the key patterns and processes used by the above practitioners through a specific process known as modelling led to a refining of their understanding of the very nature of how they achieved their results.

The Structure of Magic, they state: "We have tried in the best way we know how to show some of the many patterns that therapists of every school have in common. We never had the intention of starting a new school of therapy; we wished, rather, to start a new way of talking about therapy so that the similarities of different schools approaching the task of helping to change could be understood" [p. 195].'

'So, how do we show how we, as gay men, have felt able to take NLP and use it positively? And how can NLP be of benefit to lesbians, gay men and bisexual people?'

'A case study, I think, will best illustrate this. Coming out is, I would guess, one of the most problematic and frequent issues I encounter. If it's an identity-level issue, a client can really grow once it's sorted out. For instance, one client I had wanted me to tell him he was straight. By paying careful attention to his language patterns I could hear both his gay aspect and a part that was terrified of his gay self being "found out". Given NLP's perspective on maps I talked and worked with both these parts of my client.'

'How did you do that?'

'We agreed that the first step was for him to admit his internal conflict. He didn't understand this so I asked which part caused him most distress. Without hesitation he said the part of him that was terrified. I then asked him if he loved the part of him that was terrified – he didn't. So I said that, if I could show him that this part had a positive intention for him, could he then love that part? He said maybe.'

'This is where the presupposition that "every behaviour has a positive intention" comes in.'

'That's right. I talked to his terrified part as if it was a real person, asking what its positive intention was, and what was it trying to achieve by being terrified? It answered that it was keeping my client safe because, if my client admitted he was gay, he would lose everything. So I congratulated that part on its intention and my client also agreed this sounded sensible. I then asked what that part ultimately wanted for my client: "Happiness", was the response. I said that was also a very sensible and sound intention. I asked that part how old it was: "ten" came the response.'

'This is a perfect example of your unconscious working: until you ask, your client doesn't know, but your client's unconscious maps all these details.'

'After about fifteen minutes my client and I discovered that, at the age of ten he had been told explicitly by a teacher that "Gay men are sad people who never have good jobs or marriages and who grow old and die alone and unloved". The ten-year-old took all this in, incorporating it into his growing internal map. This necessitated for him the creation of a separate self that would never die alone because it wouldn't grow up – ever. This man was in his late thirties, but his ten-year-old self had remained terrified that he would lose everything if he came out. Further questioning elicited the fact that his gay self was miserable because it was connected to the terrified part, but it also wanted him to be happy as a gay man. Result – conflict.'

'So what did you do next?'

'Using his whole system as he presented it to me at that time . . .'

'What do you mean by that?'

'Simply including in the process all the parts of himself he had become aware of at that point. In effect, treating him *as if* he were a collection of people. This is the systems thinking behind NLP, with a touch of the Virginia Satir family therapy approach.'

'Of course, we don't live in isolation from each other. So you valued his view of the world, his map, by accepting and working with his "internal family", his constructs.'

'Right. We then identified positive aspects in both his gay self and the rest of him. At this point I asked if there were any other parts of him that wanted to be heard on this issue. After a moment's thought he said "No".'

'This happens to me as well. I normally add a form of words which means that, if there are any other parts, they can join in as and when they want to. This gives clients permission to rebuild their map – literally change their mind as they have described it.'

'I think that's very important. Then we looked at gay men with successful relationships and jobs, and he concluded that the teacher had been wrong. I asked my client to recreate the memory of being told and then to run the memory again with the new learning of how gay men can be, given today's role models. This reduced the feeling of misery.'

'So he knew that what he was doing was working.'

'Indeed, clear evidence is so important. I then asked the terrified part to talk to the gay part and to work together to achieve the happiness they both wanted. After a few minutes' thought my client said that he no longer felt terrified or miserable and that the part identified as ten-years-old had gone, but that it wasn't missing.'

'So he had reintegrated this aspect of himself into his whole personality.'

'Exactly. In its place was a feeling of excitement tinged with uncertainty. I was then able to direct him to various social organisations that could provide further support for him to explore and develop.'

'Well done. For me, NLP works with queer issues because, proceeding from a systems way of thinking, it works with issues without labelling them. Being about wellness and how to achieve it, it does not spend its time judging and theorising on something like homosexuality, but instead looks at how homosexuality may affect our life.

'In any case, the word "homosexuality" is a nominalisation, an abstraction which means different things to different people. It began its life defining a psychiatric diagnosis and if there is one thing we aim to avoid in NLP it's diagnosing, because of the way this has of fossilising a behaviour, making it harder to work on and change.

'For some people homosexuality may solely be a matter of behaviour, like having or wanting to have sex with people of your own sex [Paalman 1990]. For others, it's about beliefs, values and preferences regarding sex and love. And for still others, it's a matter of identity, who they perceive themselves to be. It depends from what logical level [Dilts 1990] they operate as sexual beings. [see Box 5.5 and Appendix B, which illustrates logical levels from a sexual health promotion perspective].

'Much of the effectiveness of NLP comes from recognising and understanding these levels, these hierarchies of thinking at which we operate: they enable us to apprehend and integrate the structure of our subjective experience. By listening carefully to the words people use and the intonation they give to these words, you can identify from which logical level they are operating at any one time. Given that, it is so much easier to elicit what a

---

Box 5.5   Logical levels

Logical level	Example/meaning
SPIRIT	⇧ **Wherefore** I am: purest or highest form of being
IDENTITY	⇧ **Who** I am
BELIEF	⇧ **Why** I am as I am and do as I do
CAPABILITY	⇧ **How** I live and do as I do
BEHAVIOUR	⇧ **What** I do in my life
ENVIRONMENT	⇧ **Where** and **when** I do what I do

---

problem might actually be and effectively work on it. Freud was concerned about "contaminating" his clients with his ideas and constructs. This explains, I am told, why you see psychoanalysts sitting behind their client: they hope to remove their influence from the client, so as not to "lead the witness", as it were.

'In a therapeutic context, of course, like anywhere else, the therapist's own experience also has a structure. In the past this has, by and large, been a negative force for members of sexual minorities [Davies and Neal 1996], although things are changing. As NLP practitioners, we take a holistic approach with our clients, which includes and optimises the effect of the therapist on the therapy. However, to achieve this means that a neurolinguistic practitioner should be aware of any problems or concerns a therapy raised for him or herself, so that they can address and resolve it. This way a client doesn't leave the therapy with more problems than they began with, as sometimes occurs.

'You know, whether gay, lesbian or bisexual, terror or disgust at one's own sexual identity can often be traced to an unconscious belief, like "To be gay is bad, filthy or disgusting", acquired at a very early age, which we generalise to our whole life. The client may have been carrying this first association around with them, living it every day and everywhere. Identifying this first association and re-accessing it from a new perspective and with a new insight (e.g. "Gay men can be as happy and successful as anybody else", or "It's how I choose to live as a gay man which really matters") can enable conclusions based on the original association to be dismissed as "out of date", or plain irrelevant and a new, resourceful conclusion to be put in its place. Many problems I have worked with were linked to very negative emotions connected to "I" statements, which Gestalt therapists would call introjections, along the lines of "I can never be a success", "I will never find a partner", or "I hate myself".

'Hence, when we see clients, one of the things we do is to identify these and when they were acquired. The processes we carry out are especially effective at disentangling negative emotions from the actual experience, lifting years of internalised self-fulfilling disgust, so that the person is able to learn anew from this experience. Once we have done so, we can enable them to bring into consciousness new, more beneficial, more affirming learnings. These new learnings are then used as a base on which to build. They become incorporated into the client's whole map, thereby removing consequent damage to mental *and* physical health. This is especially relevant in the field of psychoneuro-immunology: the mind/body system. I understand that studies in the psychology of long-term survivors of HIV show that they may not have such negative self-beliefs.[2]

'Of course, it may be that the client prefers the original negative message and stays with that: better the devil you know. Or they may fear to lose whatever positive intention was hiding behind the behaviour. This, in turn, would suggest a different, perhaps subtler unresourceful message to resolve and another way to go about enabling resolution, no matter how unconscious it may be. Ultimately, the aim is to become in rapport with your unconscious mind, so the whole of you pulls in the right direction, instead of being at loggerheads. The really useful thing is that, as a therapist, I don't need to know who or what has caused the negative emotion to be generated or what the event actually entailed. The client can hold that themselves. Using the ideas behind rapport and behavioural flexibility I can ask all sorts of bizarre questions which enable *them* to find out.'

'That's what I always find fascinating: since our filters appear to exist and function regardless of personal desires, all this processing *is* free of content.'

'Indeed, although content remains important, NLP is about *how* you put your ideas together (i.e. *process* and *structure*) rather than *what* exactly those ideas are or the "story" contained within any memory or experience (i.e. *content*).'

'And it is because NLP is structure- and process-oriented that it is very quick and effective, as NLP therapy does not delve into the content of memories, or only in so far as they are directly relevant. It takes time to analyse content and often to little effect.'

'Whereas playing with the format of a memory can make a hell of a difference! Think about how poor a document can look in one format or font and superb in another. Likewise think how different a film looks watched on the big screen or on the television and a piece of music sounds from a tinny radio or a top of the range system. We call these minimal differences in the formatting of our experience *submodalities* [Bandler and MacDonald 1988]. These have actually been shown to encode the *meaning* of any particular experience as good or bad and the work we do enables us to recode, to reformat these submodalities. Hence the term programming.'

'Having given some background and practical examples I think that we really need to relate this to the process of NLP, especially to where the so-called "four pillars of NLP" [see Box 5.6] come into play.'

Box 5.6   The 'four pillars of NLP'

Rapport: this is the quality of the relationship between yourself and those around you. In the therapeutic context, it is the degree to which therapist and client understand and trust each other. The quality of the understanding is dependent on the responsiveness and trust shared between participants.

Outcome orientation: this is being clear about what it is that you want. If you don't know, being clear that you don't know is the first step to finding out. Without a clear goal there is no way of measuring achievement or change.

Sensory acuity: the ability to perceive with accuracy exactly *what* is being expressed, and *how*, through language, voice, and body language. As with rapport this applies as much to self as to other. It's a classic feedback loop: both positive and negative information is useful only if it can be recognised. All the senses can be used: after all, you know full well when your favourite drink or food is 'off'. Can you say the same about your relationships?

Behavioural flexibility: having a variety of choices open to you and providing these for people that you meet. You may have noticed how crabs in a bucket will never get out because each one has a programme that is unlikely to alter. Some people always make the same mistakes whereas others duck and dive with life. It's a matter of choosing and recognising you have choices.

'Yes, of course. First, the therapist will need to establish good *rapport* [O'Connor and McDermott 1996], not just with the conscious mind of the client, but especially with their unconscious. NLP's perspective on the "conscious" and "unconscious" aspects of our mind informs much of what we do. We choose to believe that the unconscious mind is simply that aspect of you that you're not aware of at any particular time, including that which runs your body, whereas the conscious mind is just that aspect of you which is self-aware. For instance, you may know your own home telephone number, but only when you want to give it to somebody will you be consciously aware of it. Where is it the rest of the time?'

'Encoded in a network of neurones which have not been fired?'

'Possibly. What's important to know is that, at all times, the information is present but not activated. Similarly, a computer is far more active than just what we can see on the screen. The activity behind the screen can be likened to the unconscious part of our mind, although we're far more complex than computers. Unlike computers, our "software" and programming continuously modifies our "hardware" and vice versa. Compared with the unconscious, our conscious mind is very limited: studies in the 1950s showed that the conscious mind can only cope with seven items of information, plus or minus two, at any one time [Miller 1957], which has led some people to compare it to "a very tight sphincter"!'

'No comment! It might go some way towards explaining why people take "consciousness-expanding" drugs, although what they actually do is to modify the properties of the unconscious, which is, after all, actually in charge of memory, learning, perception, behaviour and emotional states [Hall 1995].'

'If all these were within the control of your conscious mind, somebody could tell you: "Be happy, now!" and you would be. This is not often the case, so NLP has developed many processes which operate through this unconscious activity, to enlist its support, for the benefit of our clients, understanding and manipulating our internal mental structure.'

'Who does the manipulating: the practitioner or the client?'

'Ultimately, the client does or should do, through the tools and resources which the practitioner enables him or her to identify within.'

'How is the practitioner going to achieve that?'

'By using rapport skills, meeting people at their map of the world and making any changes which respect that world view. In this manner, clients can achieve what they want. Otherwise you won't get anywhere. After all, rapport has to have a purpose, otherwise why bother? It needs to be done with sensitivity and respect, and with utmost flexibility. If you impose your map on clients, it won't work.'

'By purpose I take it you're referring to *pacing* and *leading*: appropriately matching the type of language of the person, their tonality, their body language, to establish rapport? You then, utilise the rapport you achieve to lead the client from their unresourceful state to one they would like to be in, which will enable them to achieve their outcome and, ultimately, to cope and thrive in a changing world. It's about real experience, after all. If a therapist has unresolved conflicts, these might show in their beliefs and behaviours and be picked up by the client.

'The degree of rapport a therapist achieves with him or herself defines the degree they can achieve with clients. Rapport is also therefore about achieving that sense of internal balance, which we call congruence.'

'That's right. Congruence is a concept NLP adopted from person-centred therapy. I wonder how many of us are in rapport with ourselves and how many are still fighting within? So many of us have internalised the homophobia inherent in our society. If you don't love yourself, how can you expect to love other people, or be aware that other people love you?'

'Of course. Another secret for successful rapport is to have clear and open channels: by these, I mean both your hardware filters: eyes, ears, skin, nose, mouth, etc. and your software, cognitive filters, such as beliefs and values, which also "colour" and "shape" your map of the world. By becoming aware of them and how they influence your communications with others, you can learn to set aside those that interfere with excellent rapport, at least during the process of therapy. This sounds easy but, by and large, tends to be possible only after training.'

'We call being aware of these inputs "exercising our sensory acuity". In any case, all that we as therapists (or human beings), actually ever know of a person's state is their behaviour and external physiology: it's like the visible part of an island, what's above the surface. We *calibrate* the person, observing and listening to their behaviour, describing it in sensory-specific terms and refraining from using evaluative language, like "the corners of his mouth turned up" instead of "he smiled".'

'That's right. If you use evaluative language you "mind-read" others, attributing to them thoughts and feelings they may or may not have. What happens inside their heads, their internal representation, is just guesswork, albeit educated: sometimes it's bang on, other times it's way off the mark, even with people we know very well. So, when working with a client, it is just as important to consider their physiology and behaviour as it is to imagine what internal processes might go on inside them – i.e. their filters and internal representations. When the internal representation seems fixed and unable or unwilling to change, then varying the physiology can prove an effective means to creating a change.

'As a result, we can equally well operate from the "body end" or the "mind end" of the person, or both. We believe that mind and body are one system, constantly influencing each other in feedback loops within the system. Mind that matters, matter that minds.'

'Whether we are aware of it or not, we are part of systems and have systems operating within us.'

'That's right: so, whichever way we do it, we ultimately aim to enable you to understand the relationships you have with yourself, with other people and also with the world in general and to refashion these if they don't achieve what you want.'

'And we endeavour to ensure that these relationships are in harmony, sustaining and supporting each other, thus ensuring the "ecology" of the system, instead of undermining it or taking others over.'

'Congruence again?'

'It's inevitable: after all, our *ecology frame*, our awareness of consequences, is the defining element in the system and we, as practitioners, owe it to our clients to be congruent ourselves, so that we can be at our most effective with them.'

'And the NLP presuppositions [see Box 5.7], which form the interface where theory and application meet, are our operating assumptions.'

'This brings us back to identifying the key issues for good practice the editors wanted. As a bisexual, a lesbian, a gay man, or anyone else in therapy – NLP or any other type – you need to know that the therapist: understands and respects your model of your world (rapport); works with you to set realistic, clear and attainable goals (outcome orientation); shows

> **Box 5.7 Some key NLP presuppositions**
>
> - Individuals operate from their internal maps rather than from external reality.
> - Mind and body are one system.
> - Rapport is about meeting individuals at their map of the world.
> - Recognising responses requires sensory channels that are clean and open.
> - The meaning of a communication is the response that you get.
> - There is a positive intention for you behind everything you do.
> - There is also a context in which every behaviour has value for you.
> - We continuously process information through our own senses.
> - There is no failure in communication, only feedback.
> - I am in charge of my mind, and therefore of my results.

that they have listened to what you have to say and taken notice of how you feel (sensory acuity); and is able to change their views and ideas when you bring in new information and can make use of whatever information you're giving them, verbal and non-verbal to enable you to achieve your goal (behavioural flexibility).'

'You know, it sounds like we're going to expect a lot of our audience.'

'That's right. It's because we *presuppose* they can do it, otherwise why bother? Why do you think you'd buy a book such as this if we didn't stretch you a little?'

'So, how are we going to present it exactly?'

'Ooops, I haven't thought of that yet.'

'And there is such a lot more we haven't talked about, like some key processes.'

'Anyway, it's too late, we've run out of space.'

'Oh, well, didn't they say they were going to do another book?'

Appendix A

This mission statement was reached after discussion with other gay participants of our master practitioner training course, February–June 1995, where NLP enabled us to identify the following goals in relation to our gay peers:

- To enable gay people to come out with comfort and confidence at home, at work and within their local community.
- To empower gay people to address issues of discrimination constructively.
- To enable gay people to identify their own personal response to HIV and AIDS, whatever their health status.
- To enable gay people to identify resources within themselves to deal constructively and elegantly with issues which may be perceived as threatening their gay identity.
- To invite gay people to consider how each, in their own way, can contribute to the flourishing of an ecological gay community, both within itself and as part of a multicultural society.

Appendix B

Table 5.1 Health promotion matrix in relation to sexual health

Identity: I am . . . Who?	*Beliefs, convictions and values: I think/feel that . . . Why?*	*Capabilities and skills (or lack thereof): How?*	*Behaviour and activities (or lack thereof): I do . . . What?*	*Environment (space and time): Where? When?*
Man/woman age	**In relation to self**	Dynamism	Sexually active	Home
Child	Loved	Curiosity	Taking drugs	School
Boy/girl	Happy	Safer sex	Violence (sexual, emotional, physical)	Workplace
Teenager	Esteem	Safer drug use	Drinking	Prison/young offenders institute
Gay/lesbian	Value } By self or others	Assertiveness	Working	Youth centre
Bisexual	Worth }	Skills	Employment	Hospital
Pregnant	Confidence }	Qualifications	Mobility	Clinic
Homeless	Respect }	Talents	Teaching	Surgery
Parent	Comfortable	Receptiveness	Caring	Pharmacy
Drug user	Necessary	Planning ahead	Treating	Abroad
Hiv positive	Useful	Knowledge	Parenting	Away
Married	OK	Learning difficulties	etc.	Leisure setting
Divorced	Deserving	Physical disability		Convivial setting
Bereaved	Tolerant	Active		Street
Son/Daughter	Attitudes	Injecting drug use		Time of the day/week/month/year
Disabled	**In relation to others**	Dependent use		Community
Handicapped	**In relation to the world**	Recreational use		Hostel
Black	etc.	English as first/second language		Pub/clubs
Foreigner		Mobile/transient		Recreational
Asian		etc.		Sporting settings
Catholic				Saunas/massage parlours
Moslem				Remand centre
Single				Youth detention centre
Sex worker				Police
Offender/Criminal				Genito-Urinany medicine
Soldier				Family planning
Haemophiliac				Army camp
Smoker				Ambulance
etc.				etc.

The reasons which may lead a person to take risks in general and in matters of sexual health in particular can be viewed as forming a matrix dependent on:

- environment, in space, time or both;
- behaviour and activities, or lack thereof;
- capabilities and skills;

- beliefs, values and attitudes, which can either limit or broaden our horizons;
- identity, or who we see ourselves as being;
- spirituality/connectedness (not covered here).

The arrow of priority on this table is from identity to environment in a decreasing order.

Therefore, depending on the outcome sought, some initiatives tend to concentrate on one dimension of the matrix to the expense of the others. Thus, in the context of HIV, a person can say: 'I'm not gay, not a drug-user' (identity), 'therefore I'm not at risk' (belief), while the subject of sexual health concentrates more on capabilities (empowerment, self-esteem, etc.), behaviour (having sex, taking drugs, etc.), or environment (risk situations, etc.). These latter 'logical levels' may be easier to alter, but the underlying attitudes may remain if the higher levels are not also attended to.

Notes

1 Meta-programmes are unconscious sorting processes through which we distinguish, filter and organise sensory inputs in order to sustain our internal reality and identity. They exhibit themselves as behaviours or in the words that we use. Meta-programmes are not 'right' or 'wrong', they are the processes by which we maintain our subjective view of the world.
2 'Living Proof' (1995), London. A conference for long-term survivors of HIV (Confidential Communication from one of the conference attendees.)

References

Bandler, R. (1995) Trainer's training manual. Course handout, San Francisco, CA.

Bandler, R. and Grinder, J. (1975) *The Structure of Magic*. Palo Alto, CA: Science & Behavior Books Inc.

Bandler, R. and MacDonald, W. (1988) *An Insider's Guide to Sub-Modalities*. Cupertino, CA: Meta Publications.

Bridoux, D. (1997) NLP for gaymen and bisexual men: a millennium project for the gay community, *Rapport*, 35: 43–8.

Cameron-Bandler, L. (1985) *Solutions*. Moab, UT: Real People Press.

Capra, F. (1996) *The Web of Life*. London: Harper Collins.

Davies, D. and Neal, C. (eds) (1996) *Pink Therapy: A Guide for Counsellors and Therapists Working with Lesbian, Gay and Bisexual Clients*. Buckingham: Open University Press.

Dilts, R. (1990) *Changing Belief Systems with NLP*. Cupertino, CA: Meta Publications.

Dilts, R., Grinder, J., Bandler, R. and De Lozier, J. (1980) *Neuro-Linguistic Programming*, Vol. I. Cupertino, CA: Meta Publications.

Hall, M. (1995) *Meta-States*. Grand Junction, CO: Empowerment Technologies.

James, E.T. (1995) *Time-Line Therapy Training Manual*. Kona, HI: Advanced Neuro-Dynamics.

Korzybski, A. (1933) *Science & Sanity*. Lakeville, CT: The International Non-Aristotelian Library Publishing Company.

Miller, G. (1957) The magical number seven, plus or minus two: some limits on our capacity for processing information, *Psychology Review*, 63: 81–97.

O'Connor, J. and McDermott, I. (1996) *Principles of NLP*. London: Thorsons.

Paalman, M. (ed.) (1990) *Promoting Safer Sex*. Amsterdam/Lisse, Netherlands: Swets & Zeitlinger.

Person-centred therapy

Introduction

The person-centred approach is one of the most commonly practised therapeutic approaches in the UK and has long been one that lesbian, gay and bisexual clients and therapists have engaged with. This chapter explores some of the reasons for this and some of the conflicts between the theory and how the theory is actually practised.

I start with a history and a critical examination of the central tenets of person-centred theory – the six necessary and sufficient conditions – and proceed from there to offer some guidance towards developing affirmative practice with clients using the person-centred approach.

A brief history

The founder of the person-centred approach was Dr Carl Rogers (1902–87). He was a disciplined scientist and scholar, as well as a prolific writer, teacher and practitioner (for biographies see Kirschenbaum 1979; Thorne 1992). The approach has variously been known as 'client-centred therapy' and 'non-directive therapy' – somewhat a misnomer but a name initially given to the approach by Rogers to try and differentiate it from more directive or interpretative therapies of the time.

Rogers' work found great popularity during the 1960s and 1970s, culturally times of great change in sexual politics and civil rights. Carl Rogers was open minded, and he 'made no distinction about, nor placed any judgements on the gay experience, reinforcing gay life as a potentially satisfactory and acceptable way of being' (Knopf 1992: 52). He was known to have lesbian, gay and bisexual colleagues working alongside him long before the declassification of homosexuality by the American Psychiatric Association in 1973. His own non-judgemental attitude and ability to 'prize' and value individuals, along with the fact that the person-centred approach eschewed diagnosis and notions of pathology, meant many lesbian, gay and bisexual people found a home within it.

Those therapists who were lesbian, gay and bisexual mostly chose to keep their sexuality a discreet affair, and were not politically active in their communities. Some were brought up in the 1930s and 1940s, which we know were difficult times to be openly gay. By the time Rogers' work had achieved its great popularity these few lesbian, gay and bisexual therapists were well established in their careers and one can imagine had found their own ways of dealing with their sexuality as entirely a personal and private affair.

The decision of leading practitioners not to focus any of their work on gay affirmative therapy is a loss to the profession. My own view is that this is a result of their own internalised homophobia and shame, due to external heterosexism, which made it hard for these practitioners to come out and be open, rather than to inherent negative attitudes within the approach.

Whereas now it is possible to be 'out' as a lesbian, gay or bisexual person-centred therapist in many settings, this is still a fairly recent phenomenon. Establishing a career and reputation often means putting one's sexuality on the back burner. It's difficult to have a 'coming out' crisis later on in one's career (see Siegel and Lowe 1994, and Isay 1996 for examples). One can only speculate how some of these closeted person-centred practitioners were able to work effectively with such a significant part of them shut off from awareness.

A search through person-centred literature shows very few examples of heterosexist thinking and practices. Indeed, sexuality *per se* has regrettably been largely ignored by person-centred theory (Schmid 1996). Rogers barely mentioned homosexuality in his prolific career as a writer. There are relatively few references to it, and when he does discuss lesbian, gay and bisexual people he does so in an entirely respectful way, making no judgement about them.

A small piece of evidence for supporting Rogers as gay affirmative is his reference to a hypothetical homosexual client in his major theory published in 1959. Rogers writes in his definition of congruence: 'Thus he [*sic*, the client] discovers that one aspect of his experience if accurately symbolized, would be hatred for his father; another would be strong homosexual desires. He reorganizes the concept he holds of himself to include these characteristics, which would previously have been inconsistent with self' (Rogers 1959: 206). His work with this client demonstrates Rogers was able to prize homosexuality in his clients and respond to a gay client just as he did any other client.

Absence of gay affirmative literature

There is then a lacuna in the literature of person-centred therapy and counselling regarding homosexuality. Only recently has the subject begun to be covered (Knopf 1992; Davies 1998). It is interesting to speculate why this has been the case. For the most part I believe (as I indicate above) that it has come about because lesbian, gay and bisexual therapists have not chosen to write and publish their experience and ideas on working with clients. A further reason is that in the literature of a number of other approaches, in particular the psychodynamic traditions and those derived from them, homosexuality was seen as evidence of pathology. The person-centred approach abstains from this, and it may be that there was thought to be no need to write about this client group – that there was nothing extra to know or do. I believe this is a somewhat naive view – that the person-centred approach can be all things to all people, and that no special knowledge, skills or awareness is necessary to work with lesbian, gay and bisexual clients. There is a tendency to see the approach in universalistic terms. I have heard it said 'that all person-centred practitioners are non-judgemental and would never oppress anyone, or behave in any way that is discriminatory'. I challenge this view, and hope that this chapter shows this assumption to be superficial in the extreme, at best causing a great disservice to clients.

How homosexuality is perceived of explained

There is no person-centred theory of homosexuality. The person-centred approach has not spent energy in developing a theory of sexuality in the broadest sense of the word. One contribution (Schmid 1996) seeks to develop a solely person-centred theory rather than borrowing from other schools. Schmid views sexuality as a central component of the actualising tendency. The actualising tendency is a core concept of the approach, which can be described as the striving of the organism for wholeness. Self-actualisation is essentially the positive drive towards congruent expression of the self: 'Sexuality is part of human nature. It can be understood as an expression of the actualising tendency. Accordingly sexual needs, wishes and activities are actualisations of the sexual potential of a person' (Schmid 1996: 86). Schmid believes sexuality should be considered as potentially constructive and trustworthy. If someone believes himself or herself to be lesbian, gay or bisexual, then this is the striving of the actualising tendency towards congruence. Coming out is a constructive tendency towards wholeness and fulfilment of the person's potential.

While the approach abstains from diagnosis, it is clear that some lesbians, gay men and bisexuals experience mental health distress, usually from living in a society which pathologises same-sex love. Research from the London based lesbian and gay counselling service Project for Advice Counselling and Education (PACE) (McFarlane 1998) and the national mental health charity MIND clearly describes some of these experiences.

Only comparatively recently has any work been published from within the person-centred approach positing theories of the development of mental illness (Speierer 1990). Speierer identifies five risk factors for psychological illness. One of these – incongruence between societal and organismic values – clearly has a relevance to lesbian, gay and bisexual people. He posits a way of understanding mental illness that has incongruence as a central construct. Speierer suggests it is possible to see the origins of all psychiatric illnesses as connected in some way to incongruence between the person and their environment. It is the breakdown of people's coping strategies or recognition of this incongruence that causes illness to develop and come to attention through symptomology. The remaining four risk factors (non-socially caused capacity for congruence and incongruence; psychopathogenic relationships between children and their significant others as well as all persons in relationships of dependency; poor ability to compensate and poor possibilities of compensation of incongruence; and life-change events) can also be seen to feature among lesbian, gay and bisexual people who develop mental health problems. Space does not permit a full explanation of his model but Speierer's work is worth following up.

How has history informed practice?

In Britain, large numbers of counsellors have been trained in the person-centred approach. One of the largest British courses (metanoia) has traditionally had sizeable cohorts of lesbian, gay and bisexual counsellors in training. This stems partly from the fact that some of the founders defined themselves as lesbian, gay or bisexual; and partly from the fact that the agency was located in London, and its reputation grew among lesbian, gay and bisexual people. A number of other London-based training courses in the person-centred approach have also actively sought to attract students by advertising in the gay press. Given this interest in recruiting lesbian, gay and bisexual people into counsellor training it is lamentable that few courses include much beyond some basic exercises on attitudes and self-awareness to prepare their students (straight and gay) to work effectively with clients.

The assumption should not be made that because a course has lesbian, gay and bisexual people as students or faculty members it is better able to prepare such trainees for clinical work with lesbian, gay and bisexual clients. Substantial changes in curriculum development are necessary before knowledgeable and skilled practitioners will serve clients.

What unique theoretical contributions and techniques does the person-centred approach offer?

In the first place, the person-centred approach is not a technique, and therefore it might be said that it has no 'magic' to offer clients. This in itself is its strength. The act of one human being prepared to listen to, and become involved in understanding, the experience of another can on its own be very healing. Most therapists, of whatever theoretical model, know about the three core conditions of the person-centred approach (empathy, unconditional positive regard and congruence). However, it is often naively assumed that the person-centred approach is only suitable for basic counselling and if you want to do 'proper' psychotherapy then you have to retrain in another model. Fortunately this is now being challenged by newer psychotherapy training programmes and writing which demonstrate some of the unique contributions the approach has to offer in working at depth and with people in severe mental health distress (see Speierer 1990; Warner 1991, 1998; Prouty 1994; van Werde 1994; Mearns 1996).

Rather than the ubiquitous three core conditions, Rogers actually proposed six conditions that are essential for constructive change to occur. He hypothesised that 'no other conditions are necessary. If these six conditions exist, and continue over a period of time, this is sufficient' (Rogers 1990: 221).

Despite the simplicity of these six conditions they can be very difficult to apply in practice. I shall take each condition in turn and illustrate some of what therapists wishing to practice within the person-centred approach need to be aware of. I expand on this in a more detailed form elsewhere (Davies 1998), with suggestions for experiential exercises and education that I cannot include here.

Condition 1

The first condition states that 'two persons are in psychological contact' (Rogers 1990: 221). Rogers states it is important that 'each person makes some perceived difference in the experiential field of the other. Probably it is sufficient if each makes some "subceived difference"' (p. 221). Therapists establish this first condition at the point of pre-contact, during the initial stages of contact and as a result of the client's requests for disclosure of the therapist's sexual orientation.

There is some evidence (Budd 1994; Lemma 1996) that clients begin to form a relationship with the therapist prior to meeting them face to face. Publicity material, the reputation of an agency, and reputations gleaned from other clients or colleagues are all relevant to the information gathering and careful checking out that many clients report. It is also likely that the client may have tried to establish the therapist's sexuality and attitudes to lesbian, gay and bisexual people prior to making the initial contact. This may account for some heterosexual therapists feeling that they rarely see gay clients, and others seeing many people from sexual minorities.

Therapists need to consider how they present themselves during the initial contact with clients, reflecting on the different perceptions and subceptions clients might have of them. What difference does a therapist's sexuality make to how he or she makes contact, and how the client makes contact? At a subceived level what does the working environment say about the therapist? How might another person perceive the therapist? As heterosexual? Gay? Married with or without children? What sort of pictures hang on the walls? Is the counselling room a book-lined study? If so, what might this say? Are there books that are positively connoted to homosexuality visible on the shelves? (This might be perceived as permissive.) In an attempt to demonstrate valuing other therapeutic models, might some of the books come from, for example, a traditional psychoanalytic tradition that describes lesbian, gay and bisexual people pathologically? I refer to some best sellers like Laufer and Laufer (1984) and Malan (1979), rather than modern gay affirmative analytic texts such as Isay (1989, 1996), or O'Connor and Ryan (1993). What sort of magazines are in the waiting area and what might these say about the therapist or the agency?

Many lesbian, gay and bisexual people have a highly developed sixth sense or 'gaydar' and scan for visible and implicit references to the therapist's sexuality and attitudes. It is often important for clients to know their therapist's sexual orientation. This is rarely as simple as wanting to know whether the therapist can identify with the issues the client is presenting. Some therapists might experience this desire to 'know' as an intrusive invasion of their personal life, or assume that if they say they are heterosexual then the client will not want to work with them. Aside from this being the client's right to choose, it might be that the client is also attempting to establish psychological contact with the therapist, by 'being in personal contact with each other' (Rogers 1990: 222).

Sexuality and sexual orientation are often seen as a private matter. Lesbian, gay and bisexual people might sometimes say 'What I do in bed is my own affair'; while heterosexuals may say a variation of 'I don't mind homosexuals as long as they don't flaunt it, or force it down my throat'. A therapist is encouraged to treat everyone the same, and fear of complaint arising from a breach of equal opportunities policies can cause therapists to strive to be politically correct when working with people from minority groups, when they still have their own views and unconscious prejudice. The avoidance of difference and denial of cultural variables can be very damaging for the therapeutic relationship. Clients may spend a lot of time trying to work out the therapist's real frame of reference, and look for subtler signals of genuineness or incongruence. Incongruence in particular detracts from the precondition of psychological contact (Singh and Tudor 1997).

Condition 2

The second condition states that 'the first person, whom we shall term the client, is in a state of incongruence, being vulnerable or anxious' (Rogers 1990: 221). Rogers explains that incongruence is 'a discrepancy between the actual experience of the organism and the self picture of the individual insofar as it represents that experience' (Rogers 1990: 222). Much of society has sought to distort the 'self picture' of lesbians, gay men and bisexuals through its labelling of same-sex love and affection variously as sinful, perverted and sick. The colonialisation of lesbian, gay and bisexual mental health has created a vast number of casualties. Some of the 'therapies' have included neurosurgery, electric shock therapy and brainwashing through to intensive regular, long-term psychoanalytic psychotherapy. Wise clients may well be suspicious or defensive around a therapist until it has been demonstrated that the therapist is trustworthy and skilled.

Condition 3

The third condition states that 'the second person, whom we shall term the therapist, is congruent or integrated in the relationship' (Rogers 1990: 221). Rogers describes therapist congruence in this way: 'It means that within the relationship he [sic] is freely and deeply himself, with his actual experience accurately represented by his awareness of himself. It is the opposite of presenting a façade, either knowingly or unknowingly' (p. 224). He makes it clear that maintaining congruence is not always easy or comfortable and 'includes being himself even in ways which are not regarded as ideal for psychotherapy' (p. 224). This level of integration makes enormous demands of therapists in terms of their self-awareness. Tudor and Worrall (1994: 198) take this point further: 'It is likely that if as therapists we consistently ignore or deny some of our feelings and experiences we will, out of awareness, communicate such unassimilated or partially accommodated material to our clients'.

Therapists have a responsibility to undertake a rigorous re-examination of their attitudes to lesbian, gay and bisexual people – it is not uncommon for therapists to feel comfortable with just one of these three groupings, and yet uncomfortable with others. A heterosexual woman therapist shared how she felt fine with gay men, but felt afraid of being around 'butch dykes'. Another therapist, a gay man, said he did not 'believe' in bisexuality, and wished 'they' would 'make up their minds'.

Therapists wishing to work well with lesbian, gay and bisexual clients clearly need to have done a considerable amount of personal work on themselves. For all therapists this work includes re-examining the negative messages they have received about homosexuality and lesbian, gay and bisexual people, as well as reaching a deeper understanding of their own sexuality and sexual attractions.

For heterosexual therapists it may also be helpful to explore what Clark (1987) refers to as one's 'homosexual component' – that part of most of us that recognises same-sex attractions, whether in fantasy or through actual behaviour. For lesbian and gay therapists, it is important to explore the corollary of this, their 'heterosexual component' – to come to a greater understanding of their own attraction to people of a different gender to their own and their reasons for choosing not to act on this. This awareness is important in helping to address biphobia, and may increase their comfort with their own homosexuality. For example, some lesbians and gay men have a defensive response to being around the other gender. This avoidance can also lead to stereotyping and prejudice towards the opposite sex, which is clearly unhelpful when working with this section of clients.

I take it as axiomatic that it is only possible to accompany someone in working at depth if there has been a similar experience of working at depth oneself (Tudor and Worrall 1994). Heterosexual therapists are more likely to bring to their practice of therapy the issues their own therapist has worked on with them, their experience of heterosexual clients, and their reading from the vast array of textbooks and novels on issues connected with heterosexuality. It may be extremely difficult for lesbian, gay and bisexual clients (including therapists-in-training) to explore their sexuality in depth – especially any negative or shameful feelings about it – with a heterosexual therapist, for fear of judgement or titillation. In my experience it is more likely that deeper exploration is more easily done in therapist-client dyads of the same orientation.

Lesbian, gay and bisexual therapists may therefore find it more difficult to trust the responses of their heterosexual therapists to them. They may have to translate aspects of their life and culture for the therapist and censor certain issues on which they fear they may be judged. One unfortunate consequence of this is that they in turn may be less well equipped to serve their own communities, including their heterosexual clients, especially when the use of self is paramount, as it is in the person-centred approach.

Heterosexual therapists may be less personally motivated in their own therapy to work on their attitudes and beliefs around homosexuality, preferring to prioritise other issues of greater personal significance. They may be less inclined to make time to learn more about lesbian, gay and bisexual psychology issues and to stay current with lesbian, gay and bisexual community issues. This avoidance inevitably results in their clients receiving a lower quality of care. There is clearly a role for both training institutions and supervisors in ensuring that gay affirmative therapy issues are fully addressed. Rogers himself indicated that therapists needed such training when he said:

> It seems desirable that the student should have a broad experiential knowledge of the human being in his [*sic*] cultural setting. . . . Such

knowledge needs to be supplemented by experiences of living with or dealing with individuals who have been the product of cultural influences very different from those which have molded the student.

(Rogers 1951: 437)

It is clear from Rogers' earlier description of congruence that to successfully work with lesbian, gay and bisexual clients, therapists need to feel comfortable with their own sexuality, including homosexual feelings and attraction. Therapists may choose not to act on these feelings, but they need to reflect on the reasons for the choices they make. One trainee therapist explained that while she had some same-sex sexual experiences well into her early twenties, she felt she ought to settle down and get married because she wanted children, and her parents would have difficulty in accepting a lesbian daughter. It is highly likely that her external locus of evaluation and conditions of worth had a negative impact on any work she did with clients. Another student, a heterosexual male supervisee, explained how he found it extremely difficult to empathise with his gay male client when he spoke of his relationship with his partner. Because of this trainee therapist's upbringing, which included a fairly tough, hypermasculine family and school life, the idea of two men being in a deeply intimate, sexual relationship was too threatening to contemplate. The supervisee had pushed any possibility of same-sex feelings out of his awareness to the extent that he felt revulsion when working with this client. He discovered he felt not only uncomfortable but also unsafe, working at a deep level in an intimate emotional relationship with this gay man, and was unable consequently to enter the 'relational depth' required for effective person-centred therapy (Mearns 1996). Therapists working within the person-centred approach need to reflect on their sexual histories and current sexuality.

It is not only heterosexual therapists who need to work on feeling comfortable and integrated in their sexuality. Lesbian, gay and bisexual therapists have not escaped the insidious and relentless barrage of anti-homosexual propaganda. They are perhaps likely to have experienced this more negatively than heterosexual colleagues, since it has greater personal significance for them. The internalisation of this hatred and prejudice can grow in some people like a cancer and become 'intra-psychically malignant' (Forstein 1988: 34). It is practically impossible for a person to grow up in society and not to have internalised society's negative messages about sexuality (Davies 1996). To work effectively, lesbian, gay and bisexual therapists also have to look carefully at their homophobic residues and defensive beliefs.

Condition 4

The fourth condition states that 'the therapist experiences unconditional positive regard for the client' (Rogers 1990: 221). One of the myths of western society is that homosexuals abuse children and young people, that it is homosexuals who have uncontrolled libidinous drives, and want to have sex any time, anywhere, with anyone. How difficult is it for therapists to offer unconditional positive regard to clients when such an atmosphere surrounds them? Person-centred therapy underlines just how important it is to experience, not just convey, unconditional positive regard for the client.

For example, imagine a gay male client (19) tells the therapist that his new lover (15) wants to try anal sex. The client is anxious about the legal implications, as the current age of consent in Britain for gay men is 18. How might the therapist be feeling? What might they be thinking? By offering unconditional positive regard might this be seen as affirming, or in legal terms inciting, the commission of a criminal act (Cohen 1992)? Might there be concerns that the young lover is being 'exploited' by this client? If the roles were reversed, and the client was 15 and said that he wanted to penetrate ('make love to') his 19-year-old lover, would the therapist's feelings be any different?

Can a therapist offer unconditional positive regard to a client if every cell in their body is repulsed by the idea of anal sex? It is not an adequate justification to use congruence as a reason for conditionality – 'my behaviour is how I am'. Some practitioners may believe the person-centred approach requires therapeutic neutrality. To affirm feelings of attraction or desire, for example, may imply an endorsement or approval that is out of context with the unconditionality of the approach, in that a therapist may end up affirming 'positive' behaviours and not affirming 'negative' ones. It is my view that 'neutrality' in this respect does not convey positive regard (warmth, love, prizing) and is not sufficient to counteract the negative internalised messages of shame and self-loathing which inevitably reside in most people at some level. Therapists need to be watchful of putting a liberal façade on their negative beliefs, especially where they go out of their way to demonstrate their enthusiasm and 'warmth' for their clients by unsolicited hugging and sugary ebullience. Clearly congruence is missing here.

Furthermore, therapists need to be watchful for the 'love the sinner, hate the sin' type of attitude expressed by some so-called 'Christian counsellors':

Gay clients have no desire to be confronted by therapists who warmly offer to help them make the best of a poor situation. In fact, such an attitude is one of the subtler forms of homophobia. Therapists who are unable to accept homosexuality as a positive and potentially creative way of being should recognise this fact and not take on gay clients: their fear, anxiety and ambivalence will inevitably be conveyed to their clients.

(Woodman and Lenna 1980: 14)

Therapists holding negative views of homosexuality have an ethical responsibility to work on these attitudes prior to working with clients. The recent revisions to the British Association for Counselling (BAC) *Code of Ethics and Practice for Counsellors* (1998) make it clear that anti-discriminatory practice is a basic requirement for ethical practice:

Counsellors must consider and address their own prejudices and stereotyping and ensure that an anti-discriminatory approach is integral to their counselling practice.

Counsellors work in ways that affirm both the common humanity and the uniqueness of each individual. They must be sensitive to the cultural context and worldview of the client, for instance whether the individual, family or the community is taken as central.

Counsellors are responsible for ensuring that any problems with mutual comprehension due to language, cultural differences or for any other reason are addressed at an early stage.

Counsellors have a responsibility to consider and address their own prejudices and stereotyping attitudes and behaviour and particularly to consider ways in which these may be affecting the counselling relationship and influencing their responses.

(British Association for Counselling 1998: paras A.2, B.2.1, B.2.3, B.2.4 respectively)

Condition 5

The fifth condition states that 'the therapist experiences an empathic understanding of the client's internal frame of reference and endeavours to communicate this experience to the client' (Rogers 1990: 221).

Lesbians, gay men and bisexuals are a cultural minority with a long history of being oppressed and stigmatised because of their choice of sexual partners. While they may sometimes have the possibility of being able to hide who they are for short periods, which, for example, black people do not have, black parents affirm the cultural identity of their children, and this is seldom the case for lesbian, gay and bisexual people. Most African-Caribbean people nowadays have a collective consciousness of the history of slavery and oppression because of their colour. Many are hypervigilant as a result. Lesbians, gay men and bisexuals have a collective consciousness of being thought of as 'mad, bad and dangerous to know.' They too have a hypervigilance to maltreatment and prejudice.

In order to establish empathy, the therapist needs to understand something of the environment in which lesbian, gay and bisexual people live; the prejudice they experience daily; the constant decisions about whether to come out, to whom and how and the possible consequences of this; the risk of violence lived with; the possibility of having their home damaged because of being gay; the possible career implications of coming out, etc.

An analogy I developed some years ago and have used in training workshops to describe the shift in frames of reference required by heterosexual therapists, is that my gayness is akin to my being born speaking a different language. I am capable of thinking, speaking and behaving in 'Heterosexual'; I used to be almost fluent in it, but it is not my mother tongue. My mother tongue is 'Gay', and I think, feel and behave more spontaneously and naturally in that language. When I am in the 'country' of heterosexuals then everything I think, say and do has to go through an internal translator, which can reduce my spontaneity, especially with emotions. It can result in my being quite guarded and defensive. Translating takes a lot of energy, which is why I need time with my own 'people' to rest and recuperate.

It is equally important for all therapists to be acquainted with current issues and the different perspectives that are part of the lesbian, gay and bisexual communities: for example, models of relationships (open and closed, multiple and single); attitudes to sex; coming out to parents and at work; issues around body image and lifestyle; drug and alcohol use; spirituality; and religious issues. This knowledge means therapists can be more empathic to what the client is saying, as they become more familiar with the different gay perspectives on such issues, and as they set aside their own assumptions.

Condition 6

The sixth condition states that 'the communication to the client of the therapist's empathic understanding and unconditional positive regard is to a minimal degree achieved' (Rogers 1990: 221). I would suggest therapists reflect on the following questions alone and in supervision: How can a therapist know whether their empathic understanding and unconditional positive regard are communicated to their clients? How do they show warmth and understanding? Do they need to consider any other ways in which they can convey these conditions to lesbian, gay and bisexual clients? How do they know if the client is actually receiving their empathic reflections and unconditional positive regard? How well can they 'audit' their work with clients?

A further suggestion is that therapists record their sessions and seek consultation from lesbian, gay and bisexual therapists and supervisors who have been trained to work with this population (see Chapter 4). Audiotaping is probably the most reliable method for assessing how well therapists are working with their clients (Mearns 1997). Historically, Rogers was the first person to make routine use of audiotaping and analysing his sessions in supervision, and therapists would be well served by following his lead.

Conclusion

The person-centred approach has much to commend it for working in an accepting and affirming way with lesbian, gay and bisexual people. Therapists who have faith in the actualising tendency can actively seek to promote a climate where clients can discover their own inner truth and wisdom. The development of this congruence between their inner and outer experiencing leads to clients feeling able to withstand the stresses of living in a homophobic culture. Nevertheless, working in this gay affirmative way from within this approach is not as simple as it may appear. Person-centred therapy is far from being simplistic. It makes many demands on the person of the therapist. A high degree of self-awareness and personal development is necessary if one is to work effectively. While the person-centred approach clearly has theoretical advantages, in that there has never been any tradition of pathologising the experience of clients, practitioners wanting to work within the approach alongside lesbian, gay and bisexual clients clearly have a great deal of work to do if they are to remain true to Rogers' ideals.

Guidelines for good practice

- Therapists need to uncover the messages they have received about lesbian, gay and bisexual people and understand how these have influenced them in their practice.
- Therapists need to be aware of their own sexuality, and how they feel about it.
- Therapists need to work towards developing an attitude of empathic understanding, unconditional positive regard and a striving for congruence with regard to their own sexual feelings, desires and potentials.
- Therapists need to become familiar with the range and diversity of lesbian, gay and bisexual cultures, lifestyles and community issues; and stay current in their knowledge through reading, socialising with lesbian, gay and bisexual friends, etc.
- Therapists need to understand more about some of the specific psychological issues that affect the functioning of lesbian, gay and bisexual people in society and become familiar with particular clinical issues through supervision, reading, training courses and conferences.

Acknowledgements

My sincere thanks to colleagues for feedback on earlier drafts of this chapter, in particular to: Keith Tudor, Fiona Purdie, Alan Frankland, Pete Sanders, Irene Fairhurst, Margaret Warner and Peggy Natiello. Also to my friends Philip Britton and Tom Southern for providing a nurturing space in which to write. Finally to my partner Lee Adams for his enduring love and support.

References

British Association for Counselling (1998) *Code of Ethics and Practice for Counsellors*. Rugby: BAC.

Budd, S. (1994) Transference revisited, in S. Budd and U. Sharma (eds) *The Healing Bond*. London: Routledge.

Clark, D. (1987) *The New Loving Someone Gay*. Berkeley, CA: Celestial Arts.

Cohen, K. (1992) Some legal issues in counselling and psychotherapy, *British Journal of Guidance and Counselling*, 20(1): 10–26.

Davies, D. (1996) Homophobia and heterosexism, in D. Davies and C. Neal (eds) *Pink Therapy: A Guide for Counsellors and Therapists Working with Lesbian, Gay and Bisexual Clients*. Buckingham: Open University Press.

Davies, D. (1998) The six necessary and sufficient conditions applied to working with lesbian, gay, and bisexual clients, *The Person-Centered Journal*, 5(2): 111–24.

Forstein, M. (1988) Homophobia: an overview, *Psychiatric Annals*, 18(1): 33–6.

Isay, R.A. (1989) *Being Homosexual: Gay Men and their Development*. Harmondsworth: Penguin.

Isay, R.A. (1996) *Becoming Homosexual: The Journey to Self-acceptance*. New York: Pantheon Books.

Kirschenbaum, H. (1979) *On Becoming Carl Rogers*. New York: Delacorte Press.

Knopf, N. (1992) On gay couples, *The Person-Centered Journal*, 1(1): 50–62.

Laufer, M. and Laufer, E. (1984) *Adolescence and Developmental Breakdown*. New Haven, CT: Yale University Press.

Lemma, A. (1996) *Introduction to Psychopathology*. London: Sage.

McFarlane, L. (1998) *Diagnosis Homophobic: The Experiences of Lesbians, Gay Men and Bisexuals in Mental Health Services*. London: PACE.

Malan, D. (1979) *Individual Psychotherapy and the Science of Psychodynamics*. London: Butterworth.

Mearns, D. (1996) Working at relational depth with clients in person-centred therapy, *Counselling*, 7(4): 306–11.

Mearns, D. (1997) *Person-Centred Counselling Training*. London: Sage.

O'Connor, N. and Ryan, J. (1993) *Wild Desires and Mistaken Identities: Lesbianism and Psychoanalysis*. London: Virago.

Prouty, G. (1994) *Theoretical Evolutions in Person-Centered/Experiential Therapy: Applications to Schizophrenic and Retarded Psychoses*. Westport, CT: Praeger.

Rogers, C.R. (1951) *Client-Centered Therapy*. London: Constable.

Rogers, C.R. (1959) A theory of therapy, personality and inter-personal relationships, as developed in the client-centered framework, in S. Koch (ed.) *Psychology: A Study of a Science*, vol. 3. New York: McGraw-Hill.

Rogers, C.R. (1990) The necessary and sufficient conditions of therapeutic personality change, in H. Kirschenbaum and V.L. Henderson (eds) *The Carl Rogers Reader*. London: Constable.

Schmid, P. (1996) Intimacy, tenderness and lust – a person-centered approach to sexuality, in R. Hutterer, G. Pawlowsky, P.E. Schmid and R. Stipsits (eds) *Client-Centered and Experiential Psychotherapy*. Frankfurt: Peter Lang.

Siegel, S. and Lowe, E. (1994) *Unchartered Lives: Understanding the Life Passages of Gay Men.* New York: Penguin.

Singh, J. and Tudor, K. (1997) Cultural conditions of therapy, *The Person-Centered Journal*, 4(2): 32–46.

Speierer, G.W. (1990) Towards a specific illness concept of client-centred therapy, in G. Lietaer, J. Rombauts and R. Van Balen (eds) *Client-Centred and Experiential Psychotherapy in the Nineties.* Leuven: Leuven University Press.

Thorne, B. (1992) *Carl Rogers.* London: Sage.

Tudor, K. and Worrall, M. (1994) Congruence reconsidered, *British Journal of Guidance and Counselling*, 22(2): 197–206.

van Werde, D. (1994) An introduction to client-centred pre-therapy, in D. Mearns (ed.) *Developing Person-Centred Counselling.* London: Sage.

Warner, M. (1991) Fragile process, in L. Fusek (ed.) *New Directions in Client-Centred Therapy: Practice with Difficult Client Populations* (monograph series 1). Chicago: Chicago Counseling and Psychotherapy Center.

Warner, M. (1998) A client-centred approach to therapeutic work with dissociated process and fragile process, in L.S. Greenberg, J.C. Watson and G. Lietaer (eds) *Handbook of Experiential Psychotherapy.* New York: The Guilford Press.

Woodman, N.J. and Lenna, H.R. (1980) *Counseling with Gay Men and Women: A Guide for Facilitating Positive Lifestyles.* San Francisco: Jossey-Bass.

Psychoanalytic psychotherapy

Introduction

The psychoanalytic world is undergoing change with regard to its understanding of lesbian, gay and bisexual people. It may have taken a long time, but the psychoanalytic community is being influenced by other disciplines – among them feminism and postmodernism. Lewes (1995) is of the view that these influences have affected practice and personal attitudes, but left theory relatively untouched. This has created a need to review psychoanalytic theories of development, and there are a few writers who have done this – Lewes (1995) from a predominantly Freudian stance, and Isay (1989) who discusses the experience of the gay male child and the response he evokes in his parents. Both of these revisions concern gay men's development, and are American publications. In terms of lesbian development, Rohde-Dachser (1992), and Deutsch (1995) represent the American contribution. O'Connor and Ryan (1993) offer the most comprehensive review of developmental theory and raise what must be the most challenging trend in psychoanalytic thinking, postmodernism, urging us to radically rethink the role of developmental theory in our analytic work. Postmodern thought is inviting psychoanalysis to abandon fixed and rigid definitions and models (see Domenici and Lesser 1995) and this goes to the heart of psychoanalytic theory.

There can be no doubt that psychoanalysis lacks a history to be proud of when it comes to its relationship with homosexuality. As Ratigan (1998: 59) puts it, 'why should any sane person undertake a form of therapy which has a history of seeing a core aspect of the human person as deviant, perverted or sick?' In this chapter I briefly review the history of this relationship and note some current more hopeful trends. I explore the unique contributions of the psychoanalytic approach in the hope that the reader will see that, notwithstanding the unfortunate history, this way of working and understanding has a great deal to offer the lesbian, gay or bisexual client.

Historical overview

No exploration of such a history can omit Freud. Lewes (1995) and May (1995), to whom the reader is directed for a fuller discussion of Freud's contribution, both note a great deal of ambiguity in Freud. About one thing he seemed very clear – his position on the legal and moral issues. Freud was against treating homosexuality as a criminal activity. In 1930 he signed a public appeal to decriminalise homosexuality in Austria and Germany and in a response to a question about homosexuality in *Die Zeit*, he wrote:

> I am . . . of the firm conviction that homosexuals must not be treated as sick people, for a perverse orientation is far from being a sickness. Would that not oblige us to characterise as sick many great thinkers and scholars of all times, whose perverse orientation we know for a fact and whom we admire precisely because of their mental health? Homosexual persons are not sick.
>
> (Freud 1905a: 5)

Perhaps Freud's most famous statement on the subject comes from a note he wrote to an American mother of a gay man in 1935:

> I gather from your letter that your son is a homosexual. I am most impressed by the fact that you do not mention this term yourself in your information about him. May I question you, why you avoid it? Homosexuality is assuredly no advantage but it is nothing to be ashamed of, no vice, no degradation, it cannot be classified as an illness; we consider it to be a variation of the sexual function produced by a certain arrest of sexual development. Many highly respectable individuals of ancient and modern times have been homosexuals . . . It is a great injustice to persecute homosexuality as a crime and cruelty, too.
>
> (Freud [1935]1951: 786)

However, in these last two quotations we can see the ambiguity: many take exception to homosexuality being called a 'perverse orientation' and the statement that it is 'produced by a certain arrest of development' is at the root of a view of homosexuality as pathological. This raises the complex question of the relation of homosexuality to psychopathology. I believe it is helpful to see this as a continuum – from one end, seeing homosexuality *in itself* as a psychopathological entity, through seeing homosexuality as a *feature* of other pathological conditions, to the other end where no necessary connection is seen between a person's sexual orientation and psychopathology. Lewes (1995) suggests that Freud advanced statements located in all three positions. As an example of a statement located at the 'no necessary connection' end of the continuum, Freud's correspondence with Ernest Jones in 1921 is perhaps surprising. It concerns Jones' letter to Freud informing him that it had been decided to reject the application of a 'manifest homosexual' for admission into his psychoanalytic society on the grounds of his acknowledged homosexuality. Freud's reply was co-signed by Otto Rank:

> Your query, dear Ernest, concerning prospective membership of homo-sexuals has been considered by us and we disagree with you. In effect we cannot exclude such persons without other sufficient reasons, as we cannot agree with their legal prosecution. We feel that a decision in such cases should depend upon a thorough examination of the other qualities of the candidate.
>
> (Freud [1921]1977: 9)

It is lamentable that psychoanalytic training institutions have ignored this view in their subsequent exclusion of openly gay or lesbian candidates, a situation that has begun to change only in the last 20 years.

Freud, however, leaves us in no doubt that the 'natural' outcome of psychosexual development was heterosexual object choice for both pleasure and procreation: 'One of the tasks implicit in object choice is that it should find its way to the opposite sex' (Freud 1905b: 95).

Lewes (1995) draws out four separate aetiologies of homosexual development in Freud, all of which carry implications for pathology in varying degrees. With regard to lesbian development, Freud's main contribution is 'The psychogenesis of a case of homosexuality in a woman', published in 1920. It should be remembered that this is a single case study, so care should be taken not to apply Freud's conclusions universally. Nonetheless, Freud makes some interesting points. He remarks that 'one must remember that normal sexuality too depends upon a restriction in the choice of object' (1920: 151), and warns the reader 'not to form too simple a conception of the nature and genesis of inversion, and to keep in mind the universal bisexuality of human beings' (1920: 156–7). However, it is from this paper that Freud's notorious statement comes: 'she changed into a man and took her mother in place of her father as the object of her love' (1920: 158). This became the classic understanding of lesbian object choice.

Even if we leave aside all of Freud's explicit comments on homosexuality, there is a key aspect to his theory of sexual development which has formed the linchpin of subsequent pathologising of gay and lesbian object choice – the Oedipus complex. How analytically oriented psychotherapists view and use the Oedipus complex is of fundamental importance in working with all clients, I believe. It leads us to what Horrocks (1998) describes as a confusion between correlation and causation: analytic thought has been criticised for seeming to be occupied with *why* someone is gay, lesbian or bisexual, rather than exploring the *how* of being hetero-, homo- or bisexual. Other writers from a postmodernist perspective have felt that notions like the Oedipus complex are obsolete and create a view of sexuality that is fixed for life. Schwartz (1995) argues for a severing of the tie between the erotic and the gendered body. Lewes (1995) wants to retain the classical developmental ideas, but offers a fascinating reworking of the Oedipus complex which, by exploring the vicissitudes of identification and object of desire, he shows to have 12 equally valid outcomes (6 homosexual, 6 heterosexual) rather than the one 'successful' heterosexual outcome.

In Freud's writings there exist paradoxes, contradictions and conundrums. Domenici and Lesser (1995) write of his ground-breaking dismantling of the connection between both the sexual instinct and the object, and the sexual instinct and the aim: 'If there is no natural object and no natural aim' they write, 'then deviations from genital intercourse cannot be called perverse' (1995: 2). Freud's theory of innate bisexuality shook the culture he lived in and offers the possibility of viewing sexuality in a much more fluid and mobile way.

It is fair to say that Freud did not have 'a view' on homosexuality, but many views, some of which are hard to reconcile. However, the analytic community, after Freud, demonstrated a difficulty in either letting the ambiguity stand, or developing his structural work to harmonise clearly with his *open* views, such that by 1962 the perceived 'expert' on male homosexuality, Bieber, was able to say 'all psychoanalytic theories assume that adult homosexuality is psychopathologic' (Bieber *et al.* 1962: 18), and not provoke a storm of protest.

To detail the developments that took place in analytic thought over the years in between Freud and this statement is outside the possibilities of this chapter – the reader is again directed to Lewes (1995). I wish to make two general points only.

First, the shift in the 1930s and 1940s from Oedipal level conflicts to the primitive oral stage made an impact on theories of homosexuality. What Freud had called the constitution (offering little hope of conversion) was now viewed as 'pre-Oedipal development' and therefore amenable to analysis and change. There is of course a concomitant supposition – that if the origin of homosexuality occurs at an earlier stage of development, the greater is the psychological disturbance. This is seen in the work of Socarides, for example, who wrote: 'The homosexual is ill, and anything that tends to hide that fact reduces his chances of seeking and obtaining treatment . . . if he were to achieve social acceptance it would increase this difficulty' (Socarides 1963, cited in Isay 1989: 4). Interestingly, May suggests that the movement to pre-Oedipal concerns which characterised the British school, meant that they did not have to focus on homosexuality as pathology (May 1995). There is a difference in the histories of the relationship between homosexuality and psychoanalysis in Britain and in the USA. In America there seems to have been a more overtly hostile and pejorative tone in psychoanalytic writing following Freud (see Lewes 1995; Isay 1996). Perhaps this is the reason why so much more contemporary, enlightened writing is coming from the USA at present.

Second, another development of relevance was the questioning of the assumption that human beings were innately bisexual (Rado 1940). If this aspect of Freud's theory is discarded, there can be no such thing as innate homosexual desire; homosexuality becomes, according to Rado, a remedial substitute for intimidated heterosexuality. Rohde-Dachser (1992) comments that Bieber took up this idea in his study published in 1962. This study will be known to some readers for its conclusion that male homosexuality is *caused* by a certain family constellation: close-binding, intimate mothers and detached, hostile or rejecting fathers whom the patient hated or feared during childhood. The study has been extensively criticised (see Lewes 1995) but has been powerful nonetheless.

There are a number of points that should be made about the psycho-analytic approach to homosexuality. First, O'Connor and Ryan (1993) make the point that according to Freud's (1920) theory in 'The psychogenesis of a case of homosexuality in a woman', choice is based on repudiation. This is part of a wider criticism, which is based on the notion that homosexual choice is a reaction *to* something, rather than a choice *for* something.

Second, Domenici and Lesser (1995) draw our attention to the 'copulo-centric' nature of psychoanalytic theory. By this they mean that it must regard non-procreative sexuality as perverse. This was part of the Judaeo-Christian inheritance that prevailed in the late nineteenth century, and Weinberg (1972) cites this as a significant factor in homophobia.

An additional point is made by both Domenici and Lesser (1995) and O'Connor and Ryan (1993). In Freud's theories of male and female homo-sexuality, there is a split between identification and desire. The above writers draw attention to the setting up of these as binary opposites – one cannot *have* and *be* the same sex at the same time – and wish to challenge this assumption.

All the contemporary writers considered make the point that, since openly gay and lesbian people were barred from psychoanalytic training, there were few gay and lesbian analysts. This means that nearly all the writing (until the late 1980s) has been from analysts writing from their *clinical* experience, rather than their *personal* experience. Lewes sees some connection between the way women were treated by classic psychoanalytic theory (a bias towards regarding women as essentially inferior) and the treatment of gay men (seen as flawed and defective because they shared certain psychic characteristics with women!) However he sees the history of the thinking on both of these as radically different. From the start, there were women analysts who elaborated, challenged and qualified the psychoanalytic view of femininity (Horney 1932; Deutsch 1944; Thompson 1947; Bonaparte 1953; and later Mitchell 1974 among others). In contrast to this, the theory of homosexuality has not until now permitted its objects to participate in its formulation.

I conclude this section with a brief overview of the contemporary field of writing in the area of psychoanalytic thought about homosexuality. Schwartz (1995) bands contemporary writing on gay and lesbian issues into three broad groups. First, those like Socarides, Trop and Stolorow, who he describes as pathologising and disparaging; second, those involved in the work of psychobiology, Friedman in particular. This group sees sexual orientation as determined biologically, which Schwartz criticises on the basis that it leaves out mobility of object choice. Lewes (1995), however is keen to hear and reflect on the research findings of this group, and suggests that the increase in biological research will lead psychoanalysis to choose between two alternatives: either psychoanalysis can *account* for sexual orientation (with constitution merely influencing the *mechanisms* which determine sexual development); or psychoanalysis can merely describe what *kind* of homosexual or heterosexual a person will develop into (as constitution is shown to determine sexual orientation).

In Schwartz's final group, he includes writers such as Isay and Lewes and I would add Cornett, together with O'Connor and Ryan. These articulate a non-pathologising view of homosexuality, and address the prevalence of homophobia in society, within the psyche, and in the consulting room. Lewes' (1995) work details the complex history of psychoanalysis and homosexuality, and offers a new interpretation of the Oedipus complex. Isay's (1989, 1993, 1996) contribution is markedly different, addressing the gay man's experience of growing up, and being in therapy. Cornett (1993, 1995) writes particularly from a Kohutian perspective into which he has integrated existential dynamic theory, and offers technical considerations as well as theoretical. O'Connor and Ryan (1993) write from a more postmodern standpoint, and challenge psychoanalysis to criticise itself and rethink many of its suppositions.

The unique contributions of the analytic approach

Perhaps the most valuable contribution of the approach is that it offers a rich understanding of human experience. Although psychoanalysis has been guilty of at best an unexamined, at worst an abusive and punitive, response to the gay, lesbian or bisexual person, it has also given us the tools with which to understand these responses. It is tragic that psychoanalysis lacked the capacity to self-reflect upon its attitudes in the past, particularly when the intellectual understanding of them is clearly at its elbow. There is a wealth of work concerning homophobia (e.g. Weinberg 1972; Hopcke *et al.* 1993; Young-Bruehl 1996); its causes in terms of the internal world of the individual, how it is translated into a societal and cultural phenomenon through projection and institutional dynamics. Not only this but psychoanalysis can offer an understanding of how this homophobia then becomes internalised by a person through the mechanisms of identification and introjection, and seeks to explain the consequence of this in terms of shame and self-hatred on the part of the gay, lesbian or bisexual person, or distancing, judging or attacking behaviour on the part of those who identify as straight. Indeed, the analytic approach stresses the *internal* working out of homophobia and pays far less attention to the *external* manifestations of homophobia in societal and institutional terms. It is hoped that this balance may be redressed. The approach further enriches the concept of homophobia via the understanding of bisexuality, to suggest that each of us will have internalised homophobia whether we identify as gay or straight. As Freud famously believed, everyone is capable of making a homosexual object choice, and in fact has made one in their unconscious. For gay, lesbian or bisexual people, internalised homophobia will result in shame and self-hatred (about which more below), and behaviour such as the denigration of gay culture. For heterosexuals, internalised homophobia manifests itself in the kind of structural prejudice we are all too aware of and in smaller more interpersonal ways (a silence in regard to gay or lesbian colleague's partnerships, for example). The impact of homophobia on the straight person's internal world may include a repression of feelings of love and tenderness for those of their own sex, through fear and shame.

I believe a major contribution of the psychoanalytic approach to be the emphasis on shame and self-hatred which is the gay, lesbian or bisexual person's inheritance of growing up in a homophobic world. Isay (1993), Malyon (1993), Gair (1995) and Buloff and Osterman (1995) all write sensitively and thoughtfully about internalised homophobia. A widely regarded strength of the analytic approach is the emphasis on the experience of early life. Gair (1995), in an exploration of shame and social stigma which comes about through the 'profound absence of mirroring of lesbian orientation' (p. 121), shows not simply how shame is engendered, but also the mechanisms by which it is perpetuated internally by the client. Frommer (1995) discusses the emotional defences formed to protect the self from injury when growing up in a homophobic setting. These, in my experience, are often what constrains and isolates the client in adult life. For example, a gay patient protected himself with a grandiose defence, believing himself better, superior to others. This was a comforting and retaliatory way of dealing with the alienation he felt from a young age, but cut him off from sources of nurture and emotional contact, including those in his new and potentially affirming relationship.

Frommer (1995) stresses that it is vital that the therapist has insight into the psychic consequences of growing up gay, and has worked through their own introjects. Gair (1995) outlines strategies for therapists seeking to work with the impact on 'self-cohesion' of shame. A concept she draws on is one central to working psychoanalytically – that of containment. She stresses the need for the therapist to be able to tolerate induced shame, to act as a container for all the intolerable feelings associated with shame, and to make emotional contact with the shamed parts of the client's identity. This challenges the therapist to deal with their own shame, too, whatever their sexual orientation. Gair encourages the therapist to work with the defences of shame – again a central analytic concept – and shows that the therapist will need to have an awareness of how homophobic shame might be defended against. She cites many examples of this, including the patient believing that she may be able to hide from the external oppressor while not recognising she cannot hide from the internal one. Like Frommer, Gair points out the need for the therapist to engage with the lesbian client in identifying the social, cultural, environmental and familial elements that have produced shame in her. Clearly, there is then a need for therapists to be *aware* of these things, and of their part in them, whether real or perceived. Frommer emphasises the importance of the therapist first working through their own introjects from society – this is not simply an awareness of them, but a real commitment to working with them. Elsewhere (Wheeler and Izzard 1997) I have discussed the importance of counsellor training addressing this.

Internalised homophobia is not only about shame however – it can represent the 'shadow side' of a client's sexual orientation; the aspects of it that the client finds unsatisfactory or disappointing. Isay makes the point that 'at some point in every intensive therapy, every gay patient expresses unhappiness and dissatisfaction with his homosexuality' (Isay 1993: 31). This has certainly been the case in my practice. A lesbian woman in her thirties spoke with regret and longing about the relationship she had with a man in her early twenties. She felt that it had been so much easier then, and wished for many of the aspects of a heterosexual relationship she had valued. She found it frightening that she began to dream about the man, and that in her dreams she was having enjoyable heterosexual sex.

I will come to my response to this material when I have addressed what feels like the most contentious contribution of this approach in a book about affirmative therapy. This is the concept of neutrality. Ratigan (1998: 64) gives a summary of the distinctive quality of a psychoanalytic therapy:

> Psychoanalysis and psychoanalytic psychotherapy are attempts to construct a bounded mental structure in which the analyst or therapist is neutral (or as neutral as can be achieved); emotionally available or attuned to what the patient is consciously and unconsciously attempting to do with them within the structure of the therapy . . . There is no reassurance and there is no affirmation.

It may be worth pointing out that 'emotionally available' in the analytic model refers to the quality of openness on the part of the therapist. We have a commitment to allowing the patient to make an emotional impact on us at the deepest level, and to thinking about this in terms of a communication by the patient. The analytic therapist puts himself or herself at the disposal of the patient, to be caught up in the drama that is the patient's internal world. There is, however, an emphasis on containing and processing the drama by the therapist, *not* acting it out.

The provision of this neutral space is deliberate, with the intention that it becomes an arena in which the patient's way of relating to him or herself and others can emerge and be seen and experienced. Psychoanalytic psychotherapy pays attention to the intra-psychic processes as well as the interpersonal, and seeks to interfere with these as little as possible so that they can be seen clearly. This way of working is particularly concerned with the least acceptable parts of ourselves and is perhaps more concerned with 'truth' than change, as it seeks to bring more and more of a person's hidden self into the light and bring about a way of relating to the self and other(s) which does justice to the grim reality of the human condition.

Key in this approach is the provision of mental space 'in which to think, free from pressure from the psychotherapist implicit in both the homo-sexuality-as-pathology model and the gay affirmative model' (Ratigan 1998: 66). While all contemporary writers here mentioned would espouse a gay affirmative stance, 'which begins with the premise that homosexuality is not perverse, and that it is homophobia that is pathological' (Horrocks 1998: 15), there is some questioning in the analytic literature of the assumed superseding of neutrality by a gay affirmative stance *in the room*. 'For an analytic therapist or psychoanalyst, gay affirmation smacks too much of special pleading' writes Horrocks (1998: 38). Having a gay affirmative therapist may present a block to exploring the negative feelings about being gay or lesbian, he contends. Similarly, Shelley (1998) believes that the shift from an 'illness model' to an affirmative model is a 'reaction to', rather than a 'working through' of the preceding illness model. 'The word affirmative seems to lack a kind of dialectic, or better yet, a reflexiveness within its uni-dimensionality. Affirmative means certitude, an absolute 'yes', with synonyms for affirmative including: unequivocal, undeniable . . . sure and absolute' (Shelley 1998: 8). Shelley argues that affirmative is not the best word to describe therapeutic work from a non-pathology position, thinking that it might antagonise other non-pathology positions, such as 'the stance of neutrality taken in psychoanalytic practice' (p. 8). Ryan comments that 'the extent, depth and resilience of feelings of shame and self-hatred – the hallmarks of internalised homophobia – are not sufficiently appreciated in the understandable desire to provide more affirmative therapy than has hitherto been available for lesbians and gay men' (Ryan 1998: 56).

There is widespread agreement among analytic writers that neutrality is more helpful than affirmation. Isay (1993: 33) interprets neutrality in a helpful way; as an:

> undeviatingly uncritical, accepting therapeutic stance in which thought-fulness, caring, and regard for the patient are essential. By so doing I am not underestimating the value of the questioning, uncovering, and usual interpretative work of any analytic or dynamically oriented therapy. Nor am I advocating the unquestioning acceptance of the patient's views and value. Rather, I am attempting to demonstrate that an attitude of positive regard makes analytic work possible because it enables the patient to express and analyze negative transference distortions from both the past and the present.

Cornett, in discussing Isay's work, refers to the conception of neutrality as a 'state of non-judgemental curiosity. The analyst or therapist maintains an interest in and curiosity about the patient's internal life' (Cornett 1995: 95). Cornett maintains that curiosity and condemnation are mutually exclusive – an interesting point on which to reflect. He also states that true curiosity (a desire to understand the patient's world in all its complexity) precludes judgement and leaves no room for the imposition of values by the therapist. In the example from my own practice given above, I felt it was important to respond to the client's material with curiosity, allowing her to fully explore where the negative feelings about her identified orientation were coming from and to allow her to acknowledge losses she was in touch with about her lifestyle. I would say 'gay affirmation' may have inhibited the client in this particular regard, however I do think that the capacity of the client to bring such material into the therapy partly depends on the creation of a safe environment. Deutsch (1995: 32) writes about 'a neutrality that includes recognition of reality: prejudice against lesbians is pervasive in the culture and in analytic relationships'. I believe that as analytic therapists we strive to balance a commitment to neutrality *alongside* awareness of the impact of the real world. Frommer (1995: 77) emphasises this: 'A major function of the psychoanalytic endeavor with patients who are homosexual must include an examination and deconstruction of the social context – the culture's contribution to both the analyst and the patient's internalised heterosexual bias and homophobia'.

One lesbian patient seemed closed off to the impact of homophobia in her workplace and family relationships, preferring to see it in terms of her own lack of self-esteem. It did not seem to me to be an abandonment of neutrality to point out to her that she was ignoring the very real prejudice in her external world. However, as a true analytic therapist, I had to complete the intervention by commenting that this perhaps was because it saved her having to be in touch with the prejudice in her internal world.

Earlier I commented that the therapist must be prepared to acknowledge her or his own part in the shame-inducing contexts in which clients grow up and live their lives, *whether real or perceived*. As analytic workers, we need to be prepared to tolerate and contain the negative projections of our clients that is transference, without giving in to the desire to correct their perceptions of us. Ryan (1998) points out that the therapist, at some point in the therapy, will 'stand for' society, and will be required to endure the discomfort of being experienced by the client as a representative of the very worst that society can do. There is no doubt that being seen or experienced as homophobic, no matter how sure we are that it is transference, is acutely painful, and the urge to reassure or correct the client's perception is strong. I am not sure myself that I have always stayed firm on this, and have given in at times to a collusive fantasy that homophobia is 'out there', and cannot be within either of us. I do not think however that this is ultimately useful. Ryan makes the very important point that the willingness to be used as a transference figure of this kind will only be useful to the client if the therapist 'is not actually homophobic in her conduct of the therapy' (Ryan 1998: 55). This cannot be stressed enough – the experience of any kind of transference needs to maintain an 'as if' quality, such that there is a part of the client which knows at some level that this therapist is actually *not* the embodiment of all the oppression and hatred that they have suffered. An approach that communicates accepting and valuing of the client's choice will be essential here. I recall work with a lesbian client. She entered therapy from the very first moment with a concrete expectation that I would be homophobic, that I was rejecting of her and secretly labelling and diagnosing her. Her hostility was a testament to her suffering at the hands of a homophobic world. Many clients do enter therapy with this painful expectation – particularly in analytic work where the renowned historical antipathy of the model is often being carried into the room with the client – and the therapist needs to work hard to create an alliance in which the client can experience and acknowledge to some extent the genuine valuing of their object choice.

But can neutrality really exist in practice? A therapist may be able to adopt a neutral, non-homophobic stance with patients externally, but what is going on internally? The psychoanalytic model has a contribution to make here that illuminates *all* practice, of whatever model. Frommer's (1995) work in particular clarifies the need for practitioners to examine their emotional stance with regard to clients:

One might think that a de-pathologized view of homosexuality would naturally result in a neutral stance, but it is a mistake to assume, however, that the analyst operates from a position of *emotional* neutrality regarding the patient's homosexuality merely because s/he adopts a *technically* neutral stance towards it.

(Frommer 1995: 68, italics added)

Frommer explores the power of heterosexist bias in the therapist, seeing it as different from a homophobic countertransference (what psychoanalytic writers term the emotional experience in the therapist in response to the client). Heterosexist bias is about the way in which looking at the world from a heterosexual point of view imbues all associations, theory, thought and responding, and is present even when the therapist does not view homosexuality as pathological. Heterosexist bias, Frommer claims, may account for a distance between therapist and client, where respect cloaks a hesitancy to enquire deeply about the client's same-sex desire, a point made by Ryan (1998) in a discussion about therapists' anxieties in working with lesbian patients. She maintains that the erstwhile pathologising approach of classical analysis has produced a swing to a 'hands off' approach, characterised by 'a failure to enquire into the precise nature and details of a patient's lesbian desires and experiences, analytic blind spots, defensive displacements of analytic interest and uneasy silences' (Ryan 1998: 49).

What is needed then is an awareness of the power of values, which communicate themselves whether we are conscious of it or not. Gould (1995), in a discussion of working with lesbian clients, states that an aware therapist is aware that she is *always* making value judgements, and can then be on the lookout for those which pertain to her lesbian clients: 'Is she trying to influence them to be more "acceptable" lesbians, less out, less butch, less unconventional in appearance or behavior, less "promiscuous"?' (Gould 1995: 14). Gould points out that the aware therapist knows that she has needs in regard to, and is challenged by, all patients and again pays special attention to the situation with those who identify as lesbian, gay or bisexual. If the therapist is a lesbian, she will need to ask: 'Do I need my lesbian clients to be "healthier" than they really are, in order to feel better about myself?' Whether the therapist is gay or straight, he or she will need to ask themselves: 'Do I need my patients to adopt a lesbian identity?' if they are uncomfortable with a more fluid approach to sexuality.

Values around child rearing will need to be explored (Hargaden and Llewellin 1996): in my own practice, a lesbian client whose partner became pregnant needed space to explore her feelings about becoming a father/ mother herself. She saw herself taking on more of a father role. It was important for me to ask myself 'What do I really feel about parenting? Is my espousal of a separation of biological sex and parenting function more than politically correct talk?' Gould also emphasises that the questions will constantly need to be asked 'How open am I to receiving my clients' loving and sexual feelings towards me?' and 'How open am I to experiencing sexual feelings towards my patients?' Erotic transference and countertransference is a topic which struggles for attention in the analytic world – how much more so with regard to homosexual feelings? A male supervisee told me that he had disclosed to his gay client that he was straight. I questioned this, and in exploration it emerged that he had done so (albeit unconsciously) in order to deflect the client's possible sexual interest in him. Based on a naive assumption that gay men are 'put off' if they know someone is straight, the supervisee's statement revealed his fear of being an object of his client's love and sexual interest. Several of my lesbian clients have feared that I would *assume* that they fancied me if they spoke of any warm feelings for me – a manifestation of the cultural prejudice that inhibits much same-sex affection in our society.

Our values are also made manifest in the things that interest us and occupy us. Ryan (1998) suggests that therapists fear being seen as ignorant about homosexual lifestyles when working with lesbian clients. She points out that it is a burden for lesbians to have to enlighten or inform therapists about lesbian culture – for example, with regard to the dilemmas about coming out, or deciding to have a baby. There are two issues that emerge from this. One is that all too often therapists *are* ignorant about gay or lesbian culture. For example, in a supervision session, a therapist presenting work with a lesbian client commented that she thought the client knew she was straight. On being asked why, she replied, 'Well, I live in a big house!'

Another issue, which is raised by Ryan, is that although therapists are called on in all their work with clients to draw on their imaginative and exploratory capacities in order to empathise and facilitate the work, there seems to be an inhibition in this capacity when working with lesbian clients. This suggests that perhaps therapists do not *want* to know about lesbian experience from the inside – it is perhaps too threatening to imagine or identify with such experience, presumably for fear of what desires and envy it might stir up.

Conclusion

Psychoanalytic work with lesbian, gay and bisexual clients has had a chequered history. It has suffered from an unexamined homophobia, which has only recently begun to be explored. Training that specifically includes an exploration of the impact of homophobia is rare. Historically, analytic work has not been neutral with homosexual clients, but has openly sanctioned the application of heterosexist values. I am glad to be able to write that this has changed considerably, and although we have a long way to go, it is possible to find good analytic work which is critical of its own values and seeks to affirm the orientation of clients.

Guidelines for good practice

- It is vital to address homophobia at every level in the work with clients: the reality of prejudice, invisibility and oppression in the external world;

the experience of growing up gay, and the impact of the homophobic world and family on the child's development; the creation and perpetuation of internalised homophobia, particularly shame and self-hatred.

- It is essential that therapists have sufficiently worked through their own shame such that they can contain and work sensitively with that of others.
- It is necessary that therapists have a robust awareness of the extent and impact of homophobia in our society.
- It is absolutely key that the therapist has confronted their own internalised homophobia, and become comfortable with their own homosexuality if they identify as heterosexual and their heterosexuality if they identify as gay or lesbian (Davies 1996, 1998). The importance of this cannot be overstressed – unless this is done any recommendations for good practice will come to nothing.
- Unless the therapist is continually working to raise their awareness and work through their unconscious homophobia they will be unable to provide neutral space that goes beyond technical correctness, nor will they be open and able to tolerate the sexual desire – their own and their clients' – which is part and parcel of the work. Neither will that practitioner be able to allow their gay, lesbian or bisexual clients to see and experience them as a representative of the homophobic world as they transfer their hostile experiences onto the therapist to work with them *in vivo*. Nor, I believe, will therapists be able to provide a safe space for a client to face their own negative feelings about their sexuality, and in addition, therapists will not be able to use their imagination creatively to enter the gay, lesbian or bisexual's world empathically.
- Unexamined homophobia will lead the therapist to either neglect or show a voyeuristic interest in the client's sexual activity. If internalised homophobia is not being dealt with in the therapist, that therapist will be employing defence mechanisms ever more strenuously as the client tries to venture into areas of experience which threaten the therapist. This will result in a severe impoverishment of the relationship, will re-oppress the client, and impair the work.
- Counselling and psychotherapy training courses must provide arenas where students can explore their own sexualities and become increasingly aware of their sexual prejudices, in addition to raising their awareness of the impact of living in a homophobic society.
- The individual therapist can, however, increase their awareness of diverse lifestyles through an involvement in gay, lesbian or bisexual cultures – magazines and papers, novels, films and events. However, there is no substitute for warm relationships with those who have different lifestyles from our own, who will point out the assumptions which betray us, and challenge and stretch us by being people we share our lives with, not characters 'out there' who remain distant, or worse, invisible.

References

Bieber, I., Dain, H., Dince, P. *et al.* (1962) *Homosexuality: A Psychoanalytic Study of Male Homosexuals.* New York: Basic Books.

Bonaparte, M. (1953) *Female Sexuality.* New York: International Universities Press.

Buloff, B. and Osterman, M. (1995) Queer reflections: mirroring and the lesbian experience of self, in J.M. Glassgold and S. Iasenza (eds) *Lesbians and Psychoanalysis: Revolutions in Theory and Practice.* New York: The Free Press.

Cornett, C. (ed.) (1993) *Affirmative Dynamic Psychotherapy with Gay Men.* Northvale, NJ: Jason Aronson.

Cornett, C. (1995) *Reclaiming the Authentic Self: Dynamic Psychotherapy with Gay Men.* Northvale, NJ: Jason Aronson.

Davies, D. (1996) Towards a model of gay affirmative therapy, in D. Davies and C. Neal (eds) *Pink Therapy: A Guide for Counsellors and Therapists Working with Lesbian, Gay and Bisexual Clients.* Buckingham: Open University Press.

Davies, D. (1998) The six necessary and sufficient conditions applied to working with lesbian, gay, and bisexual clients, *The Person-Centered Journal*, 5(2): 111–24.

Deutsch, H. (1944) *The Psychology of Women.* New York: Grune and Stratton.

Deutsch, L. (1995) Out of the closet and on to the couch: a psychoanalytic exploration of lesbian development, in J.M. Glassgold and S. Iasenza (eds) *Lesbians and Psychoanalysis: Revolutions in Theory and Practice.* New York: The Free Press.

Domenici, T. and Lesser, R.C. (eds) (1995) *Disorienting Sexuality: Psychoanalytic Reappraisals of Sexual Identities.* London: Routledge.

Freud, S. (1905a) Brief, *Die Zeit* (Vienna), 27 October: 5.

Freud, S. (1905b) Three essays on the theory of sexuality, in J. Strachey (ed.) *The Standard Edition of the Complete Psychological Works of Sigmund Freud* (24 vols), Vol. 7: 123–245. London: The Hogarth Press.

Freud, S. (1920) The psychogenesis of a case of homosexuality in a woman, in J. Strachey (ed.) *The Standard Edition of the Complete Psychological Works of Sigmund Freud* (24 vols), Vol. 18: 145–72. London: The Hogarth Press.

Freud, S. ([1921]1977) Letter (to Jones), *Body Politic*, May: 9.

Freud, S. ([1935]1951) Letter, *American Journal of Psychiatry*, 107: 786.

Frommer, M.S. (1995) Countertransference obscurity in the psychoanalytic treatment of homosexual patients, in T. Domenici and R. Lesser (eds) *Disorienting Sexuality: Psychoanalytic Reappraisals of Sexual Identities.* London: Routledge.

Gair, S.R. (1995) The false self, shame, and the challenge of self-cohesion, in J.M. Glassgold and S. Iasenza (eds) *Lesbians and Psychoanalysis: Revolutions in Theory and Practice.* New York: The Free Press.

Gould, D. (1995) A critical examination of the notion of pathology in psychoanalysis, in J.M. Glassgold and S. Iasenza (eds) *Lesbians and Psychoanalysis: Revolutions in Theory and Practice.* New York: The Free Press.

Hargaden, H. and Llewellin, S. (1996) Lesbian and gay issues in parenting, in D. Davies and C. Neal (eds) *Pink Therapy: A Guide for Counsellors and Therapists Working with Lesbian, Gay and Bisexual Clients.* Buckingham: Open University Press.

Hopcke, R.H., Carrington, K.L. and Wirth, S. (eds) (1993) *Same Sex Love and the Path to Wholeness.* New York: Shambala.

Horney, K. (1932) The dread of women, *International Journal of Psychoanalysis*, 13: 348–60.

Horrocks, R. (1998) Historical issues: paradigms of homosexuality, in C. Shelley (ed.) *Contemporary Perspectives on Psychotherapy and Homosexualities*. London: Free Association Books.

Isay, R. (1989) *Being Homosexual: Gay Men and their Development*. Harmondsworth: Penguin.

Isay, R. (1993) On the analytic therapy of homosexual men, in C. Cornett (ed.) *Affirmative Dynamic Psychotherapy with Gay Men*. Northvale, NJ: Jason Aronson.

Isay, R. (1996) *Becoming Gay*. New York: Henry Holt.

Lewes, K. (1995) *Psychoanalysis and Male Homosexuality*. Northvale, NJ: Jason Aronson.

Malyon, A. (1993) Psychotherapeutic implications of internalized homophobia in gay men, in C. Cornett, (ed.) *Affirmative Dynamic Psychotherapy with Gay Men*. Northvale, NJ: Jason Aronson.

May, R. (1995) Re-reading Freud on homosexuality, in T. Domenici and R.C. Lesser (eds) *Disorienting Sexuality: Psychoanalytic Reappraisals of Sexual Identities*. London: Routledge.

Mitchell, J. (1974) *Psychoanalysis and Feminism*. Harmondsworth: Penguin.

O'Connor, N. and Ryan, J. (1993) *Wild Desires and Mistaken Identities: Lesbianism and Psychoanalysis*. London: Virago.

Rado, S. (1940) A critical examination of the theory of bisexuality, *Psychosomatic Medicine*, 2: 459–67.

Ratigan, B. (1998) Psychoanalysis and male homosexuality: queer bedfellows? in C. Shelley (ed.) *Contemporary Perspectives on Psychotherapy and Homosexualities*. London: Free Association Books.

Rohde-Dachser, C. (1992) Male and female homosexuality, *International Forum of Psychoanalysis*, 1: 67–73.

Ryan, J. (1998) Lesbianism and the therapist's subjectivity: a psychoanalytical view, in C. Shelley (ed.) *Contemporary Perspectives on Psychotherapy and Homosexualities*. London: Free Association Books.

Schwartz, D. (1995) Current psychoanalytic discourses on sexuality: tripping over the body, in T. Domenici and R.C. Lesser (eds) *Disorienting Sexuality: Psychoanalytic Reappraisals of Sexual Identities*. London: Routledge.

Shelley, C. (ed.) (1998) *Contemporary Perspectives on Psychotherapy and Homosexualities*. London: Free Association Books.

Thompson, C. (1947) Changing concepts of homosexuality, *Psychiatry*, 10: 183–9.

Trop, J. and Stolorow, R. (1992) Defense analysis in self psychology: a developmental view, *Psychoanalytic dialogue*, 2: 427–42.

Weinberg, G. (1972) *Society and the Healthy Homosexual*. New York: Anchor Press Doubleday.

Wheeler, S. and Izzard, S. (1997) Psychodynamic counsellor training: integrating difference, *Psychodynamic Counselling*, 3(4): 401–17.

Young-Bruehl, E. (1996) *The Anatomy of Prejudices*. Cambridge, MA: Harvard University Press.

Psychosynthesis

A contemporary overview

Psychosynthesis has been enjoying a growth in popularity in recent years as a mainstream psychotherapeutic approach. Compared to other 'schools' it is relatively small, written about less and, given its explicit focus on the spiritual nature of self-identity, considered somewhat dismissively by some of the more hard-nosed psychological disciplines. This changed in the 1980s and 1990s as other schools became more receptive to the idea that spiritual life has an important bearing on psychological and emotional well-being and growth.

Like most therapeutic schools today, psychosynthesis is rich with differences of style and approach reflecting an evolving discipline. Originally developed by Roberto Assagioli, an Italian psychoanalyst (1888–1974), it began in Italy and was developed significantly in California in the three decades after the Second World War, from where it was brought to Britain in the early 1970s. According to Firman and Russell (1992: 2), psychosynthesis is 'one of the earliest forerunners of both humanistic psychology and transpersonal psychology, even preceding Jung's break with Freud by several years'.

Although contemporary psychosynthesis in Britain and some centres in Europe came out of the Californian stable, there are increasing links being forged with some of the older schools. Broadly speaking, we can talk of a distinction between traditional, or classical, psychosynthesis and integrative psychosynthesis – the latter being more common in Britain and the Netherlands.

Psychosynthesis has never been purely a therapy. It is a way of looking at people, systems and change, which has application to education, politics, management and creative development. However, with the emergence of the United Kingdom Council for Psychotherapy (UKCP) in the 1990s, the main emphasis in training in this country has been on psychotherapy, with academic recognition at Masters level. Within UKCP, psychosynthesis, along with other approaches such as core process therapy, sits within the Association for Accredited Psychospiritual Psychotherapists – the first grouping to gain independent recognition.

For lesbians, gay men and bisexuals, a psychospiritual basis to understanding the psyche has a number of advantages. First, one of the traditional assumptions in orthodox psychoanalysis – that human character and identity should be looked at primarily from a neurotic standpoint – has not been prominent, given that our model of what constitutes psychopathology is radically different. Second, many lesbians and gay men, although suffering psychologically or emotionally in life, have an explicitly spiritual awareness and context for living indicated by large numbers working in the healing professions, the artistic and performance worlds and in religious institutions. Assagioli, although saying nothing about same-sex relationships, by implication saw homosexuality within the negative psychoanalytic conventions of his day: 'Concerning results, we can state that the best ones have been achieved in the cure of psychosomatic disorders, phobias, and homosexual tendencies' (Assagioli 1993: 234).

In practice, the culture within psychosynthesis has been open-minded. This is not to say that homophobia, oppression or ignorance are not found within psychosynthesis culture even today, but merely to make the point that the environment has not been locked into normative assumptions about what constitutes a healthy self, since each soul is held to be following its own path to self-development. Gigante (1988: 202), commenting on psychosynthesis and gay sexuality says:

> The gay person willing to explore beneath the self-hatred often finds a message of purpose, of goodness, and of perfection in the very fact of Gayness. From images of the Wise Old Being, from Jesus, from the sun, comes the message of needing to be both a student and a teacher, of needing to learn some important lessons and ready to teach some important lessons by virtue of being a gay person in an ostracising society. Many sense that their gay sexuality is a choice for the incarnating soul (or some other higher being) for specific purposes.

The ethos of psychosynthesis may have more in common with certain tolerant spiritual cultures such as some versions of Buddhism, progressive Christianity and Judaism, and Native American traditions. Given that increasing numbers of 'out' lesbians, gay men and bisexuals are training, the future can only continue to look brighter. At the time of writing, what is generally lacking within psychosynthesis – although it is probably not alone in this – is a developed theoretical treatment of sex and sexuality in general. Lesbians and gay men have the opportunity to be at the fore-front in developing theory rooted in personal and collective experience and in advancing change in institutions through our presence and continued dialogue.

Psychosynthesis in a nutshell

Psychosynthesis, in common with all other therapeutic endeavours, is a response to what might be called 'the human condition'. Figure 8.1 represents four aspects of this predicament. Implicit in this diagram is the recognition of paradox. Life is complex, with contradictory and often competing needs and demands. Acceptance of this complexity sets the scene for appreciating the fullness of human beings without prejudgement of what is a right or appropriate way to live, as each person needs to come to terms with the complexity of life in their own way. At every point, we are posed with choices that vary in their degree of appropriateness. For the most part, the aspect of this predicament that we meet as therapists, at least when people come to us for the first time, is the suffering. Therapy is but one way of tackling suffering, complementary to but distinct from other pursuits such as medicine or politics. In responding to suffering, the hallmark of psychotherapy is the attention given to the psychological or inner world.

Therapeutic schools differ on certain fundamental points. The first concerns the degree to which the state of the psychological world is primary and causal to the experience of suffering in the world. In this respect, psychosynthesis holds that the psyche has a profound impact on both an individual's immediate world and the society in which that person is embedded, which is recognised as having a reciprocal effect on the development of the inner world.

The second point concerns speculation on the origin, development and manifestation of psychological life. In this, psychosynthesis is distinct from many other therapies. The psyche here is not just an arbitrary collection of drives, instincts or developmental forces (what we call the 'lower unconscious'), or merely the result of our upbringing. It is also fashioned from the start by what might be called 'transpersonal qualities' emanating from the source of being or 'the Self' (what we call the 'higher unconscious') which, according to Assagioli (1993), include the potential for altruistic love, genius, states of contemplation, illumination and ecstasy. This all shapes our developmental path in a particular way. We might say that the combination of our drives and developmental forces, working in conjunction

Figure 8.1 A map of the human condition

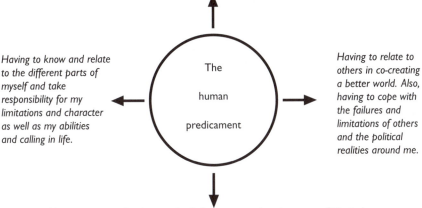

with the manifestation of those qualities which are divine or transpersonal, constitutes 'the will'.

According to one training school: 'The Will is a central concept in psychosynthesis and is seen as an essential impulse towards wholeness and synthesis' (IPL, undated). It is easy to see how, in a historical context, homosexuality might have been viewed purely from the standpoint of the lower unconscious as the result of, say, unresolved Oedipal conflicts. When we start to imagine that the expression of same-sex attraction might contain a transpersonal dynamic, this changes radically the perception of homosexuality as a phenomenon. Viewed in this way, attention shifts from homosexuality as, primarily, a source of inner psychological suffering (unresolved complexes), to a view where the way the environment has responded becomes foreground.

Figure 8.2   A model of the person

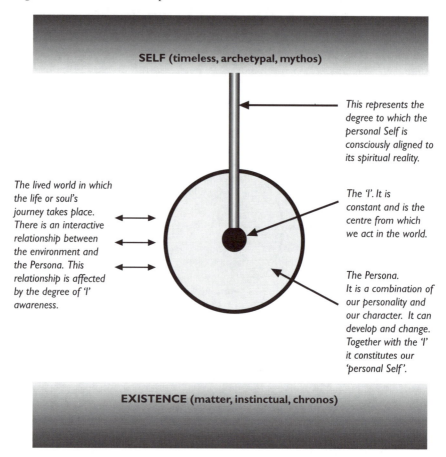

A psychosynthetic model of the psyche

The Persona, the 'I' and the Self (see Figure 8.2) illustrate some 'building blocks' of the psychosynthesis landscape. One of the most fundamental distinctions is between what we call the Persona and the 'I'. The Persona is that aspect of someone that we usually meet in everyday life – the person we know – a combination of personality and deeper character. Generally speaking, although the Persona tends to be stable for long periods of life, it undergoes subtle or sometimes radical transformations at times. An example is when someone experiences a change in sexual orientation and 'comes out'. It seems that their whole relationship to the world and themselves becomes radically different. Attitudes to family and friends, politics and even their own body, change. The 'I' however is that aspect of a person that is beyond change – it just is. An analogy would be the centre spindle of a vinyl record turntable. While we can see the record turning, the spindle remains relatively still. Although we may experience its presence – every living person has an 'I' – it has no tangible substance.

In this way the 'I' is comparable to the 'no-self Self' or state of egolessness found in Taoist or Buddhist traditions. In practical terms it can be experienced through the self-reflective writing of a daily journal, or in meditation. We can discern the presence of the 'I' sometimes in people's coming-out stories. Whenever someone reports 'I always knew I was lesbian, ever since I was very young' we can detect the presence of the 'I' – the one who has always known and does the telling.

Where people differ, however, is in the degree to which they have developed 'I-awareness'. This may best be described as a 'sense of Self' or sometimes more commonly as 'presence of mind'. For example, in HIV prevention work, it is common to find that someone has had unprotected sex, knowing full well the risks, but has given way to impulse. We might say that, at that moment, they lost their sense of Self. Psychosynthesis places great value on helping clients discover, or rediscover, their 'I-awareness' because this is the centre from which one can purposefully direct one's will, thus making and enacting life choices. Although 'I-awareness' may well involve the use of one's mental thinking capacities, it is essentially a place where body, feelings and mind are moved to act in unison in a congruent and authentic way. In addition to reflective questions, practical techniques such as writing and drawing, meditation and guided fantasy are used.

Figure 8.2 illustrates a further feature of the psychosynthesis model: the degree of connection or alignment between the 'I' and the Self. This is sometimes difficult to comprehend, let alone explain. Basically, it concerns the degree to which we are able to act consciously in service of our values or our interconnectedness with others. Three types of example can demonstrate it. One is in a vocational life choice to devote one's energies to the service of others, such as the care of those living with AIDS. A second is in terms of how we handle a delicate situation – say, where someone we do not find sexually attractive makes persistent advances. How do we refuse the other with care, respect and dignity in a spirit of compassion and harmlessness? This principle is called 'right relating', which is similar to the 'I-Thou' principle of the philosopher Martin Buber (1937) and can also be seen in the work of Carl Rogers (1961). A third illustration is in the maintenance of faith – a sense of something both within and beyond our individual selves. This need not be religious, but it is certainly spiritual and, as such can be the basis of developing a sense of stability and tranquillity in one's world.

The point about each of these three illustrations in relation to the 'I-Self' connection, is that it does not come from any 'superego injunction' or

Figure 8.3 A model of the psyche

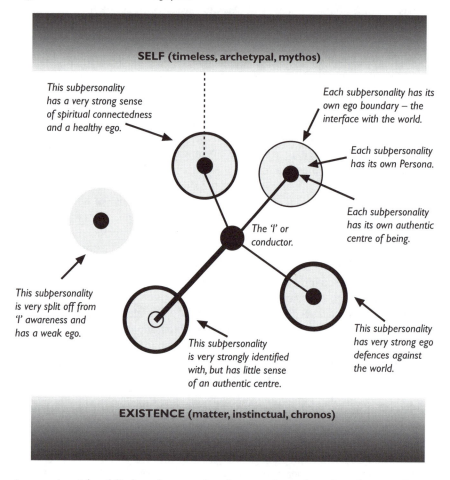

imperative 'should', but from a deeply experienced and authentic choice about how to live and act in the world. This capacity can take many years to develop. In psychosynthesis, we would see this as integral to the psychotherapeutic process, not ancillary to it.

Subpersonalities and the ego

Another building block in psychosynthesis is the concept of subpersonalities. Although this is comparable to the idea of parts in Gestalt and, to some extent, ego states in transactional analysis, there are some significant features central to the theory and practice of psychosynthesis. Figure 8.3 shows many of the important features of subpersonalities.

Although as a whole they make up the Persona, subpersonalities function, effectively, as mini-Personas in their own right, each with an authentic and relatively timeless centre. This is important because we might be tempted to exclude ones we do not like or approve of from the personality system, and ally or 'identify' with the ones we like. For example, we might have an inner 'judge' who disapproves of our sexual practices. It might be tempting to cut off from this subpersonality. In psychosynthesis, we listen to the deeper, authentic message of this subpersonality whose function may well be to protect us from harm. Then, in dialogue with other subpersonalities (such as the adventurer, the rebel or the playful child) we can come to an acceptable arrangement. The authenticity of each subpersonality comes from two sources. The first is the Self, or archetypal realm. The easiest way of understanding archetypes is from the mythic stories of gods and goddesses who represent different energies or qualities of spirit. The second source comes from the instinctual realm – our drives for protection or survival and the satisfaction of biological and emotional needs. To a large extent, the culture we come from, and particularly our homes of origin, may emphasise, cherish and encourage, or neglect and abuse certain aspects and features of our subpersonalities. So, a large task of therapeutic work is to sort out the authentic voices from the socially conditioned ones – something that is crucial to gay people growing up in a largely unsympathetic environment – and to help us come to terms with the complexity of our subpersonality system.

From Figure 8.3, a further feature can be seen: the ego. 'The ego', of course, is a term common to virtually all therapeutic traditions, including psychoanalysis, and some spiritual disciplines as well. However, unlike other modalities, in psychosynthesis the development and maintenance of a secure or healthy ego is not the end goal of therapy. From our perspective, the ego is a psychological and emotional containing structure that allows the Persona and the 'I' (along with its component subpersonalities) to survive and function in the world. The ego helps us recognise what is us and what is not us – where, say, my needs begin and those of my partner end.

We can talk of weak egos (where someone wants to merge entirely with us), rigid egos (where someone is terrified to let anyone get close to them) or healthy, flexible egos (where someone can be assertive without being aggressive). A distinctive possibility within the psychosynthesis model is that the ego is not, and need not, be uniformly developed across all areas of one's Persona. One subpersonality may have a well-developed ego (e.g. my professional side) whereas another may experience being more vulnerable (e.g. my romantic or sexual side). This is important, because subpersonalities have 'ages and stages' – some are old and familiar to us; others are young and new and need to be nurtured, protected and developed. For example, when an adult, professionally successful individual comes out as gay in mid-life, they may want nurturing and protecting and the chance to experience those young or less-developed parts of themselves.

A further feature of the concept of the ego in psychosynthesis is that, in order to be open to new experience, particularly in terms of the 'I-Self' connection, it is not too helpful to have an overly strong ego. An analogy is a medieval city with strong town walls – when the city wants to develop, and there are no longer external threats of invasion, the walls need to come down in places. An example is a lesbian client who presented a 'tough' Persona to the world as a protection from early wounds. Eventually, she learned to soften these ego boundaries, giving way to a much softer nature. More profoundly, a relaxation or transcendence of ego boundaries often opens the psyche to experiences that are called 'transpersonal' which can be moments of great insight, inspiration and creativity. Such experiences are taken very seriously and are handled carefully so as not to be confused with those experiences of weak or non-developed ego boundaries, which would be more appropriately treated as psychotic or disturbed. Examples from history include visionaries such as Hildegard of Bingen.

More commonly, a transpersonal quality goes hand in hand with an undeveloped or 'prepersonal' character trait or limitation. Hal Zina Bennett describes a friend whose 'spiritual mission in life takes her into hospitals all over the world, where she counsels people with critical illnesses and offers strength to those who are dying', yet she 'feels that she is terribly inadequate as a human being' (1987: 76–7). He observes 'the great contradiction is that what some might perceive as her limitations are the root of a kind of expansiveness of character that allows her to succeed in a task where only a very few ever do' (1987: 77–8). An example from therapy is a gay man whose problem was an extreme obsession with tidiness and cleanliness. In exploring the deeper meaning of this 'perfectionism', it was found that he also had a most sublime appreciation of beauty and perfection in art. The task of the therapist was to help the client see beyond the literalism of the presenting symptom to a more profound message, thus providing an opportunity for resolution.

The context of psychosynthesis therapy

Some thoughts on the nature of journeys

We are now in a position to look more closely at what we call the 'context' of psychosynthesis therapy, concerned with the soul's healing. Essentially, we work with life journeys, of all kinds. Psychosynthesis therapists used to be known as 'guides', the idea being that we accompanied our clients, emotionally, psychologically and to a limited extent, spiritually, along their path in life, particularly through times of transition or crisis. We often call this journey the 'soul's journey', using the term in a non-religious way to suggest that the personal Self is in some way a vessel of consciousness that undergoes transformations and learnings during the course of a lifetime.

This role is analogous to that of Virgil or Beatrice in Dante's *Divine Comedy*. Dante's journey begins in what we might now term 'mid-life crisis': 'Midway this way of life we're bound upon / I woke to find myself in a dark wood / Where the right road was wholly lost and gone' (Luke 1989: 4).

Such moments of life crisis or transition often appear quite ordinary and mundane – such as being made redundant from a job – but they may set in train a whole series of psychological and emotional changes that force the client to face certain issues. Such issues may be found by bringing into consciousness feelings and perceptions that seem new and unfamiliar. The converse also happens, when what appears as a deep psychological problem that has been diagnosed medically as a 'pathology', requires practical, outwardly directed changes. Coming out as gay might be a case in point. It can be argued that medical science (particularly psychiatry and some psychoanalytic approaches) and orthodox religion have created more emotional crises for lesbians, gay men and bisexuals than they have helped to heal or solve.

What makes psychosynthesis rather different from other stances is the perspective it holds on the nature of 'pathology'. From a conventional, normative standpoint, a healthy individual might be one who seems problem-free, with a good upbringing, and able to get on with life in a relatively smooth, untroubled way. This is reflected in the values, aspirations and treatments meted out by most helping professions. From a psychospiritual viewpoint however, it is natural to face deep questions in life, where certain crises are just as likely to provide creative opportunities as remain defeative scenarios. Perhaps the biggest failure is never having to wrestle with oneself and life or, worse still, never having lived true to one's spirit and nature. Thus it follows that, for a gay person to stay firmly in the closet through fear and shame is quite pathological from a psychospiritual standpoint, whereas to face oneself and the world is healthier. From this viewpoint the suffering of symptoms and illnesses – psychological or physical – is an expected and 'normal' phenomenon, and is not to be viewed as a life failure. The struggle and search for meaningful solutions or the capacity to sit with and 'suffer suffering' is a healthy response to an incarnated life. Similarly, the capacity to seek joy – whether outwardly through people, activities or things, or inwardly through one's emotional and spiritual resources – is equally a valid and authentic response to life.

In psychosynthesis, the life journey is worked with from two perspectives – or, if preferred, two stories. I call these 'the incarnational journey' (or the journey into form) and 'the redemptive journey' (or the journey towards wholeness). At any one time during therapy, one of these journeys may be foreground, providing the explicit context for the work, with the other is background, providing the implicit context. Although for convenience these two journeys are described separately here (see Figures 8.4 and 8.5), they are frequently closely connected, often in a paradoxical way. For example,

Figure 8.4 The incarnational journey

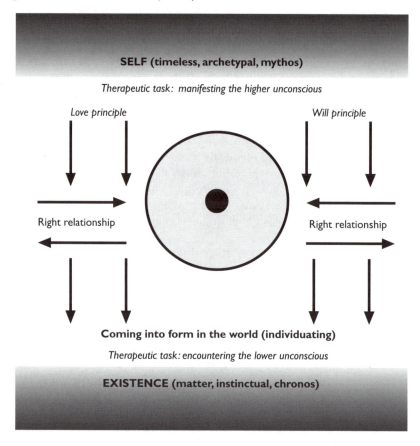

a client who has never learned to cook bakes a cake for the first time. There is satisfaction at finding a form for a new experience, which then creates a sense of wholeness.

The incarnational journey

We are always being born – or at least we are always in a process of becoming. Perhaps our biological birth is the most powerful experience of all, setting the scene for the way in which other 'mini-births' throughout life happen for us. In psychosynthesis, this process of becoming is thought to start with an oceanic experience of oneness within the mother's womb, through a symbiotic relationship where we are part merged with mother and part separate, to a fully-fledged experience of distinctness which, as life progresses, constitutes our individuality. Different parts of us – the

Figure 8.5   The redemptive journey

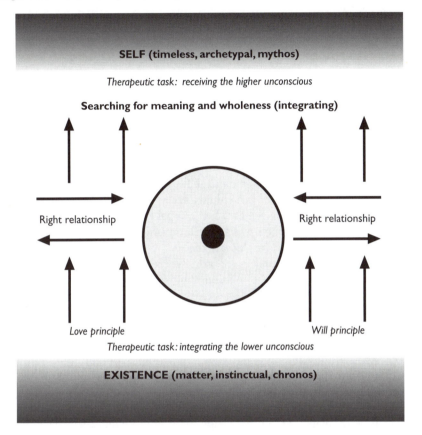

subpersonalities – go through this process at different times and rates and often in an unconventional order.

In more traditional developmental (and psychosynthesis) models, it has been assumed that there are appropriate chronological or existential ages for specific subpersonalities to come into their own. For example, we talk of the 'rebel' subpersonality as being typically constellated in adolescent years. If this does not occur, this is seen in some way as a personality deficit. From my clinical observation, I believe that in our complex post modern culture these age-related stages are not nearly so fixed. A person may be opening to their playful child subpersonality for the first time in old age, or connected to their inner 'wise old person' in childhood. For lesbian, gay and bisexual people, this can be a very important point. Given that we often lack role models or 'human mirrors' at crucial stages in our social development, we tend to discover our adolescence later. An example is a 33-year-old divorced man who, having recently come out as gay, started to go to clubs, changed his wardrobe and opened himself to a variety of exciting sexual encounters. It might be argued that a by-product of a socially and sexually competitive commercial scene has been that more lesbians, gay men and bisexuals stay connected to a sense of youthful vitality far longer than might have been the case in previous generations.

Where psychosynthesis tends to be in general agreement with other therapies – including psychoanalysis – is in identifying early infant relationships as having a significant impact on the pace and style of personal development – our conditioning. A good deal of modern psychosynthesis practice has been influenced by the object relations theory of child development, prominent in Britain since the middle years of this century. This has given us great insight into working with, say, early sexual or violent abuse, where aspects of the 'inner child' get damaged and shut down early in life and need to be revived later, or individuals act as if they are very 'grown up' sexually when in fact they are not. It is the pace and style of our early conditioning that is determined by early relationships, rather than our nature itself. James Hillman, in his 'acorn theory', criticised what he calls 'the parental fallacy' often found in therapy, where there is confusion between early conditioning or 'object relations failure' and our individual nature, character or calling which he claims emerges as largely a separate phenomenon: 'The more my life is accounted for by what already occurred in my chromosomes, by what my parents did or didn't do, and by my early years now long past, the more my biography is the story of a victim' (Hillman 1997: 6).

Right from the start, a small child is self-initiating in terms of which 'objects' in its social or physical environment it chooses to bond with or alienate itself from. This point is important, because it alleviates gay people from the old adage 'My mother made me a homosexual'. It is easy to see how analysts of old fell into the causation trap. If their gay clients seemed highly neurotic and disturbed, it might not have occurred to them that it was the society in which they had to live and function that created the disturbance and defined the pathology rather than any particular failure in early object relationships. So, in this incarnational journey, the psychosynthesis therapist is working first to help identify subpersonalities which are emerging; second to facilitate the development, strengthening or loosening of ego boundaries; and third to guide the client into discovering and accepting the significance, usefulness and expression of these subpersonalities in daily life. This process additionally involves working with two principles in tandem (love and will), the former reflecting self-nurturing, compassion and acceptance, the latter reflecting choice, action and self-responsibility.

An important feature that is not to be overlooked is the respect we give to perceived blocks, ego defences and 'resistances'. We see these as purposeful and meaningful. Thus we hold that this process of becoming has its own timing and wisdom – usually unconscious – and trust that a person will open to whatever they need when the time is right. Much of this work is intuitive, recognising that the unfolding of the psyche is a mystery. Not everybody is ready for deep exploratory work that involves the uncovering of the lower unconscious. For example, someone with generally fragile ego boundaries might not be able to cope with a journey into Dante's inferno. Also, someone with very rigid ego boundaries might not be able to make much use of such a process.

The redemptive journey

Human beings search for meaning and purpose in life. Quite what that means is different for everyone. Often this creates a sense of alienation, either from the world or from parts of oneself. Sometimes such issues, if not fully or consciously articulated, manifest as depression. More commonly, they manifest in a deep questioning of identity and a desire for 'something more' which, Moody and Carroll (1998: 28), echoing Assagioli, have charted as a number of stages beginning with 'the call':

> The urge to find deeper purpose in life, if heeded and encouraged, unfolds in a sequence of stages that exerts a slow but sure metamorphic effect on the adult personality. In the end, one who has passed through these stages emerges as a more fulfilled and self-realized individual. These stages of the soul are the foundation for a new map of life.

Often, the desire for something more gets sublimated into the material world: obsessive drinking, sex or shopping. What remains hard to articulate or eludes discovery is a sense of completeness or what might be called that 'heaven within'. Such issues can become problems at certain times in life: 'mid-life' is one. There is a growing awareness that life is finite and the question of what needs to be done, or what cannot be put off until tomorrow, sits not quite so easily. This is accompanied by the self-question, 'Is this all there is?' A metaphor frequently used in psychosynthesis training is to compare the Persona and achievements to a house: 'When I was a teenager, I lived in my parents' house; in my twenties, I built my own house; in my thirties I lived in the house that I built; and in my forties, I decided to burn the house down and start again'. This is a time of challenging who one is, sifting through what is useful to keep and what to discard. Psychosynthesis is especially suited to guiding people through these confusing questions and giving form to the next manifestation of ourselves. An example is a gay man who at the age of 50 allowed himself to fall in love for the first time. Such questions do not occur only in mid-life, although this is a very common time. One of the lessons of AIDS, in the early days when many young people found themselves faced with the prospect of a premature death, was that such profound questions can be posed at any time, brought on by any sudden shift or change in life circumstances.

At a community level too, gay people started asking more questions about the meaning of things such as love, commitment and faith. A general deficiency in otherwise affirmative therapeutic thinking about gay people in my view is the neglect of those existential and psychospiritual issues faced in mid-life and beyond. The emphasis has tended to be on the coming out process. Issues and choices around aloneness, partnership and community are vital to explore in therapy, not least because conventional cultural guidelines are generally based on the requirements of heterosexual family partnership. However, as these models are becoming less useful, we are seeing far more non-gay people tackling the same issues. Perhaps, lesbian, gay and bisexual people, having had to face questions of aloneness and identity more prevalently, have much to offer.

In psychosynthesis this quest for meaning and wholeness is worked with by drawing into awareness and everyday usage images and forms that come from or evoke the higher unconscious. For example, we make use of guided fantasy, internal images of 'the wise person' and creative methods such as writing, drawing and meditation. As with the incarnational journey, we work with the subpersonalities, making conscious how they manifest the principles of love and will. Although psychosynthesis is not a spiritual discipline itself, we encourage clients to develop and take an interest in a spiritual discipline of their own, whether or not this might be aligned to any specific faith. We also encourage clients to discover and nurture creative or community pursuits – anything from gardening to volunteer work – which may foster a sense of centredness and spiritual nourishment.

The redemptive journey is rather like a journey home – not particularly to our home of origin, but to a home of spirit. For lesbian, gay and bisexual people, one of the tragedies of the wider western culture and of those therapies or religions which have pathologised us, is that we have been sold a lie: that we have no spiritual home, no positive archetypes and thus no authentic redemptive journey is possible. Perhaps no other group in history has had to live with such a message. Fortunately, we know now that not every culture has been like this. For example, according to Grahn (1984), Williams (1986) and Roscoe (1988), many Native American tribes have had positive archetypal myths and characters reflecting same-sex attraction and identity, which has been duly reflected in the affirmative attitudes taken towards gay or transgendered people.

Although western culture does not particularly offer many gay-affirming archetypal figures, psychosynthesis can help foster various life paths and destinies that speak to archetypal callings. In my work I have encountered several: the healer or shaman, the artisan, the adventurer and, for gay men, the 'male mother'. There may be many more: the purpose here is not to typecast or stereotype, but merely to note how common it is to find lesbians, gay men and bisexuals directing their life energies into certain vocations which offer a distinctly devotional aspect. These 'stereo-archetypes' are, interestingly, noticeable in other cultures such as the Native American tradition, typified in the form of the *berdache* or two spirit people.[1] The healer or shaman is relatively obvious: caring professions such as nursing, social work, religion and the therapies. Artists, writers, craftspeople and performers might represent the artisan. The adventurer might be found within, say, the travel industry or communications technology. The 'male mother' (is there a counterpart of the 'female father'?) takes us across gender divisions and raises issues about same-sex parenting. Male mothers can be found in teaching, therapy and childcare. A question that the reader might explore is the degree to which these patterns are a result of our social conditioning or are authentic self-choices.

In summary, both the incarnational and the redemptive journeys share the concern for authenticity in life – whether this authenticity takes us into the experience of our suffering, the expression of joy, or the will to make radical life changes.

The dynamics of the therapeutic relationship: working with the authentic and the 'false' self

The emphasis on authenticity and 'I-awareness' is a central theme that affects both the style of working and the nature of the therapeutic relationship with the client. As signalled earlier, one of the hallmarks is trust and respect for the process, particularly regarding the so-called defences the client might have and that usually exist for a good reason.

In the training of therapists, great emphasis is placed on the here-and-now awareness and perception of such things as body language, shifts of energy and quality of interpersonal contact – perhaps no differently from, say, a Gestalt therapist. Emphasis is also on the quality of verbal interventions and other strategies, ensuring that they are in keeping with the contextual journey of the client. Figure 8.6 illustrates this process. The therapist, by sensitive enquiry, helps to establish and bring into awareness those needs, values, beliefs, anxieties and aspirations which are real and authentic to the client, while exploring and dispelling those features of psychological life that are based on projection and introjection, denial and splitting. The client, in return, is encouraged to bring their own self-reflective processes to bear in expressing what is deeply valued and needed and to own and take responsibility for their emotional life. Often the client presents what is called a 'false self', which may consist of socially conditioned or adaptive behaviours which reflect early or core wounding. Although the therapist respects the client's current need to display this 'false self', it is also seen as important to help the client become more aware of what is happening.

Figure 8.6   The authentic mirror

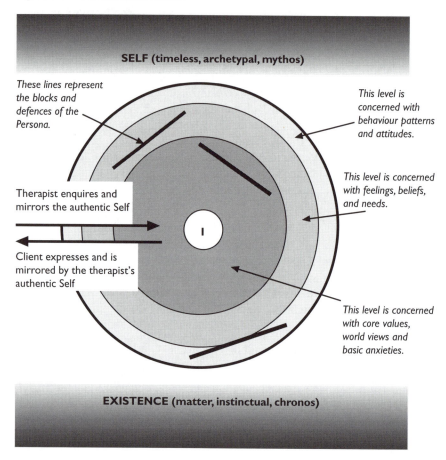

An example might be when a client consistently speaks of people only as sex objects. The therapist here might gently challenge whether the client experiences any feelings about the other as a real person.

Arguably, lesbians, gay men and bisexuals have been 'core wounded' in particular ways, perhaps in very early childhood by the 'rejection' of the same-sex parent. This often plays out, for example, in the difficulty many lesbians and gay men experience in terms of trust and intimacy in relationships. However, this is not to say that non-gay people are not wounded too. A paradox is that in the playful and enjoyable acting out of roles in the commercial gay scene, certain aspects of the core wounding, in terms of presenting a 'false self' may in fact be exacerbated. For example, the cultivation of a very 'macho' image may, unintentionally, make someone seem unapproachable.

Figure 8.7   Four modes of therapeutic relationship

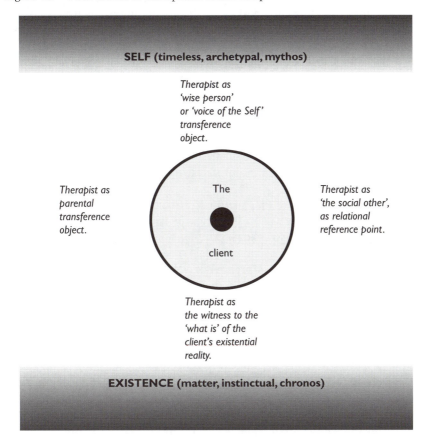

Transference in psychosynthesis

Given that the primary function of the therapeutic relationship is 'I awareness' and authenticity, the handling of transference (the feelings the client experiences in relation to the therapist) and its converse the counter-transference (the feelings the therapist experiences in relation to the client) is different from that found in conventional psychodynamic approaches. It must be said that the therapist is not always a direct 'stand-in' for a past parental figure. However, where the work is clearly of an early 'object relations' kind, this may be so. In most other cases, the therapist represents other types of relationship, depicted in Figure 8.7: the 'voice of the Self' (the projected 'wise person'), a form of transference, not necessarily parental; the 'social other', working interactively to simulate a microcosm of the social world; or the witness to the life story of the client, standing for what we call the 'what is' (naming things for what they are, stripping away illusions about what is not real or realistic). It follows that one of the objectives of the therapeutic relationship is ultimately to own projections so that the transferences are made redundant. Taking responsibility for one's projections rather than playing into them is thus an important goal in owning and coming to terms with one's own existential pain.

As the therapist does not always represent a 'past parent', it is not necessarily the case that a lesbian or gay client requires a gay therapist, or even a member of a specific gender. However, at certain times in the therapeutic work, it may be helpful to work with one 'parental representative' rather than another. At others, it is enough to work with an experienced and aware therapist who has some appreciation of the lived worlds of gay people.

It is of great importance that the therapist accepts the legitimate fears of gay clients that by the very process of therapy itself they can be re-wounded through being pathologised. For example, normative assumptions about appropriate sexual practices vary among therapists. This presents a difficulty in distinguishing when a preference for many sexual partners is compulsive rather than nourishing. From a psychosynthesis perspective, it is perhaps of importance that a therapist appreciates the spiritual dimension, which sets the context for the life journey of a gay person.

Towards a psychosynthetic understanding of same-sex attraction

Finally, I suggest a perspective on same-sex attraction, as viewed from a psychospiritual rather than a 'neurotic' perspective. This is referred to in Figure 8.8. From an incarnational and redemptive perspective, we might regard life as being experienced along a continuum, with an experience of wholeness and connectedness at one end and individuality, separateness and a sense of fragmentation at the other. Life exposes us to both extremes at times, with various degrees of each in between.

We might suppose that sexual attraction also functions along such a continuum, ranging from attraction to sameness to attraction to difference. I believe that this holds true for heterosexuals as well as for lesbian, gay and bisexual people. Biological gender itself may ultimately prove to be a 'red herring', as we are attracted (or repelled) by intra-psychic qualities in the end: I might find myself relating to the man-within-the-woman or the woman-within-the-man. We all search for 'the beloved' and find it in the most unusual places and in the most unlikely of people!

What also holds for heterosexual as well as lesbian, gay and bisexual attraction is the power of the image of the divine held in the mirror of the other. The end of the spectrum at which one holds up a mirror to catch the

Figure 8.8 A model of sexual attraction

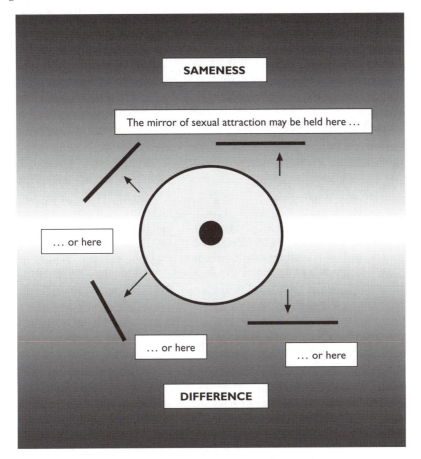

SAMENESS

The mirror of sexual attraction may be held here ...

... or here

... or here

... or here

DIFFERENCE

image of the divine is possibly a moveable feast. For lesbians and gay men that mirror is placed near the top end of the spectrum. This gives them a particular advantage and a particular disadvantage (relative to heterosexually attracted people). The advantage is that gay people have potential access to an experience of the beloved in the form of knowing sameness in a profound way through sexual union. The disadvantage is that gay people may get fixated on that image in a very narcissistic way. It may be hard in relationships to distinguish between a state of union with the other (a redemptive journey experience) and a state of undifferentiated merger with the other (an incarnational journey experience). Wilber (1996) has highlighted the difficulty for the therapist in distinguishing such pre-personal and trans-personal experiences. This is indeed a mixed blessing. It might explain why most psychoanalysts have maintained (and some no doubt still do) that homosexuality is essentially a narcissistic disorder. What they do not appreciate is the 'other side of the coin', that homosexual experience is also privileged to certain spiritual gifts. Unless psychology includes the spiritual dimension, this larger picture will be missed entirely and we fall back into the quagmire of pathology. One of the most useful therapeutic tasks a therapist can undertake with a lesbian or gay client who happens to be struggling with a sexual relationship is to sort out which aspects of the relationship belong to the incarnational journey, and which belong to the redemptive journey – and where they might find coexistence.

Note

1 '*Berdache* was a derogatory term European colonizers used to label any Native person who did not fit their narrow notions of woman and man. The blanket use of the word disregarded distinctions of self-expression, social interaction, and complex economic and political realities. Native nations had many respectful words in their own languages to describe such people . . . However, cultural genocide has destroyed and altered Native languages and traditions. So Native people ask that the term *two-spirit* people be used to replace the offensive colonial word' (Feinberg 1996: 21).

References

Assagioli, R. (1993) *Psychosynthesis: A Manual of Principles and Techniques.* London: Aquarius/Thorsons.

Bennett, H.Z. (1987) *The Lens of Perception.* Berkeley, CA: Celestial Arts.

Buber, M. (1937) *I and Thou.* Edinburgh: T & T Clark.

Feinberg, L. (1996) *Transgender Warriors: Making History from Joan of Arc to Dennis Rodman.* Boston: Beacon Press.

Firman, J. and Russell, A. (1992) *What is Psychosynthesis?* Palo Alto: the authors. (Obtainable from: 459 Hawthorne Avenue, Palo Alto, CA 94301, USA).

Gigante, M. (1988) Psychosynthesis and gay sexuality, in J. Weiser and T. Yeomans (eds) *Readings in Psychosynthesis Theory, Processes & Practice*, vol. 2. Toronto: Ontario Institute for Studies in Education.

Grahn, J. (1984) *Another Mother Tongue: Gay Words, Gay Worlds.* Boston: Beacon Press.

Hillman, J. (1997) *The Soul's Code: In Search of Character and Calling.* London: Bantam.

IPL (Institute of Psychosynthesis, London) (undated) *Prospectus of the Institute of Psychosynthesis, London* (c.1995).

Luke, H. (1989) *Dark Wood to White Rose: Journey and Transformation in Dante's Divine Comedy.* New York: Parabola.

Moody, H.R. and Carroll, D. (1998) *The Five Stages of the Soul: Charting the Spiritual Passages That Shape Our Lives.* London: Rider.

Rogers, C. (1961) *On Becoming a Person: A Therapist's View of Psychotherapy.* London: Constable.

Roscoe, W. (ed.) (1988) *Living the Spirit: A Gay American Indian Anthology.* New York: St Martin's Press.

Wilber, K. (1996) The pre/trans fallacy, in K. Wilber (ed.) *Eye to Eye: The Quest for the New Paradigm.* Boston: Shambhala.

Williams, W.L. (1986) *The Spirit and the Flesh – Sexual Diversity in American Indian Culture.* Boston: Beacon Press.

Social constructionist and systemic therapy

Introduction

This chapter explores some of the ideas from systemic, narrative and social constructionist therapy practices, and looks at how these ideas might apply to therapeutic work with lesbians, gay men and bisexuals. It identifies and contextualises some of the social, political and cultural discourses which influence counselling and psychotherapy practices.

Social constructionist therapy sets the individual or couple and their problems in a relational context of conversation and social discourses – be it with a partner, friends, family, school, workplace or culture. Therapeutic practice centres around enquiry into people's description of their experiences so as to create opportunities to know how to overcome difficulties by elaborating and reconstructing therapists' and clients' stories.

Building on developments in systemic therapy, social constructionist therapy does not work with the notion of a pathology in an individual or social system (for example, a *'dysfunctional* family' or a *'disturbed* individual') but rather with how the description of the problem arises and how it may be a problem in itself. More attention is paid to the language we use and to the consequences of ideas we construct with each other. Social constructionism is concerned with meaning-making *between* people and the contexts in which the meaning arises which might influence the accounts we develop to describe our circumstances. A key hypothesis proposes that people are recruited into particular stories by more dominant discourses at the expense of other descriptions which might be differently useful.

From our perspective as women, as lesbians and as therapists, social constructionist therapy offers some political and ethical coherence as a way of practising therapy and thinking about practice. Our work takes place in a variety of community settings, most significantly, in The Pink Practice, a lesbian and gay systemic and social constructionist counselling and psychotherapy practice that has been established for ten years. We regard social constructionist therapy as offering a coherent framework for therapeutic work with lesbians, gay men and bisexuals because it pays attention to practices of power and challenges assumptions about pathology, sexuality, gender and life choices. It strives to promote a reflexive, co-constructive working relationship in which therapist and client(s) can deconstruct the assumptions in the stories each brings and reflect on the effects of those ideas.

Locating social constructionist therapy

One way of locating social constructionism is to separate psychotherapeutic theories into one of three paradigms: scientific psychotherapy, humanistic or essentialist psychotherapy and critical psychotherapy (see Table 9.1). Some practitioners draw on ideas from more than one paradigm.

Scientific psychotherapy is based on the model of science with the modernist objective of uncovering the *truth* about an individual. There are theories of personality or of perception – whether bio-genetic, socio-biological or formed in the course of one's life – which are used to identify, interpret and challenge the client's behaviour and ideas in order for the therapy to be effective. There are two interweaving bodies of knowledge: the first

Table 9.1 Paradigms in psychotherapy

Theoretical approach	Ideological assumptions	Theoretical propositions	Method	Data
Scientific psychotherapy	Human beings are biological beings	Human beings develop unhealthy patterns	Analyse and interpret patterns	Internal pathology
Essential/ Humanistic psychotherapy	Human beings are essentially good	Human beings have to find their authentic self	Unconditional positive regard for relating of experience	Own experience
Critical psychotherapy	Realities are created through conversation	Problematic stories emerge in relationships where stories are limiting/ limited	Co-constructive enquiry	Old and emergent descriptions of experience

describes the development of personality or perception and attendant pathological symptoms and the second describes the working methods of the approach.

Essentialist or humanistic psychotherapy lays less emphasis on personality and pathology and more emphasis on an idea of a *true* inner self, an essence. The self is seen as existing in its own right but its healthy functioning is seen as being dependent on achieving *authenticity* in relationships in the social world. The body of knowledge comprises a description of working methods, a philosophy of authenticity and respect for the client and for their own interpretation of their experience.

Critical psychotherapy questions the ideology behind professional and personal theories locating these stories in their wider discourses. The notion of the 'individual' is seen as a social construction. People are seen as products of a social world *and* participants in a social world whose discourses, cultures and relationships are the contexts for the creation of meaning. Persons are understood as having many selves, which are fluid and emergent and vary between contexts and over time. The 'body of knowledge' is also fluid and emergent. It draws on relationship and communications theories, which influence a variety of working methods, designed to explore the creation of meanings and their perceived effects. There is an emphasis on the need for a reflexive relationship between hidden ideologies and the practice of psychotherapy.

Social constructionist therapy is a practice of critical psychotherapy.

The implications of these approaches need to be considered when working with lesbians, gay men, bisexuals or any group of people in order that clients and therapists can be mindful of the ideological context for therapeutic conversations. Leppington (1991: 95) suggests:

> Different practices construct different forms of 'empowerment', for example, which only sometimes consists of liberating one's own voice and telling one's own story, as well as also having that story have positive material consequences for changing the cultural context in accordance with one's own and others' negotiated interests.

Social constructionist therapy exists – OK?[1]

Social constructionist therapy is a radical practice that arises out of a critical evaluation of power relations as exhibited in the social world, and how they can reproduce themselves in therapy. It is an unsettling practice that invites the most questioning, tentative and fluid of relationships with therapeutic theories. The pivotal principle through which one explores the circular and recursive relationship between theory, ideology and practice is reflexivity. It takes social constructionism as its ideological framework and it draws on practices from systemic and narrative therapy using ideas from:

philosophers (Jacques Derrida, Michel Foucault and Ludwig Wittgenstein); communications theorists (Barnett Pearce and Vernon Cronen); systemic therapists (Gianfranco Cecchin, Mara Palazzoli Selvini, Luigi Boscolo, Laura Fruggeri and other Milan colleagues; Virginia Goldner, Peggy Penn, Kenneth Gergen, Harlene Anderson, Harold Goolishian, Tom Andersen, David Epston, Michael White and Karl Tomm); and psychologists (John Shotter and Celia Kitzinger). Social constructionism is not to be confused with constructivism, which we understand as drawing on more biologically derived ideas of cognition and perception as developed by Humberto Maturana, Francisco Varela, cyberneticist Gregory Bateson and Lynn Hoffman among others. The ideas of constructivism have played a significant role in the path to social constructionist therapy.[2]

Social constructionist therapy can be considered a very queer practice (drawing as it does on the significant contributions of three gay philosophers and a lesbian psychologist) in its attempts to disrupt the course of power relations through recognising the influence of dominant discourses and attempting to deconstruct them. Some social constructionist concepts that feature significantly in therapy include:

- Social context is foregrounded over a notion of an individual's internal world.
- There is a shift from a notion of 'knowledge' to ethics.
- Human beings are seen as meaning-generating.
- There is a concern with the relationship between meanings and actions and the social contexts within which these arise.
- Meaning depends on context. We act out of and into contexts.
- Identity is continually being co-constructed in different contexts.
- Language is seen as expressing *and* constructing our experience.
- We make sense of our experience through the narratives available to us.

The emergence of a social constructionist therapy

The systemic influence

Many ideas described in this chapter evolved out of the early teachings and practices of family therapy, in particular that of the work of the Milan school in developing *systems theory*.

The concept of working with a person in their social system – a family, a related network – arose out of a recognition by psychoanalysts working in Milan (Selvini *et al.* 1980) that an individual's problems often returned after being discharged into their family from psychiatric hospital. They developed the hypothesis that the family was in some way responsible for the cause and maintenance of an individual's problem and so chose to treat the family and not just the individual.

While it is still common practice to offer therapy to the identified client and whoever they wish to bring to the therapy – for example, a partner, friend, family or colleagues – it is also considered perfectly viable to work with an individual systemically without anyone from their social system being physically present.

In the mid-1980s, the Milan approach became quite rigid and was criticised for being disrespectful towards clients who would often feel quite interrogated and powerless in the therapy. Early systems theory took no account of the place of power in society *nor* in therapy – this was particularly the case with regard to gender, sexuality, abuse, race and professionalism – and therefore would not have recognised the particular issues for lesbians, gay men and bisexuals nor the politics of sexuality. The influence of feminism, race politics and postmodernism on systemic therapy has resulted in a review of the therapist-client relationship and practices, with particular attention to power relations, knowledge and language.

Systemic therapists have reflected more on their own values, cultural stories about how people function and what counts as therapy. The critique of the power of the therapist, how they perform expertise and the effect of this on the client(s) has made for changes in how conversations take place in therapy. Expertise is no longer viewed as the sole domain of the professional nor knowledge as belonging to the expert.

The influence of postmodernism

Postmodernism has critiqued the notions of universal truths, scientific method and objectivity. This has opened the way for therapists to develop a more irreverent relationship with theory and examine culturally specific ideas implicit in therapeutic stories. Therapists are invited to reflect on their own ideology, values and cultural stories, which not only influence their practice but also are being re-created through it.

Fundamental assumptions and basic principles can be difficult to spot because they are thought of as 'common sense' and lie most comfortably in the taken-for-granted ideas of a person's everyday life (Leppington 1991). A danger is to assume that therapeutic methodologies are free of those same assumptions and that there is a 'neutral' space for therapists (see Chapter 7). In a social constructionist framework, the therapists are seen as inevitably acting out of their own deeply held beliefs, cultural bias and experience. All participants in therapy will, mindfully or otherwise, be drawing on stories about what it means to be a 'man' or a 'woman', 'gay' or 'bisexual', a 'therapist' or a 'client'.

There is an important shift in epistemological emphasis from a positivist way of knowing to a reflexive way of 'knowing'. For example, from

I know what I know because I have acquired knowledge to show the client or help them articulate what is really going on.

to

What stories am I drawing on that are bringing forth this particular description of experience?

Figure 9.1   A reflexive stance for therapy

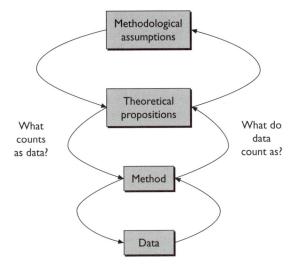

Source: Leppington (1991: 89).

Figure 9.1 shows how what we generate as 'information' (a description), how we know what we know and the context in which the conversation emerges are inseparable.

Therapy becomes a place to reflect on not only what one sees but also how one knows what one sees. If you look back at Table 9.1 and relate the different approaches to Figure 9.1, you might imagine how the range of descriptions of 'homosexuality' would vary enormously.

Social constructionism is not then a theory of human development but a way of accounting for meanings which human beings generate and a way of recognising the significance of the contexts in which these meanings arise. There are no normative behaviours that are used to identify ill health or deviancy. Being gay, therefore, would also not be assumed to have particular meanings or independent theories attached to it other than those which are brought forth in different contexts including that of therapy.

Social constructionist therapy is interested in what counts as ill health or deviancy in a particular context – for example, across culture, time or relationship – and what health or deviancy count as. It has no perspective on 'homosexuality' but rather on the culture in which the concept arises. It is less likely to ask the question

How do we account for the homosexual?

So much as

How, in a social world, do we account for the notion of a homosexual?

Further questions might be:

How, as practitioners, as clients, as lesbians, as gay men, are we influenced by the existence of discourses that theorise a 'homosexuality'?

Or

If there were no word for 'homosexuality' in our languages, in our cultures, how might we think differently about people who have same-sex relationships?

This is not to say that lesbians and gay men do not exist. It is rather an invitation to reflect on the process of naming and describing, and the consequences of those descriptions.

Discourse and sexuality

In examining descriptions, the notion of discourse is useful in understanding the contexts for the creation, maintenance and changes of meaning: 'Discourses show up in the things people say and write and the things we say and write, in their turn, are dependent for their meaning upon the discursive context in which they appear' (Burr 1995: 50).

Sexual categorisation is seen by Foucault (1976) as an invitation to participate in self-regulation, and he suggests that 'homosexuality' has been constructed as pathology in the history of psychological discourses. We speak of our sexual identity as if it is 'in our nature.' As Weeks (1991: 162) says, 'At the heart of our present is the continent of sexuality and its claim to hold the key to the truth of our individuality'.

Kitzinger (1989: 84) has created a useful critique of the role psychological discourses have played in 'structuring lesbians' experience of themselves such that lesbianism was removed from the political arena and relocated in the domain of personal pathology'. Social constructionist therapy creates some possibilities for challenging what Kitzinger describes as 'the ways in which the accounts we give of ourselves can serve to reproduce and legitimate the social order that oppresses us' (1989: 82). Sexual identity is understood as both historically created and meaningful in saying something about our relationship to dominant narratives – for example that of gender.

So in contemplating sexuality and descriptions such as lesbian, gay, bisexual, transsexual, and transgender, social constructionist interest is more likely to focus on how these descriptions have arisen, what the consequences are of describing oneself or being described in this way in different contexts, who is doing the describing, to whom and to what effect? This provides us with a more interesting and developing notion of authoring and re-authoring our story of being in relation to one another. The notion of sexual identity can operate less as a truth about self and more, as Foucault (1981: 16) has said, 'to use our sexuality to achieve a variety of different types of relationships' and 'to insist on becoming gay rather than defining ourselves as such'.

Narrative and power

The central hypothesis of narrative therapy is that people are recruited into dominant discourses that exist to maintain the imbalance of power in the world. Through communication with others, people develop stories about themselves and about society which, at times, can act as constraints. The narratives available to us influence our sense of who we are in the world.

Therapeutic conversations bring forth different descriptions of a problem and in so doing, create a notion of 'the facts'. A person's description of an experience will vary depending on the context in which the conversation is being held, on who is asking the questions, what is being asked and the consequences of the conversations in and for the broader context. This is *not* to imply that people do not have experiences independent of the therapeutic conversation, but rather that the 'diagnosis', the description of the problem we end up with, is one we have played a part in creating.

To explore what might be 'present' in a conversation but not being said, Michael White (1991) is curious about how certain stories, certain 'voices' come to dominate a person's description of their reality. He uses Derrida's ideas of deconstruction (1981) to create questions which explore these absent voices in order to bring forth accounts of why they have been silenced and to make explicit the dominant narratives in people's lives:

> Deconstruction has to do with procedures that subvert taken-for-granted realities and practices; those so-called 'truths' that are split off from the conditions and the context of their production, those disembodied ways of speaking that hide their biases and prejudices, and those familiar practices of self and of relationship that are subjugating of persons' lives.
>
> (White 1991: 27)

Therapists need to ask themselves and their clients what they are not noticing and use a collaborative process of questioning to deconstruct the taken-for-granted descriptions and clear the way for re-storying: the collaborative bringing forth of alternative descriptions which may be preferable and create more possibilities for action. This approach encourages openness and curiosity to enquire about meaning, how it is attributed, its contexts and its exceptions.

What is being described is a shift from 'knowledge' to ethics, from inter-pretation to story generation, a shift from an expert/non-expert therapeutic relationship to a co-constructive relationship where all participants' ideas have expertise (Anderson & Goolishian 1993). Therapists and clients can make ethical judgements about the possible consequences or usefulness of ideas or behaviours. Ethical decisions are neither subjective nor objective but relational.

Working methods or discursive practices?

Styles of conversing have been extensively developed since the days of early systems therapy when there was an uncomfortable imbalance of power in the way therapy was negotiated (Tomm 1984a, 1984b, 1988; Andersen 1987; Anderson and Goolishian 1988, 1993; White 1991; Epston and White 1992; Anderson 1997). Current approaches emphasise collaboration, trans-parency and reflexivity. This includes recognition of clients' 'knowledge' and expertise as well as of professional 'knowledge' and expertise. There is a shift from therapists *acting on* a client system to *acting with* a client system. Leppington (1991) suggests overcoming the dichotomy between client and therapist by replacing the notion of 'clinical tools' with 'discur-sive practices'.

Working with colleagues

A radical departure from many other forms of therapy has been the use of colleagues. The Milan team employed colleagues behind a one-way screen to help keep them on the straight and 'neutral' and to help generate hypo-theses while observing the family. Their approach has been developed and elaborated to allow for different ways of working with different clients. Many social constructionist therapists work together with colleagues in the therapy to bring forth a range of stories for client and therapist to draw on. This may cause surprise or even shock to practitioners familiar only with the culture of the therapeutic session as one-to-one. It is, of course, as personal, respectful and confidential as a one-to-one session might be and most people find the team way of working to be very accessible and engaging despite, or maybe because of, the therapists working together.

Tom Andersen (1987) has developed the practice of using a 'reflecting team' (one or more colleagues) as another way of trying to relocate expert-ise and generate empathy in the therapy team. The team can either sit in the room with the therapist and client(s) throughout the session or can come out from behind the one-way screen periodically and reflect at invited times on what they have heard. When in the same room, Andersen found that colleagues experienced more connection with the client(s) and that the ideas *and* presentation of the ideas became more respectful to the client(s). Clients have a choice of selecting from a multiplicity of stories from the reflecting team and are able to take a more reflexive position in relation to their own accounts of their experiences.

Enquiry

The practice of enquiry is central to social constructionist and systemic practice. Many questioning styles have been developed over the years to facilitate therapeutic conversation in exploring clients' and therapists' stories. Questions are generally framed to continually explore and develop or change hypotheses. The primary aim is to change the therapist's stories and not those of the client(s), with the idea that through enquiring one might be bringing forth different descriptions.

Not surprisingly, people are very comfortable with being asked questions in therapy. They often feel it facilitates the conversation so long as the therapist is pursuing a line of enquiry that the client feels is meaningful to them and their concerns.

Hypothesising

Hypothesising in advance of a session and during a session can help to generate a number of contrasting ideas about what might be going on for the client and their social system, about what has lead them to pursue therapy and the meanings that therapy might have for them. Therapists can do this by consulting colleagues or client(s) or by using a reflexive approach to their own thinking. This affords the therapist opportunities to reflect on their own stories and to avoid becoming too attached to any one idea.

A hypothesis will locate a presenting problem within the context of relationships and over time. For example, John[3] presents with a worry that he is out of control as he cannot stop having casual sex. A systemic hypothesis might be curious as to when John felt this became a problem and who might be affected by his cottaging. Perhaps something has happened that has made John review his cottaging as an unhealthy part of his life – a new partner who wants a show of loyalty in the form of monogamy; a police scare which might have jeopardised his career; a popular psychology book he has read whose central hypothesis was to pathologise uncommitted sexual contact as denial.

Circularity

Circularity is important in both the formulation of a hypothesis and in the technique of questioning. A hypothesis is based on a notion of *circular causality* which takes into account the entire social system within which the person(s) coming for therapy is located. Hypotheses which were based on a linear causality (for example, behaviour X leads to symptom Y) have been criticised for not taking into account how a social system might be contributing to the maintenance of a problem.

The systemic therapy of the Milan team developed *circular questions* (Selvini *et al.* 1980) which related to the hypothesis and located the presenting problem in the context of relationships.

Each question is usually taken from the preceding answer but is still developing and exploring a circular hypothesis. For example, in the case of John (above):

- Who is most affected by John going cottaging and in what ways?
- So when Michael and Steve look horrified with John, what does John do then?
- And when John tells them to fuck off and get a life, how do Michael and Steve respond?
- When Steve agrees that it might be fun to cottage what does Michael do?
- How does John cope with the tension when Michael and Steve row?

This example takes account of key participants in a system looking at how the presenting problems of one individual might be tied into an interwoven network of others. The principle of circular causality has been a crucial step in deconstructing the notion of the disturbed individual.

Karl Tomm (1988) has elaborated on questions as interventions with *reflexive questions*. In terms of our case example, John might be asked:

- If, one day, you found all the cottages had been closed down, what would you do? Could you cope?
- If cottaging were declared an acceptable activity for MPs of all parties, would it change your practices in any way?
- Are there any circumstances in the entire world in which you might go cottaging together?

Deconstructionist practices

Michael White and David Epston (White 1991; Epston and White 1992) have employed questions to deconstruct the dominant narratives with which people present and to bring forth alternative accounts. For example, we could ask John:

- When did you first think of your cottaging as 'out of control'?
- How did that expression come to mind?
- How come you hadn't thought of that expression about your behaviour before?
- How had you thought of cottaging before?
- What is it that you fear you might be 'out of control of' – or whom?

- How do you think your training to be a psychotherapist has influenced the idea you are 'out of control', if at all?
- Who do you think might be more alarmed by your cottaging – you or your course tutor?
- What does your particular school of psychotherapy say about cottaging?
- Who do you think it was who came up with that idea about the unhealthiness of casual sex and when was that?
- How do you think ideas about cottaging are going to change over the next ten years – in society, in your school of therapy?

This approach seeks to enquire about the contexts in which the *description* of being 'out of control' has arisen. It also takes an irreverent stance to the client's story of pathological behaviour which may be blunting the client's curiosity and limit the stories available to him.

Addressing social and cultural systems

Therapy with an individual or couple tends to privilege their own descriptions of their experiences and of those close to them. If one is going to take other stories into account and recognise the effects of powerful and excluding discourses it is important to recognise people's membership of wider social and cultural systems.

How does one bring the richness of cultural stories into therapeutic conversation while at the same time recognising the particular stories of each individual, family or social circle? What of the many other voices of older single African-Caribbean lesbians, teenage lesbian parents in Scotland, unemployed Asian gay men, divorced bisexuals living in rural areas etc.? How else can one bring forth other voices which may exist but are not heard?

Ideas and practices we have found useful in working with cultural and social experience have drawn on the social constructionist communications theory, the Coordinated Management of Meaning (CMM) (Cronen and Pearce 1980) and *wider system questions* using a *hypothetical audience* (Simon 1996, 1998) to explore the membership of specific groups. CMM describes how people act into and out of contexts and make choices according to the stories available to them. Levels of context have stories attached to them, which then have implications for what meanings get created at another level. For example, stories at a level of culture about gender might act as a context for influencing ideas about relationships; something that someone says or does may have implications for changing a person's lifelong ideas about a family story. As in Figure 9.1, all levels of context are reflexively linked and act as contexts for one another. Figure 9.2 is based on the work of Cronen and Pearce (1980).

CMM is particularly useful in helping formulate hypotheses and in pursuing lines of enquiry which relate to the influence of stories from a variety

Figure 9.2   Levels of context in CMM

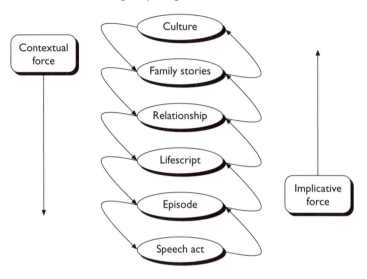

Governing story at higher level of abstraction

of contexts. For example, Jennifer, a 35-year-old African-Caribbean woman, and Usha, a 39-year-old Asian woman, had been together for seven years and wanted some consultations to explore arguments and a diminished sexual contact. The therapist is a white European lesbian of a similar age.

> *Therapist*:   And what were you thinking you might want from therapy?
> *Jennifer*:   I think we should talk about what's happening in our relationship.
> *Usha*:   [nods in agreement] We need to find out why we are no longer, er . . .
> *Jennifer*:   Having sex less.
> *Usha*:   Yes, making love less often.
> *Therapist*:   Which is it you want to explore? Having less sex or making love less often?
>   [Usha and Jennifer look enquiringly at each other]
> *Jennifer*:   They're the same things, aren't they?
> *Therapist*:   [to Usha who has not responded] Are they?
> *Usha*:   Mmm, I don't know. Not really.
> *Therapist*:   What do you think is the difference between making love and having sex?
> *Usha*:   I don't know. Mmm . . . I don't . . . I think having sex can be mechanical whereas making love feels, mmm, a bit more personal, intimate.

Therapist: Where do each of your ideas come from about what *counts* as making love or having sex?

Usha: Well, if I had done the *right* thing, and married, I would have had to have sex with my husband regularly whether I had felt like it or not. Making love is something that I would choose to do.

Jennifer: I have never thought about it like that. I just think they are the same.

Therapist: In your own family or in the African-Caribbean communities in this country, what ideas might other people have about the difference, if any, between making love and having sex?

Jennifer: Hmm. That it's just a biological thing. Although I guess men and women may have something to say on the matter. In my family, the women were the ones who were interested in sex and the men were seen, as, er, well, you know, not much use! [all giggle]

Therapist: What do you mean 'not much use'?

Jennifer: Well, they couldn't, er . . .

Usha: What? Satisfy the women?

Jennifer: Yes. They were a bit 'in-and-out'!

Therapist: How did or do either of you have access to what other women in your family or in your communities feel about sex, making love?

Jennifer: I would just listen in on my mum and her friends chatting when I was growing up.

Usha: I would too. There was a lot of laughter and I used to wonder why they were laughing so much.

Therapist: Do you laugh with each other about having sex, making love?

Usha: No. Never. It always feels quite a serious thing.

Jennifer: I'm not good at talking about those things. I just like to get on with it or forget it.

Therapist: So how do you think the women in your families would advise the two of you?

Usha: Oh, they would be very critical of me.

Therapist: For having sex with a lesbian?

Usha: No. Well, yes, but that wasn't what I was thinking about. They would feel I should fulfil my duties in a relationship.

Jennifer: Duties?

Usha: Well not duties with you, but marital duties.

Therapist: I'm confused.

Usha: Let me explain. If I were married to another Asian man, I would worry about his family thinking I was a bad wife if

I did not make love, have sex with him. In a lesbian relationship, I feel I have a choice about making love. But I resent still feeling bad for not having sex. It's like I haven't got away.

Jennifer: And I feel bad because even though I'm not with a man, I'm in the same position as other women in my family who are with men but can't have satisfying sex.

One can see here how both women are beginning to make sense of their own experiences by exploring their stories about gender from family and cultural contexts and their impact at a level of relationship.

Another way of exploring people's membership of larger social groups is the use of *wider system questions* with a *hypothetical audience* (Simon 1996, 1998). Hypothetical audience describes a group of other people who may not be physically present but who undoubtedly exist and on whose stories the therapist and client may be able to draw. Hypothetical audiences can be used to bring forth multiple descriptions or offer support for personal views that do not find support in their immediate systems.

The hypothetical audience can take many different forms. The therapist can invite the client to participate in an imaginary scenario with a group of others of whom the client might ask questions. The use of the hypothetical audience has proved useful in a practice context where clients have a strong attachment to a decontextualised description of their own difficulties, and/or where clients sometimes present as isolated with no peer group or community on whose experience or advice they might draw (Simon 1998: 43).

When co-constructing a hypothetical audience we have found it most fruitful to 'invite' a group of people who might directly relate to the client's situation. It may have been interesting to ask Jennifer and Usha some wider system questions to bring forth another audience – in this example, other lesbian couples – which would have offered a further context for exploring the meanings of sex. For example:

- If the two of you heard about a weekend workshop for lesbian couples who come from different cultural backgrounds, who have been together for over five years and who are also worried about diminishing sexual contact, what would you need to see in the workshop information that would make you decide to go?
- Suppose you did then go to this workshop, what would you be thinking on entering the workshop and seeing 150 other lesbian couples from different cultural backgrounds, who have been together for over five years and who were also worried about diminishing sexual contact?
- Imagine that the workshop facilitators asked every couple to write out how they thought their cultural origins had influenced their stories about sexual choice in relationships and then pinned them anonymously all around the hall. What sorts of stories might you expect to read up there?

- Let's suppose that next year is Year of the Lesbian Couple and at one of the events the lesbian writer you most admire is giving a lecture called 'Sex: whose idea is it anyway?' or 'Sex: myth of the white man'. If you were to go to the lecture which ideas of yours do you think might be most challenged and most supported?
- If you were to imagine yourselves presenting a workshop in five years' time to lesbians with similar concerns to your current concerns, what advice would the you-of-today be surprised to hear the you-of-five-years'-time giving them?

By using a hypothetical audience (the workshop of lesbian couples from different cultural backgrounds) with wider system questions it is possible to draw on a range of experience which might not otherwise find a voice or an audience and, hence, validation. It is also a clear intervention to create such a group, which goes way beyond that of their immediate friends, families and therapist. Individuals and couples can become mindful of themselves as members of a group that does exist albeit not immediately or visibly. In so doing, the couple is invited to relocate their experience into the more public or political arena of lesbian experience, which they can also use to find their own solutions.

Another advantage to using these questions is that the counsellor does not need to be an 'expert' in the area of the clients' concerns. On the other hand, in many situations some 'knowledge' of other groups is necessary in order to know what questions to ask.

The circulation of therapeutic stories in the lesbian, gay and bisexual communities

The therapist is in a very powerful position to influence the narratives in the lesbian, gay and bisexual communities. Counsellors and therapists are a major source of stories about how human beings 'work' and are not exempt from being recruited into dominant discourses. Being critical of dominant social and political narratives of professional institutions does not itself guarantee immunity from the very stories lesbians, gay men and bisexuals may want to challenge.

Psychotherapists and counsellors influence the language and therefore influence stories of ill health or of ability, stories of change at a personal level or an interpersonal level and, to our loss only extremely rarely, of change at a level of society. Practitioners can help to create more of a story of personal inadequacy, a story of the individual (different to individuality) or they can help to bring forth other descriptions of ability, agency, choice, social context, or stories of groups and, by implication, group experience, group history and group strength.

Members of the lesbian, gay, bisexual and transgender communities can be overheard using psychological concepts in their everyday conversations.

How often do you hear such concepts being used to positively connote someone's behaviour or choices? Too many clients present in counselling with a negative psycho-jargoned description of themselves as if this is what they felt was expected from them in therapy. In our experience, people have come to use the language of psychology or counselling to negatively punctuate a description of themselves, each other, their choices and behaviours.

What does this tell us about the discourses in which therapists are invited to participate and in which they choose to participate? And what then is the role of the therapist in the lesbian, gay, bisexual and transgender communities? Where do therapists' stories come from? How constrained is a therapist's practice by the ideas embodied by the institutions which train them and which register them? And how do we know how these constraints operate?

Queer theorists, therapists and clients are well placed to question oppressive constructs, whose interests they serve and which moral orders these ideas support. We are well placed to challenge the practices of power – the very practices which created us by giving us a name and description in the first place.

In examining our most taken-for-granted assumptions which influence our choice of therapeutic style, therapists may be further able to participate in our communities with an openness, with a preparedness to co-story with other lesbians, gay men, bisexual and transgender people. As a result we can create our own discourses and our own theories in a manner which allows therapist and client to be playful, not become so attached to theories that therapists become the custodians of fixed ideas, of truths and of exclusive expertise.

Summary

From prescription to description

There is, in social constructionist therapy, an important move towards reworking the balance of power in the therapeutic relationship. Therapeutic mystique is redundant. The therapist participates in co-constructing a conversation that is based on an idea of mutual expertise, on reflexivity, transparency and curiosity.

The role of therapist is not about curing the individual from the horrors of their past nor is it about identifying pathology for the therapist to help the client overcome. It is a storying process through conversation, which helps people to know how to go on, to find ways of making sense of their lives, so creating more possibilities. It offers the opportunity to generate ideas together about how the client's stories and the therapist's stories, how their descriptions, their language and those of other people, work for them and work against them. It recognises the context in which unhelpful accounts arise and are maintained as well as exploring the power of emergent accounting abilities and the broader contexts for them.

Social constructionist therapy lends itself particularly to work with lesbians, gay men and bisexuals because it challenges practices of power and seeks to identify the very discourses which undermine a person or a couple's choices by rendering their lived experience unable to be told.

Notes

1 With recognition to Bebe Speed's paper: 'Reality exists – OK? An argument against constructivism and social constructionism' (1991).
2 The description of social constructionist therapy in this chapter reflects some of the ideas influencing our therapeutic practice at this point in time.
3 All case examples are based on therapeutic conversations but do not describe any one person or couple.

References

Andersen, T. (1987) The reflecting team: dialogue and meta-dialogue, *Family Process*, 26: 415–28.

Anderson, H. (1997) *Conversation, Language, and Possibilities: A Postmodern Approach to Therapy*. New York: Basic Books.

Anderson, H. and Goolishian, H. (1988) Human systems as linguistic systems: preliminary and evolving ideas about the implications for clinical theory, *Family Process*, 27: 371–93.

Anderson, H. and Goolishian, H. (1993) The client is the expert: a not-knowing approach to therapy, in S. McNamee and K. Gergen (eds) *Therapy as Social Construction*. London: Sage.

Bateson, G. (1973) *Steps to an Ecology of Mind*. London: Palladin.

Burr, V. (1995) *An Introduction to Social Constructionism*. London: Routledge.

Cecchin, G. (1987) Hypothesizing, circularity, and neutrality revisited: an invitation to curiosity, *Family Process*, 25(4): 405–12.

Cecchin, G., Lane, G. and Ray, W. (1993) *Irreverence: A Strategy for Therapists' Survival*. London: Karnac Books.

Cronen, V. and Pearce, W.B. (1980) *Communication, Action and Meaning: The Creation of Social Realities*. New York: Praeger.

Derrida, J. (1981) *Positions*. Chicago: University of Chicago Press.

Epston, D. and White, M. (1992) *Experience, Contradiction, Narrative and Imagination: Selected Writings of Epston and White*. Adelaide: Dulwich Centre Publications.

Foucault, M. (1976) *The History of Sexuality: An Introduction*. London: Peregrine.

Foucault, M. (1981) Friendship as lifestyle: an interview, *Gay Information*, 7.

Fruggeri, L. (1992) Therapeutic process as the social construction of change, in S. McNamee and K. Gergen (eds) *Therapy as Social Construction*. London: Sage.

Goldner, V. (1991) Feminism and systemic practice: two critical traditions in transition, *Journal of Family Therapy*, 13: 95–104.

Hoffman, L. (1993) A reflexive stance for family therapy, in S. McNamee, and K. Gergen (eds) *Therapy as Social Construction*. London: Sage.

Kitzinger, C. (1988) *The Social Construction of Lesbianism*. London: Sage.

Kitzinger, C. (1989) Liberal humanism as an ideology of control: the regulation of lesbian identities, in J. Shotter and K. Gergen (eds) *Texts of Identity*. London: Sage.

Leppington, R. (1991) From constructivism to social constructionism and doing critical therapy, *Human Systems: Journal of Systemic Consultation and Management*, 2(2): 79–104.

Maturana, H., Mendez, C.L. and Coddon, F. (1988) The bringing forth of pathology, *The Irish Journal of Psychology*, 9(1): 144–72.

McNamee, S. and Gergen, K. (eds) (1993) *Therapy as Social Construction*. London: Sage.

Pearce, W.B. (1989) *Communication and the Human Condition*. Chicago: Southern Illinois University Press.

Penn, P. (1985) Feed forward: future questions, future maps, *Family Process*, 24(3): 299–310.

Selvini, M., Boscolo, L., Cecchin, G. and Prata, G. (1980) Hypothesising – circularity – neutrality: three guidelines for the conductor of the session, *Family Process*, 19(1): 3–12.

Shotter, J. (1989) Social accountability and the social construction of 'You', in J. Shotter and K. Gergen (eds) *Texts of Identity*. London: Sage.

Simon, G. (1996) Working with lesbian, gay and bisexual couples, in D. Davies and C. Neal (eds) *Pink Therapy: A Guide for Counsellors and Therapists Working with Lesbian, Gay and Bisexual Clients*. Buckingham: Open University Press.

Simon, G. (1998) Incitement to riot? Individual identity and group membership: some reflections on the politics of a post-modernist therapy, *Human Systems: Journal of Systemic Consultation and Management*, 9(1): 33–50.

Simon, G. and Whitfield, G. (1995) A discourse-in-progress: gay affirmative practice and a critical therapy. Paper presented at Association of Lesbian, Gay and Bisexual Psychologies Conference, University of Nottingham (http://www.pinkpractice.co.uk/papers.htm), September.

Speed, B. (1991) Reality exists – OK? An argument against constructivism and social constructionism, *Journal of Family Therapy*, 13: 395–411.

Tomm, K. (1984a) One perspective on the Milan systemic approach, Part I: an overview of development theory and practice, *Journal of Family and Marital Therapy*, 10(2): 113–25.

Tomm, K. (1984b) One perspective on the Milan systemic approach, Part II: description of session format, interviewing style and interventions, *Journal of Family and Marital Therapy*, 10(3): 253–71.

Tomm, K. (1988) Interventive interviewing, Part III: intending to ask lineal, circular, strategic or reflexive questions? *Family Process*, 27: 1–15.

Varela, F.J. (1989) Reflections on the circulation of concepts between a biology of cognition and systemic family therapy, *Family Process*, 28: 15–24.

Weeks, J. (1991) *Against Nature*. London: Rivers Oram Press.

White, M. (1991) *Deconstruction and Therapy*. Adelaide: Dulwich Centre Publications.

Wittgenstein, L. (1969) *On Certainty*. London: Basil Blackwell.

Transactional analysis

Introduction

Transactional analysis (TA) is a theory of personality and communication as well as a systematic psychotherapy for personal growth and change. The relationship between TA and homosexuality is not straightforward. Berne, the founder of TA, included in his writings pejorative references to homosexuality, which reflected the mainstream psychoanalytic thinking of the 1940s and 1950s (for example, Berne 1971: 249–54). He also emphasised humanistic-existential philosophy and phenomenological method that was part of the radical contribution of TA. There is a contradiction between his statements and the healthy existential life position summarised by 'I'm OK – you're OK, which he proposed.

Subsequent references to homosexuality in the TA literature are affirmative or non-pejorative. Many lesbians and gay men have been attracted to TA as clients and practitioners and, it seems, have been treated 'OK'. TA offers theoretical and practical features that make it an ideal base for gay affirmative therapy.

In this chapter I outline the philosophical base of TA and how this influences theory and practice; describe how homosexuality is dealt with in the TA literature; discuss various contributions of TA to theory and practice which are helpful in working with lesbian, gay and bisexual clients; and make some recommendations for gay affirmative practice.

A brief history of the relationship between TA and homosexuality

When I was asked to 'give a brief history of the relationship between TA and homosexuality saying how the latter had been perceived, explained and described and how this has informed practice' I thought all that was required was a literature review. This revealed that Berne's writing on homosexuality did not reflect how TA practitioners, in my experience, treat lesbian, gay and bisexual clients, so I asked myself: 'What attracted me to TA?' and 'Why had I "forgotten" the pejorative things Berne wrote?' The humanistic philosophy and the radical elements of TA attracted me. I 'forgot' what Berne wrote about homosexuality because it suited me to forget, because I'd read it all before, because it contradicted what excited me about TA and because it didn't fit with my experience.

This led me to consider what influences TA practice. I believe that, with respect to homosexuality at least, the underlying humanist-existential philosophy and the associated systematic phenomenology carries more weight than Berne's contradictory statements which reveal more about his historical context and homosexuality's cultural position.

Humanistic-existential philosophy and systematic phenomenology

The most consistent element in TA is the integral humanistic-existential philosophy, which places the individual at the centre of their own psychological world. Berne's potent contribution is to link this humanism with a system for understanding, describing and articulating this individual with their own frame of reference within a social and historical context.

Every human action can be evaluated according to its existential position. The four options are: 'I'm not OK – you're not OK' (the schizoid position), 'I'm OK – you're not OK' (the paranoid position), 'I'm not OK – you're OK' (the depressive position) and 'I'm OK – you're OK' (the healthy position). This is in fact Berne's elaboration of Klein (Klein 1949; Berne 1966). His addition is the healthy position as intrinsically constructive and existentially possible. Berne also added *physis*, a third drive, to the two already postulated by Freud: his mortido and libido correspond to Freud's Thanatos and Eros. *Physis* is the 'creative force of nature which makes all things grow in an orderly and "progressive" way' (Berne 1971: 98). These extensions to psychoanalytic thinking emphasise Berne's humanist philosophy.

These evaluations are not a simple positivism. They are judgements about the basic nature of people and not about their behaviour, which may well be 'not OK'. The attitude 'I'm OK – you're OK' is an essential prerequisite for practising TA and emphasises mutuality. Every therapeutic action must be consistent with this position. I can ask myself at any moment: 'If I do this, does it mean that I am OK and my client is OK?' If not I have to think about what is happening (transference and/or counter-transference) and work out something else to do. Faced with a client this therapeutic attitude should override all theory/prejudice that is not supported by the evidence.

Berne (1975a) believed the most effective way to put this into practice was the use of his diagnostic method. He required the application of four separate tools for ego-state diagnosis: behavioural information, social information, historical information, and phenomenological information. This requires the client's confirmation of the diagnosis from his or her own experience. 'Berne, by stating that the phenomenological diagnosis is the ultimate criterion for ego-state diagnosis, validates the subjective truth of a person's childhood experience' (Clarkson 1992: 69). Ego-state diagnosis is the basic tool of TA and the first thing that most practitioners are taught (after the basic philosophy) and this principle of client involvement in all diagnoses or interpretations permeates all other activities. This phenomenological part of Berne's method: 'that we can best understand the world by direct personal experience' (Stewart 1992: 20) is part of his effort to integrate both phenomenology and empiricism into his scientific method.

This has a positive implication for practice: a practitioner rigorously putting this into action would, at worst, do no harm and, at best, would understand and accept the client's frame of reference in an affirmative way.

TA, in its early years, was taken up by people with some psychiatric, analytic or psychotherapeutic background, training and experience. I hypothesise that the kind of practitioners drawn to TA in its early years were attracted by its philosophy, as I was. Gilbert (1997 in a personal communication) suggests this is largely true for the spread of TA in South Africa. Claude Steiner (1971, 1974), who made major theoretical contributions to TA, was a member of the Radical Psychiatry Collective and of the San Francisco Seminar where Berne developed TA.

TA's philosophy is an integral part of the theory and practice. Applying the method overrides diagnostic or interpretative comments made in texts. This attracted practitioners likely to value those elements and therefore to implement them. I think this helps TA feel like a safe space for lesbians, gays and bisexuals.

TA literature

The origins of TA: Berne 1947–70

Berne made eight direct references to homosexuality in five of his seven books, including confusing, incomplete revisions. These references are instructive to the extent they reflect Berne's struggle to apply his philosophy to a discussion heavily skewed by 'I'm OK – you're not OK' psychoanalytic theory. He fails to deliver a clear 'I'm OK – you're OK' statement, but does open the possibility for other TA practitioners to complete the task.

Berne first refers to homosexuality in *A Layman's Guide to Psychiatry and Psychoanalysis* (1971) originally published as *The Mind in Action* in 1947 when Berne still sought membership of the psychoanalytic establishment. He makes two remarks, almost in passing, which reflect the prevailing psychoanalytic views of homosexuality. The third and main reference is in a chapter entitled 'Alcohol, drugs, and some behaviour disorders'. Berne (1971: 249–54) devotes a section to 'What is homosexuality?'

> Many beautiful things have come out of homosexual relationships, such as some of the philosophy of Socrates. Nevertheless, happy homosexuals are uncommon. Homosexuality nearly always means a thwarted *physis* and a troubled Superego. It is contrary to the customs of our society and so makes social difficulties even under the best circumstances. Also, it is often against the law for men and therefore can lead to real disasters. Curiously enough, while nearly every American state has laws against male homosexual activities, there is none which has laws against homosexual activities in females.

These statements are almost non-pejorative and almost affirmative and don't deliver either. In his first use of 'nearly', Berne opens a small window through which homosexuality can be viewed without the automatic assumption of psychological illness. He also locates homosexual activity in its hostile context and draws attention to the inconsistency of the legal position – something lesbian and gay activists often use to illustrate the social construction of homosexuality as a problem.

Berne then gives a quite simple psychoanalytic perspective on causality and typology and some outright stereotypical prejudice. This material is unchanged from 1947 and is so contradictory to TA values that I had 'forgotten' it until asked to write this chapter.

Berne's conclusion (obviously revised) clearly demonstrates his struggle to apply 'I'm OK – you're OK' attitude to the issues:

> What is society to do with homosexuals? Their lives are confused enough as it is, and punishment is not indicated. The best thing one can do is treat them as politely as one would anyone else. They on their part, of course, should be expected to abide by the ordinary rules of decency such as apply to relationships between men and women: namely, they should not seduce minors, nor force themselves on people who are not interested in their company; they should not flaunt their desires in public by dressing in clothes of the opposite sex or otherwise; [he says this despite having a separate section in the same chapter for transsexuals and transvestites] and they should not embarrass those

around them by making love or talking about it in public. If they behave themselves and control themselves as discreetly as people with heterosexual desires are expected to do, their private lives should be no more concern of anyone else's than should a 'straight' person's. Putting them in jail often (or even usually) results only in providing them and the other prisoners with added opportunities for sexual activity. Many people nowadays feel that the laws concerning homosexual activity should be changed, as they have been in England.

(Berne 1971: 253)

It is easy today to see the prejudice in this, as we have become aware of the difference between tolerance and acceptance. I understand the comment on 'politeness' as Berne's attempt to apply his 'I'm OK – you're OK' philosophy after all the prejudicial theorising. Berne valued politeness – in the sense of being respectful and not unduly hurtful – very highly. Although Berne implied that we should not be seen to exist, he does remove homosexuality as an issue *per se*. This section most clearly reflects Berne's psychoanalytic background (he trained as an analyst for 15 years) and the prevailing views of homosexuality. It also shows the tentative and incomplete revisions that Berne made for the third edition (in 1968) and the contradictions these give rise to. Amid all the prejudice it is remarkable that the only specific instructions are to treat homosexuals politely and not be concerned in our private lives any more than one would a 'straight' person's.

Neither Berne's next major text on TA, *Transactional Analysis in Psychotherapy* (1975a, first published in 1961) nor *The Structure and Dynamics of Organisations and Groups* (1963) contain any reference to homosexuality. However, Berne makes brief, confused references to homosexuality in *Games People Play* (1968, first published in 1964), *Principles of Group Treatment* (1966), *Sex in Human Loving* (1973, first published in 1970), and *What Do You Say After You Say Hello* (1975b, published posthumously in 1972).

A valuable insight into how Berne worked is carried in this extract from Steiner's (1974) introduction to *Scripts People Live*:

Berne began to use his findings about intuition in his therapeutic work. Instead of using the notions and categories learned by him as a psychiatrist, instead of deciding that a person was, for instance, a 'severe latent homosexual' or a 'paranoid schizophrenic' [Berne] 'tuned in' to the person and gathered information by using his intuition.

For instance, a man whom he would have diagnosed as a 'severe latent homosexual' was seen by Berne's intuition as a man who felt 'as though he were a very young child standing naked and sexually excited before a group of his elders, blushing furiously and writhing with almost unbearable embarrassment'. He called this latter description of the man an 'ego image'; that is, the therapist's intuitive image of the person which in some ways describes his ego. It is important to note here that the crucial difference between the ego image and the 'severe latent homosexual' diagnosis is that the information about the ego image came mostly from his client, whereas the information about the 'latent homosexual' diagnosis would have come mostly from Eric Berne and his psychoanalytic teachers.

(Steiner 1974: 11)

This creates permission to see homosexuality in other ways, particularly those of the client's frame of reference. Steiner is describing what Berne actually did, which is more in keeping with Berne's emphasis on humanistic philosophy and his diagnostic method than with the pejorative statements he published.

TA after Berne

One of the first popular TA books after Berne was *Born to Win* (James and Jongeward 1971). In the section 'Sexual identity' the authors debunk the myth that homosexuality results from overidentification with a particular parent and say:

Homosexual behaviour can occur in people for a variety of reasons including psychological, sociological, biological, and situational circumstances. The bent [*sic*] toward homosexual behaviour is probably related to the primal feelings in the Natural Child and to the lack of adequate heterosexual adaptation. At birth infants are not programmed to know toward whom their sexual feelings should be directed. They want only to satisfy their own urges and experience their own pleasure. The Natural Child seems to be sexually non-discriminatory. The later development of heterosexual *preference* is highly influenced by childhood experiences in the earliest years.

(James and Jongeward 1971: 169)

They go on to explore how heterosexual preference develops and the effect of familial and cultural scripting on 'masculinity' and 'femininity'. Although implying that heterosexual preference is preferable (homosexuality is a 'lack'), heterosexuality is not described as 'natural' or 'preordained' but as a preference which needs specific circumstances for development. It is an early example of affirmative writing arising from the logical implementation of the philosophy and theory of TA divorced from the baggage of contemporary orthodox psychoanalysis.

In the *Transactional Analysis Journal* (*TAJ*) Aiken's (1976) article stands out. He proposes that the 'emotional suffering of gay people is due to stroke-deprivation not homosexuality; and . . . attempts by the gay minority to overthrow the injunctions that keep them stroke-deprived are prohibited and punished by police harassment, employment insecurity and social censure' (1976: 21). Collinson (1975: 8), in the *British Transactional Analysis Bulletin* identifies the primary injunction about homosexuality as: 'Don't be what you are!'

Invisibility

There are no references to homosexuality in most of the major texts: for example, Schiff *et al.* 1975; Woollams and Brown 1978; Goulding and Goulding 1979; Stewart and Joines 1987; Stewart 1989, and it goes ten years without mention in the *TAJ* between 1976 and 1986! This invisibility needs to be contextualised. I haven't space for a full history of TA but, briefly, the popularity of *Games People Play* (Berne 1968) and versions of TA like Harris's *I'm OK-You're OK* (1967) enabled the survival and spread of interest in TA throughout the world and contributed to a period of theoretical paucity. From the mid-1980s a fairly systematic effort has been made to re-establish the theoretical base of TA by thorough examination and evaluation of Berne's writing and subsequent interpretations of it. This has led to recognition of the depth, elegance and theoretical complexity of TA that had been lost in the populism.

There still is the problem of difference. It is difficult to write about difference without pathologising it. Most attempts to describe the development of homosexuality do not choose to describe the development of heterosexuality – James and Jongeward (1971) being a notable exception. The description of homosexuality becomes the aetiology of illness and therefore something to be cured. As a gay therapist I have always resisted the question 'Why am I like this?' because of the fear of being pathologised. Yet it is an interesting question. Perhaps the answer to this question and others like it can only be attempted when an overall climate of acceptance has been created and is secure enough for us to become interested in difference for its own sake and not for the purpose of 'cure'.

We also lack a language for describing difference without layering this with value. The dominant class uses difference to isolate, stigmatise, criminalise and persecute. Political strategies adopted by lesbians, gay men and bisexuals have variously played up or played down difference. Integrationist movements rely on similarities while some radical movements justify differences saying gay is better than straight. It is my experience and that of my gay clients, without exception, that our first awareness of our sexuality was of 'being different'. We need to address this difference without discounting it or making it mean more than it does.

Growing visibility

Gay issues reappeared in the *TAJ* with Simerly and Karakashian's (1989) article on working with clients who were HIV-positive or who had AIDS.

In this gay affirmative article the authors pay attention to the frames of reference of their clients and it is obviously written after extensive clinical experience. They recognise the difference inherent in their work and describe this from an 'I'm OK – you're OK' point of view. It is however, disturbing that it takes AIDS to put homosexuality back into the TA literature.

Another mark of the growing visibility of lesbians, gays and bisexuals is the way in which they are mentioned. Clarkson (1987: 83) asks: 'If Jews, homosexuals, or blacks are being persecuted in my organisation or country, how can I sustain psychological well-being in that culture?' Authors such as Massey (1990) include gay clients as case material where gayness is not an issue. Cornell (1990: 78) reviewing *In Quest of the Mythical Mate* (Bader and Pearson 1988) writes:

> I also found myself wanting more discussion on homosexual couples. The case presentation on Amanda and Jane and a brief comment in the 'Commonly Asked Questions' chapter were the only attention paid to gay and lesbian couples . . . I would like to see in this book an elaboration of the developmental perspective in relation to homosexual as well as heterosexual relationships.

Cornell (1992a, 1992b, 1992c, 1995) in his book reviews consistently highlights their relevance or otherwise to lesbians and gays. Other reviewers (Hohmuth and Borden 1992; Simerly 1993; Pelton 1994; Hochstein 1995; Vaughn 1995) also include lesbian and gay issues and perspectives. Other gay affirmative articles include English (1994) and McClendon and Kadis (1994) on the use of shame to control homosexuality, Steiner (1995: 85) and Simerly (1996). *Transactional Analysis Counselling* (Lapworth *et al.* 1993) and *Brief Therapy with Couples* (Gilbert and Shmukler 1996) are also gay affirmative in various ways.

It seems to me that the logical outcome of the integral humanistic-existential philosophy of TA, Berne's diagnostic method including the client as central, the general cultural changes that have occurred, pressure from affirmative practitioners and the growing body of writing from affirmative authors will make gay affirmative theory and practice the norm within TA.

Helpful theoretical contributions and techniques

I refer you to *Eric Berne* by Ian Stewart (1992) for a thorough, accessible description of Berne's major contributions to theory and practice, as well as a rebuttal of some criticisms of TA. Because space is limited here I must choose a few examples and describe these in detail. The risk is that this reduces a powerful system of interrelating parts to a few interesting ideas or techniques. Application of TA therapeutically requires a thorough under-standing of the whole theory. I include this warning because of the peculiar susceptibility of TA to accusations of being simplistic.

Among many significant contributions I believe the key theoretical ele-ments of TA affecting gay affirmative therapy are: accessibility of the therapy; a method rooted in observability; the systematic mapping of social forces onto intra-psychic processes; and the contribution of the stroke economy to maintaining this system.

Accessibility

One of the most visible contributions Berne made was his use of accessible language. Stewart (1992: 148) discusses the drawbacks and advantages of this extensively: 'The use of vivid concept and straightforward language has a *psychotherapeutic* purpose in itself, and one that Berne intended it to have. Namely: it helps empower the client to take an equal and active part in the process of psychotherapy' (original italics).

This accessibility is important in any therapy aiming to be gay affirmat-ive. Lesbians, gays and bisexuals have suffered at the hands of theories and practitioners, which sought to define them. TA is a comprehensive and profound tool that makes self-definition available to both practitioners and their clients.

Observability

Stewart (1992: 17) regards the essence of Berne's contribution as:

> To construct a theory that was psychodynamic in concept, yet which could be checked directly against real-world observations. . . . Other psychodynamic theorists had related their theories to real-world appli-cation of course. But none had made observability the cornerstone of their entire theory. Berne did. In my view that is his main contribution to the theory of psychotherapy.

Stewart is referring to Berne's systematic linking of several intra-psychic concepts and processes to observable phenomena – hence the definition of TA as a 'systematic social psychiatry' (Berne 1975a: 11). This is important for a gay affirmative therapy because it is insurance against prejudice. I have already outlined how Berne modified some of his comments about homosexuality. The history of TA shows practitioners in dialogue with their clients, modifying and developing theory in response. All other thera-pies probably claim something like this. The difference is that in TA the process is integral and essential to practice: over time prejudice is noticed and replaced with observable reality.

The script system

The script is a preconscious 'life plan decided in childhood, reinforced by the parents, justified by subsequent events, and culminating in a chosen alternative' (Berne 1975b: 445). The script matrix maps social forces onto individual decisions. The script system is an elegant model describing how script relates to internal experience and, in turn, the ways in which the individual shapes their experience of the world and thereby supports these original decisions. Clarkson and Gilbert (1990: 199) say TA 'integrates intrapsychic dynamics with interpersonal behaviours'. Berne (1975a: 116) called script a 'transference drama'.

Briefly, individuals react to the forces placed on them in order to survive. Every child makes decisions as to how best to do this in response to the world around them (experienced immediately through their primary caretakers). The decisional nature of this is fundamental to TA as it allows the possibility of redecision and change. A child has a range of options for responding to a situation, and genetic predispositions as well as the familial and the cultural matrix they experience will influence their unique script decision.

These script decisions will determine, in interaction with genetic restrictions and situational accidents, the destiny of the individual. Much of the rest of life will be spent putting this life plan for survival into action, gathering evidence to support it and acting in its service. The individual will live out their script, reducing their life options unless they are interfered with by a major confrontation, of which effective therapy is but one possibility. 'The script is a complete plan for living offering both strictures and structures' (Berne 1975b: 134) so, at least in part, it also protects us from continuous existential anxiety. See Berne (1975b) for a complete discussion of script.

In much TA literature the focus of script is on the family script matrix. White and White (1975) developed the overlay of the cultural component of scripting onto the familial script matrix, articulating the process by which individual families carry their own specific variant of the overall cultural script. This notion of cultural scripting as delineating the restricted view of the world carried by everybody embedded within a culture is particularly important when considering the lives of lesbian, gay and bisexual clients. Berne (1975a: 76) in discussing parental introjects (aspects of behaviour, thoughts and feelings of powerful others swallowed whole without analysis) says: 'If they are culturally syntonic [fit with generally-held views], there is a tendency to accept them without adequate scepticism as rational or at least justifiable'.

The dominant injunction (negative, restrictive script-forming message) is 'Don't exist (as lesbian, gay or bisexual)'. Every gay and lesbian client will present some strategies as evidence of this injunction and, equally importantly, every non-gay person carries these same injunctions about homo-sexuality. Unless brought into awareness this is a recipe for disaster: 'cure' for homosexuals offered by some therapists and religions is an example, however many liberal responses are subtle, but dangerous, variations. 'Don't be seen to exist' can take many forms, for example: 'It's OK to be in the closet', or 'Holding hands in the street will get you into trouble', or 'Why is it so important that you tell people about your sexuality?', all of which are, in the final analysis, merely disguised variations of 'Don't exist'.

While many other theories acknowledge the impact of the social environment on individual development, TA is primarily about this process. The script as developed by Berne (1975b) and Steiner (1974) is a cornerstone of TA theory and therapy. TA is about turning those who have been turned into frogs by their experience in the world (family and cultural scripting) back into princes and princesses.

Human hungers, strokes and the stroke economy

Berne postulated six basic hungers: stimulus hunger; contact hunger; recognition hunger; sexual hunger; structure hunger; and incident hunger. The fulfilment of these is essential for people's health and survival. TA theory understands the enormous power the provision or withdrawal of recognition has on behaviour, particularly for infants and children. From this developed the idea of the 'stroke' as the 'unit of recognition'. Initially this 'stroking' will be literal and, as an infant grows, 'symbolic substitutes' will partially take the place of physical contact: for example, a smile across a room will feed hunger for recognition. Strokes may be positive or negative, physical or verbal, and unconditional or conditional. 'I love you' is positive, verbal and unconditional. A slap across the face is negative, physical and probably conditional. A 'stroke profile' is an inventory of the kind of strokes an individual gives and receives.

Steiner (1971) introduced a radical social dimension to stroke theory with the stroke economy. He observed that an artificial economy of stroke scarcity is created. He identifies five injunctions against the free exchange of strokes: 'Don't give strokes', 'Don't ask for strokes', 'Don't accept strokes', 'Don't reject strokes' and 'Don't give yourself strokes'. Each individual carries some, or all, of these and their power will depend upon the family and culture of origin. Examples of injunctions include: 'Don't touch yourself there!' and 'Don't brag!'. Modelling of dominant cultural attitudes is pervasive – for example, as children notice their parents' reactions to stroking. Berne identified stroke manipulation as more effective in controlling human behaviour than brutality or punishment (Steiner 1974).

Scripting is created and maintained by stroking. The artificial shortage of positive strokes contributes to a felt sense that the only strokes available are those syntonic with one's script: in other words those that help to keep one's script in place. For example, clients whose script includes a basic belief that they are bad discount positive strokes counteracting this belief and, to fill the shortage, collect negative strokes which support it (e.g. interpret having casual sex as evidence of their 'bad' lust). Additionally, in the dominant culture, strokes are only available for concealing homosexuality, and any 'positive strokes received by a closeted gay must be labelled "conditional" to the extent they would be withdrawn or replaced by negative strokes if s/he disclosed his/her gayness. Stroking a closet does little for its occupant' (Aiken 1976: 23). Analysis of a client's stroke profile and economy helps identify the nature of their script. Deliberate intervention in this system can facilitate disruption of the script.

Phenomenological method

The TA diagnostic method requires the therapist not to categorise the client according to illness, but rather to use TA diagnoses such as existential life position (Berne 1975b: 85–9), life script (Steiner 1974), and ego image (Berne 1975a). All of these require active cooperation and verification by the client. In his discussion of Procrustes Berne (1975b) takes this lesson:

> The moral is, look at the ground first, and then at the map, and not vice versa . . . In other words, the therapist listens to the patient and gets the plot of his script first, then he looks in [books of fairy tales] and not vice versa. In that way he will get a sound match, and not just a bright idea. *Then* he can use the fairy tale to predict where the patient is headed, verifying from the patient (not from the book) all the way.
>
> (p. 409, original italics)

Another methodological concern of Berne was that the therapist should conscientiously self-calibrate. Questions to ask are: 'What game am *I* playing?', i.e. 'What is my transference with this client?' and 'What is my part in this client's script?' These reveal essential aspects of transference, which can guide treatment decisions.

Contracting

Contracting is fundamental to TA: defined variously in the literature, one essential is the mutuality of the process, to empower the client. One of its key contributions is aiding the surfacing of hidden agendas. This acts as a safeguard to both client and therapist: the ongoing mutual process will illuminate prejudices/introjects carried by the therapist. The therapist who is assiduous should notice these; failing that, their supervisor or the client will. The therapist is assisted and protected by the early identification of any game invitations (transference processes).

Stroke economy

Analysing a client's stroke economy is vital in assisting and maintaining any behaviour changes. A change in behaviour always leads to a change in the kind, type and magnitude of strokes available. If a client were worried about frequent anonymous sex my response would be determined by analysing his or her stroke economy. If the behaviour were fulfilling sexual hungers we would explore the meaning the client is making of their behaviour rather than concentrate on changing it. It is likely the client carries negative scripting about casual sex, or stroking, which requires decontamination through bringing the client's internal opinions into awareness. This invites the client to make choices about their own opinions, including modifying them. If, however, the client is attempting to fulfil another hunger – for example, structure or contact or excitement – then the sex may be largely unsuccessful in fulfilling the hunger, which needs another response. The client will feel anxious and may increase the behaviour in a doomed attempt to meet the underlying hunger. In this case I would aid the client to identify the particular hunger which needs feeding and to develop strategies for meeting the need directly – for example, improving levels of physical contact or finding excitement safely. Once the client meets the underlying need directly, anxiety will decrease and they will be free to choose autonomously with regard to casual sex.

Script analysis

TA offers techniques for understanding the client's drama and planning interventions to facilitate release from their script. We use the script matrix to map the social forces shaping their identity. The script matrix is the complex array of messages, and decisions the client has made. These are mapped in the form of injunctions (mainly preverbal), program (models of how to live out the script) and counterinjunctions (more script-forming messages which are mainly verbal). This work is essential for lesbian, gay and bisexual clients who have grown up in a hostile dominant culture.

Unhelpful theoretical contributions and techniques

The lack of writing about homosexuality in TA seems to reflect what I will call 'the liberal tolerance dilemma'. We don't believe it's bad, but we don't really know how to talk about and accept it. What is unhelpful in this attitude is the failure to recognise the difference inherent in homosexuality and therefore to explore, learn and write about it. Therapists need to learn about this difference so that they aren't taken by surprise by their clients or act as a force for the continued limiting of their clients' life choices. We need actively to redress this balance in the literature.

Any TA can be applied badly. This usually results from a reductionist view of the theory itself. Because of its accessibility and the power and usefulness of its concepts in various settings, TA has lent itself to oversimplified explanations and implementations, which are not embedded in theoretical completeness (Stewart 1992). Any TA concept or practice removed from its philosophical context and applied casually can be abusive. This trivialisation destroys the theoretical contribution and purpose of TA.

The TA practitioner is involved in a difficult dialogue between two ways of seeing the world: empiricism and phenomenology. This is also one of the major strengths of TA. Overemphasis on the empirical aspects will diffuse the humanistic potential of TA and increase the likelihood of a normative, and therefore heterosexist, outcome. Overemphasis on phenomenological aspects will diffuse the reality principle (Berne 1975a) and increase the likelihood of collusion in elements of script: complementary and concordant transferences where client and/or therapist each see themselves in the other (Clarkson 1992).

TA's humanism combined with Berne's systematic phenomenology which links observable behaviours with intra-psychic processes, creates a theory and practice which has many features essential for gay affirmative therapy. Specific elements of the theory and practice – for example, cultural scripting and stroke theory, offer elegant and powerful tools for understanding gay, lesbian and bisexual clients in their context, and for freeing them from the limiting scripting which they all experience.

Key issues in working affirmatively

Rather than presenting specific techniques I prefer to offer a theory of what 'working affirmatively' means that is applicable in all situations.

Decontamination of cultural scripting

Therapy with gay clients is in most respects exactly the same as therapy with other clients, but in at least one respect is very different. This is the power, pervasiveness and insidiousness of cultural scripting about homosexuality that we *all* experience although our sexual orientation will determine our range of responses to it.

The key issue in working affirmatively is a willingness to enter and explore the world of your clients from *their* frame of reference and an openness to rigorously recalibrate your judgements – i.e. to ensure you are working only from your Integrated Adult ego state.

Every one of our lesbian, gay and bisexual clients, no matter how 'sussed', carries the same cultural poisons as we do. All of my gay clients have presented with their *physis* (the creative life-force) almost crushed – the outcome of the 'Don't exist' injunction. Again this is true for many other clients too, and it is our job to engage and nurture *physis* so that clients may become fully themselves. What makes this difficult and different with lesbian, gay and bisexual clients is the power of the cultural scripting in this process, which we all, *regardless of sexuality*, have experienced too. This leads to an increased likelihood of destructive transference and counter-transference. Many practitioners, because of the general cultural onslaught against lesbians, gays and bisexuals, will not be aware of elements of that transference, even with supervision, because of the cultural imperative to eradicate homosexuality.

With respect to our clients' sexuality, to the extent that attitudes to sexual orientation are culturally created, it is *as if* we had grown up in the same family as our clients. It may be possible for a practitioner to provide therapy for their sister, but it is not recommended (and proscribed in certain ethical codes). It could only be considered if the practitioner had successfully de-contaminated their Adult (become aware of beliefs and attitudes masquer-ading as facts) and dealt with their pertinent Child issues (the feelings and decisions arising from those experiences). If we are to provide ethical therapy to lesbian, gay and bisexual clients then we need to have done the same with regard to the cultural scripting we all receive about homosexuality. Therapists, both gay and straight, may be offended by the idea that they carry homophobic scripting. It is difficult for anyone to acknowledge that it isn't enough just to *want* to be affirmative.

I believe a conscientious TA practitioner, *provided* they have schooled themselves, or been schooled, in the generalised felt experience of being different as our clients experience this, *and* have profoundly worked through their responses to the pervasive cultural scripting about homosexuality *before* they start working with clients, is then ready to meet and work affirmatively with the particular experience a gay client presents to them without doing anything special. A conscientious TA practitioner would ordinarily pay attention to all 12 guidelines for affirmative practice listed by Davies (1996: 30–4). Any client needs to be met at the point of his or her own phenomenological experience of themselves. Specifying particular strategies required for lesbian, gay and bisexual clients reduces the infinite range of experiences of self that clients bring to therapy. The key factor is the therapist's ability to freely, spontaneously and with awareness meet the client intimately and exercise the full range of therapeutic options available to them. These qualities relate to the concept of autonomy as defined by Berne.

Sexual orientation of the therapist

Davies (1996) believes the sexual orientation of the therapist is relatively unimportant. I agree, with reservations. The key element is the therapist's active engagement with their own prejudices, be they personal or cultural, and their ability to keep these out of the therapy room.

Where heterosexuality is regarded as 'normal' and heterosexuals are not forced to consider their own sexuality by social conditions which support them, it is likely that gay, lesbian and bisexual therapists will be more aware of archaic contaminations about sexuality simply through life experiences of coming out. However, being lesbian, gay or bisexual does not make one gay affirmative – sometimes quite the reverse, depending upon the route one has taken in accommodating the psychic reality of one's sexuality (see Hodges and Hutter 1977 and Adam 1978 for examples of this). Being gay affirmative requires rigorous self-examination aided by training and supervision to develop an appropriate therapeutic attitude (see also Chapter 4). Most ethical codes make some reference to practitioners assessing clients and only working with those who fall within their range of competence. This is variously defined, but several references are made to avoiding clients whose issues closely resemble one's own or who present issues that the therapist has not yet resolved for themselves. I suggest that practitioners who have not yet conscientiously examined their own sexuality (regardless of their orientation) are ethically incompetent to handle lesbian, gay or bisexual clients because of the powerful impact of cultural scripting in determining both the clients' and therapists' psychological world, and the likelihood of matching or interlocking scripting. By this I mean examining in full one's responses to the entire spectrum of social beliefs about sexuality, the cultural systems which organise this, the ways in which individuals manifest their sexuality and the world's various responses, usually regulatory, to this.

The closeted therapist

It is clear, both theoretically and ethically, that a practitioner concealing their (homo/bi) sexual identity should not work with gay, lesbian or bisexual clients. In TA terms the closeted therapist is always involved in ulterior (covert) transactions – 'It is not OK to be lesbian or gay' which supports the client's 'Don't Exist' injunction. There is a clear danger of harm to the client. In small communities there is also the likelihood of the client discovering the sexuality of the closeted therapist (see Gartrell 1984), and in my experience even London is a small community for lesbians, gays and bisexuals.

The meaning of the therapist's sexual orientation

What is certainly relevant is the meaning the client makes of the practitioner's sexual orientation. This will differ from client to client and the client will probably have several different reasons for choosing a therapist of a particular orientation. These will include overt or social level reasons as well as covert or out of awareness reasons. Discovering the client's script reasons for entering therapy with you as well as your own script reasons for taking on a particular client is an essential part of the therapeutic (and supervision) process (Berne 1975b).

Even reasons for choosing an 'out' therapist may not be simple. For example, I worked with a closeted client with carried common cultural beliefs that gay men are impotent, not 'real' men who 'can get it up with women'. Together we identified his script reason for choosing an openly gay therapist: I would be impotent in facilitating his change. My script reason for taking on this client was that he would be too difficult, which would prove that I wasn't 'good enough' and that I couldn't finish what I started. In the event his cultural introject was confronted by an out gay therapist being effective (i.e. identifying an underlying reason for his choice) which, together with other decontamination, facilitated his passage through the impasse: 'I am gay/I am not gay and don't want to be'. In this example my sexual orientation and the cultural scripting worked in our favour. The client felt safe enough coming to see a gay therapist because that meant he didn't need to change and the part of him that wanted to be gay was also comforted. When I was effective it provided a powerful confrontation to the cultural scripting as well as a permission and modelling for the gay part of the client to be powerful. This in some ways is a 'bull's-eye transaction' which reaches all ego states and so works at many different levels at once.

The therapist must be trained in and must not 'forget' the cultural scripting of homosexuality no matter what the presenting problem. They must also tread the fine line between ignoring and overemphasising the difference of lesbian, gay and bisexual clients' experience in life. TA as outlined above offers effective tools for exploring and liberating the client from the most ravaging effects of such life experiences.

Guidelines for good practice

- The therapy should be accessible.
- The therapy should facilitate self-determination/autonomy.
- The therapist must deal with all cultural issues related to sexuality before working with clients, and continue to do so.
- The therapist must be skilled in working with the internal world of the client.
- The therapeutic model should offer clients the option of emancipating themselves from their restrictive cultural scripting.
- Therapists must be aware of the meanings they and their clients make of their attitude to, and living out of, their sexualities.

References

Adam, B. (1978) *The Survival of Domination: Inferiorization and Everyday Life.* New York: Elsevier.

Aiken, B.A. (1976) The stroke economy and gay people, *Transactional Analysis Journal*, 6(1): 21–7.

Bader, E. and Pearson, P. (1988) *In Quest of the Mythical Mate: A Developmental Approach to Diagnosis and Treatment in Couples Therapy.* New York: Brunner/Mazel.

Berne, E. (1963) *The Structure and Dynamics of Organizations and Groups.* New York: Grove Press.

Berne, E. (1966) *Principles of Group Treatment.* New York: Grove Press.

Berne, E. (1968) *Games People Play.* Harmondsworth: Penguin.

Berne, E. (1971) *A Layman's Guide to Psychiatry and Psychoanalysis.* Harmondsworth: Penguin.

Berne, E. (1973) *Sex in Human Loving.* Harmondsworth: Penguin.

Berne, E. (1975a) *Transactional Analysis in Psychotherapy: A Systematic Individual and Social Psychiatry.* London: Souvenir Press.

Berne, E. (1975b) *What Do You Say After You Say Hello: The Psychology of Human Destiny.* London: Corgi.

Clarkson, P. (1987) The bystander role, *Transactional Analysis Journal*, 17(3): 82–7.

Clarkson, P. (1992) *Transactional Analysis Psychotherapy: An Integrated Approach.* London: Routledge.

Clarkson, P. and Gilbert, M. (1990) Transactional analysis, in W. Dryden (ed.) *Individual Therapy: A Handbook.* Buckingham: Open University Press.

Collinson, L. (1975) Games gays play, *British Transactional Analysis Bulletin*, 1(2): 8–14.

Cornell, W.F. (1990) Review of *In Quest of the Mythical Mate: A Developmental Approach to Diagnosis and Treatment in Couples Therapy, Transactional Analysis Journal*, 20(1): 77–9.

Cornell, W.F. (1992a) Review of *Confessions of a Psychologist: Is Physical Touch Therapeutic? Transactional Analysis Journal*, 22(3): 189–91.

Cornell, W.F. (1992b) Review of *Women and Depression: Risk Factors and Treatment Issues, Transactional Analysis Journal*, 22(3): 191–3.

Cornell, W.F. (1992c) Review of *Writing a Woman's Life, Transactional Analysis Journal*, 22(4): 243–4.

Cornell, W.F. (1995) Boundaries or barriers: who is protecting whom? A personal essay/book review, *Transactional Analysis Journal*, 25(2): 180–6.

Davies, D. (1996) Towards a model of gay affirmative therapy, in D. Davies and C. Neal (eds) *Pink Therapy: A Guide for Counsellors and Therapists Working with Lesbian, Gay and Bisexual Clients.* Buckingham: Open University Press.

English, F. (1994) Shame and social control revisited, *Transactional Analysis Journal*, 24(2): 109–20.

Gartrell, N. (1984) Combating homophobia in the psychotherapy of lesbians, *Women & Therapy*, 3(1): 13–29.

Gilbert, M. and Shmukler, D. (1996) *Brief Therapy with Couples: An Integrative Approach.* Chichester: John Wiley.

Goulding, M. and Goulding, R. (1979) *Changing Lives Through Redecision Therapy.* New York: Grove Press.

Harris, T. (1967) *I'm OK – You're OK*. New York: Grove Press.

Hochstein, L. (1995) Review of *When Boundaries Betray Us: Beyond Illusions of What is Ethical in Therapy and Life*, *Transactional Analysis Journal*, 25(2): 186–9.

Hodges, A. and Hutter, D. (1977) *With Downcast Gays: Aspects of Homosexual Self-oppression*. Toronto: Pink Triangle Press.

Hohmuth, A. and Borden, D. (1992) Review of *The Taboo Scarf and Other Tales of Therapy*, *Transactional Analysis Journal*, 22(4): 247–9.

James, M. and Jongeward, D. (1971) *Born to Win*. Reading, MA: Addison Wesley.

Klein, M. (1949) *The Psycho-Analysis of Children*. London: Hogarth Press.

Lapworth, P., Sills, C. and Fish, S. (1993) *Transactional Analysis Counselling*. Bicester: Winslow Press.

McClendon, R. and Kadis, L.B. (1994) Shame and early decisions: theory and clinical implications, *Transactional Analysis Journal*, 24(2): 130–8.

Massey, R.F. (1990) The structural bases of games, *Transactional Analysis Journal*, 20(1): 20–7.

Pelton, C.L. (1994) Review of *The Adam Principle – Genes, Genitals, Hormones, and Gender: Selected Readings in Sexology*, *Transactional Analysis Journal*, 24(3): 230–2.

Schiff, J., Schiff, A., Mellor, K. *et al.* (1975) *Cathexis Reader: Transactional Analysis Treatment of Psychosis*. New York: Harper & Row.

Simerly, R.T. and Karakashian, S.J. (1989) Psychotherapy with HIV-positive, ARC and AIDS patients: clinical issues and practice management, *Transactional Analysis Journal*, 19(4): 176–85.

Simerly, T. (1993) Review of *AIDS, Health and Mental Health: A Primary Sourcebook*, *Transactional Analysis Journal*, 23(4): 237–8.

Simerly, T. (1996) Longtime companions: gay couples in the era of AIDS, *Transactional Analysis Journal*, 26(1): 8–14.

Steiner, C. (1971) The stroke economy, *Transactional Analysis Journal*, 1(3): 9–15.

Steiner, C. (1974) *Scripts People Live: Transactional Analysis of Life Scripts*. New York: Grove Weidenfeld.

Steiner, C. (1995) Thirty years of psychotherapy and transactional analysis in 1,500 words or less, *Transactional Analysis Journal*, 25(1): 83–6.

Stewart, I. (1989) *Transactional Analysis Counselling in Action*. London: Sage.

Stewart, I. (1992) *Eric Berne*. London: Sage.

Stewart, I. and Joines, V. (1987) *TA Today: A New Introduction to Transactional Analysis*. Nottingham: Lifespace Publishing.

Vaughn, L. (1995) Review of *An End to Shame: Shaping our Next Sexual Revolution*, *Transactional Analysis Journal*, 25(2): 190–1.

White, J. and White, T. (1975) Cultural scripting, *Transactional Analysis Journal*, 5(1): 12–23.

Woollams, S. and Brown, M. (1978) *Transactional Analysis*. Ann Arbor, MI: Huron Valley Institute Press.

Index

PINK THERAPY
A GUIDE FOR COUNSELLORS AND THERAPISTS WORKING WITH LESBIAN, GAY AND BISEXUAL CLIENTS

Dominic Davies and Charles Neal (eds)

Pink Therapy is the first British guide for counsellors and therapists working with people who are lesbian, gay or bisexual. It provides a much needed overview of lesbian, gay and bisexual psychology, and examines some of the differences between lesbians, gays and bisexuals, and heterosexuals. *Pink Therapy* proposes a model of gay affirmative therapy, which challenges the prevailing pathologising models. It will help to provide answers to pressing questions such as:

• What is different about lesbian, gay and bisexual psychologies?
• How can I improve my work with lesbian, gay and bisexual clients?
• What are the key clinical issues that this work raises?

The contributors draw on their wide range of practical experience to provide – in an accessible style – information about the contemporary experience of living as a lesbian, gay or bisexual person, and to explore some of the common difficulties.

Pink Therapy will be important reading for students and practitioners of counselling and psychotherapy, and will also be of value to anyone involved in helping people with a lesbian, gay or bisexual orientation.

Reviews of *Pink Therapy* . . .

'A comprehensive British volume on lesbian and gay affirmative psychotherapy has been a while coming. *Pink Therapy*, however, has arrived, amply fills this gap, and is well worth the wait . . . A deft editorial hand is evident in the unusual consistency across chapters, the uniformly crisp, helpful chapter summaries, and the practical appendices, generous resources lists and well organized bibliographies.

I particularly liked the contributors' subtle appreciation of theoretical nuance, genuine open-mindedness to diversity of ideas, and willingness to synthesize in a pragmatic and client-oriented manner.'

> John C. Gonsiorek, Past President, Society for the
> Psychological Study of Lesbian and Gay Issues,
> (Division 44 of the American Psychological Association)

'It is all too easy for the liberal heterosexual therapist to imagine he or she has it all sewn up as far as attitudes to homosexuality are concerned. This book shows that even the politically correct, have so much to learn not just about being gay, lesbian or bisexual, but also about research into sexuality, attitudes amongst therapists, and on training courses, as well as in the development of psychotherapy and counselling.'

> Michael Jacobs, Director of the Psychotherapy and Counselling
> Certificate Programme, University of Leicester

'This book equips heterosexual therapists for gay affirmative work . . . It gave me much more knowledge and insight into being gay in our society. Extremely well researched, numerous tracks for further investigations, guidelines on relevant reading . . . the language and tone make it accessible to all except the most defensive . . . I recommend it strongly.'

> Dave Mearns, Reader in Counselling and
> Director of the Counselling Unit, University of Strathclyde

Contents
Introduction – Part 1: Fundamental issues – An historical overview of homosexuality and therapy – Towards a model of gay affirmative therapy – Homophobia and heterosexism – Working with people coming out – Part 2: Working with particular issues – Working with single people – Working with people in relationships – Lesbian and gay parenting issues – Working with young people – Working with older lesbians – Working with older gay men – Alcohol and substance misuse – Partner abuse – Religious and spirituality conflicts – Appendix 1: Resources – Appendix 2: Community resources – Appendix 3: Books for clients and counsellors – References – Index.

Contributors
Dominic Davies, Helena Hargaden, Graz Kowszun, Sara Llewellin, Dr Bernard Lynch, Maeve Malley, Lyndsey Moon, Charles Neal, Dr Bernard Ratigan, Gail Simon, Fran Walsh, Val Young.

256pp   0 335 19145 2 (Paperback)   0 335 19657 8 (Hardback)

ISSUES IN THERAPY WITH LESBIAN, GAY, BISEXUAL AND TRANSGENDERED CLIENTS

Charles Neal and Dominic Davies (eds)

Many readers of *Pink Therapy* (1996 Open University Press) found the affirmative approaches and detailed discussions there of numerous issues of particular concern to lesbian, gay and bisexual clients invaluable. This volume has twelve further areas discussed in clear and informative style by practitioners from their own professional experience and offers guidelines for good practice as well as full references and further resources. With *Pink Therapy* and *Therapeutic Perspectives on Working with Lesbian, Gay and Bisexual Clients*, from the same editors and publishers, professionals interested in treating clients from these minorities equitably will find a wealth of support, information and guidance not previously readily available.

Contents

Introduction – Issues of race, culture and sexuality – Kink therapy: SM and sexual minorities – The management of ethical dilemmas associated with dual relationships – Issues in HIV/AIDS counselling – Expressive therapy: freeing the creative self – Psychosexual therapy – We are family: working with gay men in groups – Looking both ways: bisexuality and therapy – Working with people who have been sexually abused in childhood – Long term consequences of bullying – Gay men and sex: clinical issues – Transgender issues in therapy – Bibliography – Index.

c. 224pp   0 335 20331 0 (Paperback)   0 335 20332 9 (Hardback)